THE JOHNS HOPKINS UNIVERSITY STUDIES IN HISTORICAL AND POLITICAL SCIENCE

SERIES LXXXVI   NUMBER 1
(1968)

EIGHTY-SIXTH SERIES (1968)

1. The Conservative Regime: South Carolina, 1877–1890
BY WILLIAM J. COOPER, JR.

THE CONSERVATIVE REGIME:
SOUTH CAROLINA, 1877–1890

THE CONSERVATIVE REGIME:
SOUTH CAROLINA,
1877-1890

By

WILLIAM J. COOPER, JR.

THE JOHNS HOPKINS PRESS
BALTIMORE
1968

FOR MY FATHER

ACKNOWLEDGMENTS

The assistance of many individuals and institutions made this book possible. The custodians and staffs of the research libraries cited in the bibliography helped to make my task simpler and my efforts—I hope—more profitable. I am especially indebted to E. L. Inabinett, Clara Mae Jacobs, and Jean Ligon, all of the South Caroliniana Library, who hospitably tolerated my presence and my queries for an extended period. G. G. Williamson, Jr. generously shared his intimate knowledge of South Carolina economic development, and George Tindall discussed freely his findings on Wade Hampton and his views on my topic. Stephen E. Ambrose improved my manuscript with thoughtful criticisms. Frank E. Jordan, Jr. graciously permitted me to use his unpublished materials on South Carolina primaries; Rogers E. Harrell gave me open-stack privileges in his rich legal library, a kindness that greatly expedited my work. Thomas J. Gierl drew the maps. The Johns Hopkins University, through its Dwight D. Eisenhower Fellowship in American Studies, financed the bulk of the research and the initial draft.

My appreciation to David Donald and Patricia Holmes Cooper cannot be measured. Without them, this volume would not have been started or completed.

For any inaccuracies and errors that remain I accept sole responsibility.

TABLE OF CONTENTS

LIST OF ILLUSTRATIONS

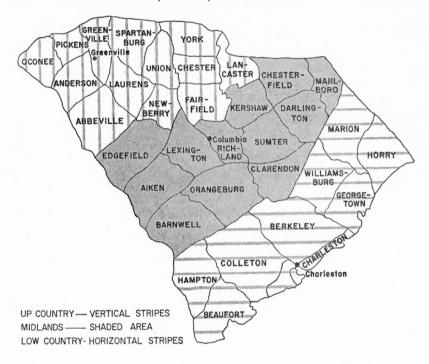

SOUTH CAROLINA (1880s)
SECTIONS, COUNTIES, PRINCIPAL CITIES

UP COUNTRY— VERTICAL STRIPES
MIDLANDS —— SHADED AREA
LOW COUNTRY- HORIZONTAL STRIPES

INTRODUCTION

The leaders of the Democratic victories that signaled the end of Reconstruction in the Southern states have become known as Redeemers, because they redeemed their states from the Republicans. Prior to 1951 when C. Vann Woodward published his influential *Origins of the New South*,[1] Southern leaders of the post-Reconstruction era were known as Bourbons—Bourbons because certain of their opponents accused them, as Napoleon did the French royal family, of neither forgetting nor learning from the past. In his revisionist study, Woodward rejected the term Bourbon as a misnomer because he found neither " obstinate adherence to the old loyalties," nor " abhorrence of the new." [2] Since then most historians have adopted Woodward's term, Redeemer, as they have accepted his basic interpretation. I choose to call these Southern leaders Bourbons because, as I hope to make apparent in this introduction and throughout the book, in at least one state they vary considerably from the Woodward portrait.

The period of Bourbon control in Southern states, which lasted from the end of Reconstruction almost to the end of the nineteenth century, has attracted little attention from historians. Although concerned with the complexities of Reconstruction and attracted by the agrarian radicalism that ended Bourbon hegemony in several Southern states, few historians have thought the Bourbon era itself to be of equal importance.

Even those writers who have not ignored the Bourbons have had little favorable to say about them.[3] Bourbons have been portrayed

1. C. Vann Woodward, *Origins of the New South, 1877–1913*, Vol. IX of *A History of the South*, ed. Wendell Holmes Stephenson and E. Merton Coulter (Baton Rouge: Louisiana State University Press, 1951).

2. *Ibid.*, p. 14, and p. 75, n. 1.

3. Most of the views expressed in this paragraph have been forcefully stated by Professor Woodward in his *Origins*. Although in this and the following paragraph I summarize the currently accepted viewpoint, I use the term Bourbon rather than Redeemer for clarity and consistency.

The most notable state studies, which for the most part support Woodward's generalizations, are: Albert D. Kirwan's excellent *Revolt of the Rednecks: Mississippi*

generally as the agents and allies of Northern business and financial interests who enriched themselves at the expense of their states. Little interested in the development of their states, so the description continues, they gave neither sympathy nor assistance to the masses of farmers gripped by depression. Fearful of the white farmers who demanded a larger share in the state government, they manipulated the Negro vote to deny the aspirations of their antagonists. According to most who have written about them, they received their just deserts in the 1890s when radical agrarians carrying the banners of the Farmers' Alliance (or Populism) ended Bourbon rule in most Southern states. Throughout the existing literature about the Bourbons runs a theme approaching the idea of conspiracy—Bourbons and their friends conspired among themselves for their own benefit, usually financial, with little or no interest in anything else.

These conspirators were planters, merchants, and professional men who, according to the literature, stood together against farmers in a division of classes.[4] This idea of class warfare underlies the entire standard interpretation of the Bourbon period. In the effort to throw out the Republicans, the Bourbons, through a bombast of rhetoric about Southernism and the necessity of preserving the white race, managed to turn farmers away from their real interests as farmers, and their appeal to racial solidarity, muting class conflict, enabled them to perpetuate their control of the Southern states. But gradually these suppressed class antagonisms reasserted themselves, and when class-conscious farmers organized to protect their interests, they overwhelmed the Bourbons in a surge of democracy.

With no intention of whitewashing the Bourbons, I believe that there are weaknesses in this generally accepted account. Certainly this neglected generation deserves a full, impartial study. Because

---

Politics, 1876–1925 (Lexington, Ky.: University of Kentucky Press, 1951), chapters i–vii; Allen J. Going, Bourbon Democracy in Alabama, 1874–1890 (University, Ala.: University of Alabama Press, 1951); and Judson Clement Ward, Jr., "New Departure Democrats in Georgia: An Interpretation," Georgia Historical Quarterly, XLI (September, 1957), 227–37.

For two competent, up-to-date historiographical essays discussing the literature on the Bourbon era, see Paul M. Gaston, "The 'New South,'" in Writing Southern History: Essays in Historiography in Honor of Fletcher M. Green, ed. Arthur S. Link and Rembert W. Patrick (Baton Rouge: Louisiana State University Press, 1965), pp. 316–36, and Jacob E. Cooke, "The New South," in Essays in American Historiography: Papers Presented in Honor of Allan Nevins, ed. Donald Sheehan and Harold C. Syrett (New York: Columbia University Press, 1960), pp. 50–80.

4. Gaston, "The 'New South,'" pp. 327–31.

Bourbons did dominate the South for a period of time, failure to take them fully into account leaves a vacuum in the historians' comprehension of Southern development. More important, the Bourbons successfully established the social and political mores which have governed Southern life almost to our own day.

To be sure, the Bourbons retained much that had existed in the South before 1861. For ante-bellum Southerners, who were firmly convinced of the justice and necessity of white rule, slavery had kept the Negro in an inferior position. With slavery abolished and the Fourteenth and Fifteenth Amendments to the Constitution guaranteeing the freedman his citizenship, the Bourbons faced the threat of a new racial alignment. It was their objective to prevent any new departure. Retaining the ante-bellum doctrine of white supremacy, the Bourbons, who used various methods in the different states, all strove to find new ways to maintain the old white dominance. With that decision and the techniques devised to implement it, the Bourbons branded the South's future.

The Democratic party, the party of redemption, became a major force in the security of white rule. By defining the Democratic party as the instrument both of white supremacy and Southern salvation, Bourbons imposed a political unity on the South far greater than that known in prewar years, when the Whig and Democratic parties had a lively competition in most states of the South until the demise of the Whig party in the mid-1850s. Yet, this seeming solidification of Southern whites in the 1880s can be overemphasized. While one party rather than two spoke for the South, the same diversity of the ante-bellum period continued under the Democratic tent, which expanded to accommodate conservatives and radicals, farmers and industrialists, and demagogues.

The ideological legacy of the Bourbons is probably more significant than race separation or a one-party system. They formed, out of the chaos of military devastation and Reconstruction, an image of a South united by bloodshed in a noble battle for independence. They paid tribute—lip service by some, conviction in others—to glories of what had existed before the war and to the nobility of the war. Some found fault with the ante-bellum South, but few discarded it. From 1880 to 1950, few white Southerners challenged the edifice built by the Bourbons. The holiness of the Democratic party and the white race together with reverence for the Confederacy and conviction of the horror of Reconstruction have, with the Protestant faith, formed the basic creed of the white Southerner.

As a way of investigating the Bourbons, I chose to study South Carolina, the home of Wade Hampton, one of the major Bourbon leaders, and of Benjamin Tillman, an outstanding agrarian who organized the movement that defeated Hampton and his Conservative associates.[5] Understanding the techniques Tillman used to gain his victory and analyzing the reasons why the Conservatives failed to meet Tillman's challenge successfully provide many clues to the nature of the Conservative regime in South Carolina. At the same time, such a comparison affords the opportunity of investigating the origins, organization, and programs of one of the major agrarian movements in the South.

In writing about South Carolina during the Bourbon period, one should be aware of conditions similar to those in other Southern states. In South Carolina as throughout the South, agriculture dominated the economy—an economy beginning to industrialize but plagued by a general agricultural depression. That depression was both cause and catalyst of agrarian movements that challenged Bourbon rule across the South. In addition to the agrarian movements, intrastate sectionalism confronted Conservatives in South Carolina as well as in Alabama, Mississippi, and elsewhere.

At the same time, certain unique features differentiated South Carolina. A heavier-than-average Negro population distinguished South Carolina from her neighbors, but more noticeable was the pervasiveness of the Negro throughout the state. Even in ante-bellum days no large areas in the state were without Negroes, and therefore the plantation system which had begun in the low country spread throughout the entire state, including Oconee county, the home of John C. Calhoun in the extreme northwestern section. And, under the influence of Calhoun, who guided the state from the 1830s to his death in 1850, South Carolina really never experienced the two-party system of the Old South. With no Whig party and a Democratic party loyal to Calhoun rather than to any national organization or platform, South Carolinians developed a fierce state pride and more political unity than did other Southerners.

In my investigations, I have found that the story in South Carolina does not fit the mold currently accepted for Bourbons; indeed, in

5. Throughout the book I use the terms Conservative, Conservative regime, and Bourbon interchangeably when referring to South Carolina. South Carolina Bourbons called themselves Conservatives (upper case) and Conservative Democrats. I am merely repeating their words.

certain respects, facts and events in South Carolina suggest that the standard interpretation of the Bourbons should be qualified or adjusted. Contrary to Professor C. Vann Woodward's characterization of Bourbons, in South Carolina they were not former Whigs; to a man they had been ante-bellum Democrats. Unlike their younger counterparts in other Southern states, few of whom had connections with the old planter class, most of the South Carolinians were over fifty years old and the scions of planters.[6]

The idea of a class conflict in which farmers battled against a clique of planters, merchants, and industrialists has little application in South Carolina.[7] The early attempts to dislodge Hampton and his friends sprang from personal and sectional differences within the state. Leading the inchoate opposition to the Hampton Democrats between 1877 and 1880, Martin Witherspoon Gary, a Harvard-educated lawyer and former Confederate brigadier, hoped to gain political prominence for himself. Gary, who accused Hampton of cultivating the Negro and making deals with Republicans, evinced little interest in farmers and certainly did not champion any suppressed lower-class agrarians. Later, in the mid-1880s, the effort by up-country elements to change the organization of the Democratic party stemmed from a long tradition of sectional hostility within the state and had nothing to do with class conflict. Editors, businessmen, and professional men led the up-country forces in their unsuccessful attempts to change party rules.

Even Tillmanism, the unmistakably agrarian movement which ended the Conservative regime in South Carolina, cannot be properly understood as an uprising of class against class. Tillman's lieutenants were educated young landowners, lawyers, and politicians, not small farmers; nor were South Carolina Bourbons chiefly business oriented, and many of them retained close ties with the land and with agriculture. Although Tillman's oratory at times bespoke radical agrarianism, his platforms demanded nothing more revolutionary than an agricultural college and control of the state Agriculture Bureau by his organization. Tillman proclaimed himself the farmers' advocate, yet drew no lines between large planters and small farmers; he even welcomed merchants, lawyers, and other non-farmers into his organization. Shunning any third party and refusing to endorse the radical portions of section-wide movements like the Farmers'

6. Woodward, *Origins*, chap. i.
7. *Ibid.*, chaps. i, iv, vii, and *supra*, n. 4.

Alliance, Tillman remained a faithful Democrat. He climbed to power on the existing party structure; to reach political ascendancy, he alternated demands for democratic reforms such as primaries with defense of the old Conservative convention system of nomination.

Unlike other Southern Bourbons, South Carolina Conservatives did not become self-serving agents and associates of Northern financial interests.[8] Realizing the poverty of South Carolina, the Bourbons welcomed industry and capital yet refused to surrender all state control. With powerful assistance from Charleston business and financial groups, the Bourbon government organized a railroad commission that gave the state some control over railroad activities. Far from acting against the wishes of their constituents, state legislators, according to my findings, often courted industry less ardently than did local communities. No one in the state, even Tillman, except in some of his more impassioned statements from the platform, foresaw any conflict between the rise of industry and the well-being of agriculture.

I do not maintain that the South Carolina Bourbons were profound economic thinkers or that they developed solutions to the state's severe economic problems. The agricultural depression revealed the thinness of Conservative economic ideas: unable to comprehend, much less relieve the situation, they tried to convince South Carolina's farmers that nothing serious threatened their livelihood. These claims Tillman attacked promptly and justly, but in turn he offered few solutions, none of which resembled programs demanded by the Farmers' Alliance.[9] Once in power, Tillman showed no more insight or initiative than had his predecessors.

Initially, the Democratic party led by Governor Hampton publicly appealed to the Negroes to become Democrats; the party awarded them both elective and appointive office. Behind this policy lay, first, Hampton's belief that a fairly moderate Negro policy would contribute significantly to the friendship he was determined to secure with the Republican administration in Washington. Second, Hampton and his associates shared the conviction that most Negroes posed little threat to their rule provided the Negroes were shown that any political alternative, such as the Republican party, was unthinkable. In addition, they tried to convince the Negroes of their good faith by allowing them to hold minor offices. A third important, yet

8. Woodward, *Origins*, chap. i.
9. *Ibid.*, chap. vii.

elusive, reason for the Hampton position derived from the Conservatives' self-assurance in dealing with Negroes. Accustomed to dominating the Negro field hand on their plantations, secure from any danger of social or economic competition from the subordinate race, the South Carolina Conservatives did not fear the Negro. After about 1880, however, South Carolina Democrats ceased trying to appeal to the Negro voters, and by the end of the decade Negroes were for all practical purposes excluded from participation in politics. Undoubtedly, removal of the threat of renewed federal intervention coupled with Hampton's relinquishing control of the party contributed to the new turn of events. It seems likely too that the prolonged, grinding agricultural depression in the state diminished the economic distance between the races and made more and more whites fearful of anything that looked like recognizing the social equality of Negroes.

While removing the Negro as a political force, the Conservative regime never erected any system of statutory discrimination that covered social relationships. My findings have supported those advanced by George Tindall and Professor Woodward that legal segregation in the South came after the period of Bourbon control.[10] To explain this delay, one must turn to intangibles—to Conservative confidence in their racial superiority along with their lack of any real concern for Negroes outside of the political sphere.

In harmony with their Bourbon brethren elsewhere in the South, Conservatives in South Carolina labored zealously to make the Democratic party the only respectable political home for white Southerners. Their gospel of Democratic solidarity proved so successful that they never faced a serious challenge from any other party. They were eventually defeated, but by a man who gained control of the very party machinery that had kept them in power. The real story of the Conservative defeat in South Carolina tells not of the success of radical agrarians nor of class conflict but of the Conservative failure to prevent Tillman from capturing the Democratic party.

Ideology, chiefly, caused the Conservative defeat. Basing their political structure not on tight organizational lines but on the influence and prominence of men in their communities and counties, Conservative fortunes, to a large degree, rested on public respect

10. George Brown Tindall, *South Carolina Negroes, 1877–1900* (Columbia: University of South Carolina Press, 1952), and C. Vann Woodward, *The Strange Career of Jim Crow*, Galaxy edition (2d ed. rev.; New York: Oxford University Press, 1966).

for individuals—more important, on the reasons those individuals could command respect. Most often this respect, approaching veneration, came to those who had served South Carolina as officers in the Confederate States Army.

The theme of the Confederacy and of times past pervaded the Conservative mind. The South Carolina Conservatives looked forward not to a better world but to a re-created one. For them, the best of all possible worlds had existed in ante-bellum South Carolina. To build anew what they revered in that commonwealth became their cardinal purpose. While ante-bellum South Carolina was their ideal, the Confederacy was their touchstone. Most of the state's Conservative leaders had led the state's forces in war. They felt that experience had proved them as leaders and as devoted sons of their state; to have been counted in gray was sufficient, in their minds, to be counted in office. When, with the years, public idolatry of the Confederacy and of the Confederate officer began to wane, South Carolina Conservatives still clung to their banners—and met their final defeat.

The picture of the South Carolina Conservative that emerges from my study casts a new light on the older view of the Bourbon and of his age. A Confederate veteran intimately bound to ante-bellum South Carolina, he expended few efforts to build any kind of New South. With no vision of a better future, his program had unity only in its loyalty to an idealized past. To search for a central thread that will make a unified whole out of economic policies and racial programs is futile, I believe. The tangible and real problems of industrialization and agricultural depression failed to challenge men thinking in the past tense. Contests for political reward within the Democratic party of South Carolina and the defense of both party and state, to them one and the same, drew forth Conservative energy and activity, but the former required no thinking about new and unpleasant matters; the latter, duty to their state, Conservatives never shirked. But energy and activity alone could not solve the state's very real problems, nor could ritual incantations about the glorious past silence criticism from a generation that had never known "the good old days" and had never ridden with Robert E. Lee. Tillman swept them from power, not because he represented a new and different class in South Carolina politics, and not because he had a new and different program for meeting the state's difficulties. He won because he spoke a new rhetoric that appealed to a new generation.

CHAPTER I

THE RETURN OF HOME RULE

I

At noon on April 10, 1877, the United States Army troops stationed at the South Carolina State House marched away from their posts. Immediately the political fortunes of the state made an about-face—Reconstruction ended, home rule began. Without demonstration from victor or vanquished, Wade Hampton, the Democratic governor, took possession of the State House. To the citizens of South Carolina, the events of that day seemed " like a quiet Sunday morning after a turmoil." [1]

Turmoil had marked the election of 1876, when the whites of South Carolina determined to regain political dominance in their state and joined together under the Democratic party banner to turn out the Republicans. Eight years of Republican control had united the thinking of white people; the sectionalism that had been so influential in state politics since the colonial period temporarily disappeared in the great effort to rid South Carolina of Radicalism. [2] Up countryman and low countryman, one-horse farmer and large planter, tenant farmer and merchant heeded the admonition of the Edgefield *Advertiser*: " Hang together like grim death. Let no side issues array you, one against the other." [3]

1. Edward L. Wells, *Hampton and Reconstruction* (Columbia: The State Company, 1907), pp. 197–98. There are numerous studies of unequal merit on South Carolina Reconstruction; a convenient introduction to them is Neill W. Macaulay, Jr., " South Carolina Reconstruction Historiography," *The South Carolina Historical Magazine*, LXV (1964), 20–32.

2. The most thorough study of South Carolina sectionalism is W. A. Schaper, " Sectionalism and Representation in South Carolina," *Annual Report of the American Historical Association* (1900), I, 237–463; also, see David Duncan Wallace, *The History of South Carolina* (New York: American Historical Society, Inc., 1934), II, 345–49, 480, and chap. lxxi; Harold S. Schultz, *Nationalism and Sectionalism in South Carolina, 1852–1860* (Durham: Duke University Press, 1950).

In dividing the state, I have followed Schaper's lead. The map in his " Sectionalism and Representation " (facing p. 245) divides the state into three sections. Occasionally his sectional lines fail to follow county lines; in such instances, to make different kinds of analyses feasible, I used county lines as sectional boundaries.

3. Edgefield *Advertiser*, July 18, 1878. Although written in 1878, these words accurately describe the conditions of 1876.

None did in the war against Republicanism—and war it was. The Democratic campaign resembled a military operation. Led by the former captains of the South's struggle for independence, the Democrats fought the election of 1876. Wade Hampton, the Democratic candidate for Governor, had been the state's highest-ranking Confederate officer. Lieutenant General Hampton's chief aides in 1876 were South Carolina's other major war leaders: Major Generals Matthew C. Butler and Joseph B. Kershaw and Brigadier Generals Martin W. Gary, John D. Kennedy, Johnson Hagood, James Conner, John Bratton, and Samuel McGowan. This similarity to a military campaign extended beyond the generals who directed the battle. Rifle clubs, local Democratic organizations normally commanded by the senior military man in each neighborhood, even had semi-official uniforms. Wearing red shirts instead of gray, the troops that had formed the ranks of South Carolina's Confederate regiments once again shouldered arms.

In this second war, the white citizens of South Carolina triumphed. Because of the fraud and intimidation undoubtedly practiced by both Republicans and Democrats in 1876, the legitimate winner will probably never be known. But the returns declared that Wade Hampton defeated Daniel Chamberlain, the Republican candidate, by 1,134 votes out of the 183,388 cast. Hampton proclaimed himself Governor, while Chamberlain, crying fraud, did the same. From November, 1876, to April, 1877, an uneasy truce marked the existence of the dual government. White public opinion in the state and the state Supreme Court supported the claims of Hampton and the Democrats; the United States Army defended the position of Chamberlain and the Republicans. Aware of the Army's primacy in the potentially explosive situation in the state, both sides courted Washington. Chamberlain told both Republican Presidents, Ulysses S. Grant and Rutherford B. Hayes, that he and the state party deserved the national administration's full support. Hampton, promising to maintain law and order and to protect both white and Negro citizens of the state, told Washington that he could not be responsible for preserving the peace should the Republican regime be maintained in power.[4] After conversations with Hampton and Chamberlain, Presi-

4. Francis Butler Simkins and Robert Hilliard Woody, *South Carolina during Reconstruction* (Chapel Hill: University of North Carolina Press, 1932), chap. xix, and Hampton M. Jarrell, *Wade Hampton and the Negro: the Road Not Taken* (Columbia: University of South Carolina Press, 1950), pp. 170–74.

dent Hayes decided to withdraw the Federal troops, and thus abandoned the Republican Chamberlain. His earnest desire to foster sectional reconciliation and his belief that Wade Hampton would maintain peace and order in South Carolina influenced the President's decision.

Standing over six feet tall and weighing over two hundred pounds General Wade Hampton, the third of his name in South Carolina, fitted the state's image of him as her matchless leader.[5] Said to be the richest man in the ante-bellum South, he had owned more than three thousand slaves and huge plantations in Louisiana, Mississippi, and South Carolina. At the outbreak of the Civil War, he organized and equipped his own regiment, the Hampton Legion. During that conflict, his ability and personal bravery raised him to Lieutenant General of Cavalry in the Confederate Army. During the war his agricultural empire collapsed; his mansion near Columbia was burned. By the end of 1868 Hampton, with personal debts of more than one million dollars, was forced to declare bankruptcy and to give up most of his land. In the year he led the Democrats to victory, he had been obliged to sell furniture and other personal property at a sheriff's auction.

Respect and admiration for Hampton existed with great unanimity throughout the state. Even when personally opposed to certain of the Governor's policies, most local politicians supported programs sponsored by the leader " they honor[ed] and love[d]." [6] " No opposition," reported the Newberry *Herald*, could stand against Governor Hampton, who was " beyond comparison; he towers far above every other man in the State in the love and admiration of the people." After the events of April, 1877, Governor Hampton proclaimed a day of thanksgiving dedicated to praising God for lifting " the Radical yoke." [7] Simultaneously, many gave thinks for Wade Hampton.

5. The biographical information in this sketch comes from Manly Wade Wellman, *Giant in Gray: Wade Hampton of South Carolina* (New York: Charles Scribner's Sons, 1949).

6. See, for example, a speech made by Thomas W. Woodward of Fairfield county quoted in William Arthur Sheppard, *Red Shirts Remembered: Southern Brigadiers of the Reconstruction Period* (Atlanta: Ruralist Press, Inc., 1940), p. 246. See also J. T. Lyon to R. R. Hemphill, May 7, 1877, Hemphill Family Papers, Duke University Library, cited hereafter as Duke. Lyon, judge of probate in Abbeville county, who opposed a certain Hampton program, said that if Hampton wanted it, " of course a small fry like myself can stand it."

7. Newberry *Herald*, April 3 and December 4, 1878; Charleston, *News and Courier*, May 25, 1877.

II

Even though the removal of Federal troops ended the Republican attempt to retain the governorship, the Republican party remained a potent force in South Carolina politics. Republicans retained control of the state Senate and the judiciary, and had a strong minority in the state House of Representatives. Because Negroes, who formed the bulk of the Republican party, outnumbered whites in the state, the Democrats faced the prospect of fighting a stronger enemy for state control.

To prevent internal bickering that might hamper the battle against Republicanism, the Democratic party decided to demand absolute unity from every Democrat in the legislature. Preparing for the special legislative session called by Governor Hampton on April 24, 1877, the cry of the Democrats became " draw tight the party lines." When former Governor Chamberlain advised the state Republican party to maintain its organization, the *News and Courier* warned the Democrats that failure " to oppose a solid front " to the Republicans meant that party would " retain a share of power and influence in State affairs." The Columbia *Daily Register* summoned the Democrats to " stand as one man, band of Spartans." House Speaker William H. Wallace declared that " caucus action is absolutely necessary for the preservation and protection of the party, and to secure the fruits of the campaign." When the Democratic legislators convened in Columbia the day before the legislature opened, they unanimously decided to abide by majority rule in a caucus, and then to act as a unit on the floor. That decision made, the Democrats stood " shoulder to shoulder " against the Republicans.[8]

Even though the Democrats controlled the state House of Representatives, they worked to eliminate as many Republicans as possible. When the special session began, the House had only 69 members— all but four Democrats—instead of the 124 directed by the state constitution. Because of the confusion and tension that followed the election of 1876, when the legislature met for its regular sessions in November, 1876, both Republicans and Democrats organized a separate House. Each House, then and now, carried the name of its Speaker: E. W. M. Mackey presided over the Republican House, while W. H. Wallace presided over the Democratic House. In its decisions validating Wade Hampton's claim to the governorship,

8. *News and Courier*, April 20, 1877; Columbia *Daily Register*, April 24, 1877.

the state Supreme Court, composed of three Republicans, had also declared the Wallace House to be the only legal House of Representatives.[9] Thus, when Governor Hampton issued the call for a special session in April, 1877, only 69 men could legally answer his summons.

When the Wallace House met on April 24, 1877, it required members of the Mackey House to appear before the bar of the House of Representatives, present their credentials, and take an oath that purged them of the contempt incurred for working against the legal House back in December, 1876.[10] The entire membership of the Mackey House, 55 Republicans, appeared; two resigned; one refused to take the contempt oath; two were expelled. When the Wallace House decided, because of irregularities on election day, to declare the 17 seats from Charleston county vacant, Democrats filled the empty seats. This maneuvering reduced Republican strength to 37 out of 124.[11]

The Democrats faced a more difficult situation in the state Senate. The election of 1876 had left the Republicans with a majority of three which they increased to six by using the same fraud argument as had the Democrats in the House, and by refusing to allow Democrats from Abbeville, Edgefield, and Laurens counties to take their seats. When the Senate met in April, 1877, Richard Gleaves, the Republican claimant to the Lieutenant Governor's chair, resigned to protest Hampton's being declared Governor.[12] Thereupon the Democrat William D. Simpson became the Senate's presiding officer and swore in four Democrats whose seats were being contested. By the end of the session, Republican resignations left each party fifteen members, with the tie-breaking vote belonging to Simpson, the Democratic lieutenant governor.[13] Between the adjournment of the special session in June and the opening of the regular session in November ten more Republican senators, including Stephen A. Swails, the president *pro tempore*, resigned.[14]

9. *State, ex. rel. Wallace* v. *Hayne and Mackey*, 8 South Carolina 367 (1876).
10. *News and Courier*, June 11, 1877.
11. The number is 37 rather than 33, because four Republicans had been in the Wallace House. Undoubtedly fraud had occurred in Charleston county because it had everywhere else. Yet in this instance, the action of the House was a Democratic device to reduce Republican strength.
12. *News and Courier*, April 25, 1877, and the *Journal of the Senate of the General Assembly of the State of South Carolina* (Special Session, 1877), pp. 5–6.
13. *News and Courier*, June 1, 1877.
14. *Ibid.*, November 28, 1877; *Senate Journal* (1877–78), p. 5; and *New York Times*, November 28, 1877.

Although when the regular session met in November the Republicans no longer contested Democratic supremacy, a possible battle for Speaker threatened Democratic unity. No Democrat opposed William H. Wallace of Union county, who had been Speaker of the House that bore his name and of the special session. But when he decided to stand for a vacant circuit judgeship, the speakership was thrown open. If, as traditionally, Charleston sponsored one of its own as a candidate, the old sectional conflict might arise again, because Wallace and other important up-country leaders supported the candidacy of John C. Sheppard, Wallace's son-in-law. In an attempt to ward off any sectional conflict, Sheppard, who was twenty-seven years old, went to Charleston to sound out the Democratic leaders there. His mission was successful. The Charleston leadership decided to back Sheppard. On December 6, the day after Wallace was elected a circuit judge, the Democratic caucus chose Sheppard as the new House Speaker.[15]

After securing the legislature, the Democrats turned their attention to the judiciary. While Republican judges sat in six of the state's eight judicial circuits, the Democrats could not feel that they had regained complete control of the state. Because the state constitution specified the length of a circuit judge's term, the legislature could not simply throw out the Republican judges, even though some of its most ardent members recommended that course.[16]

Blocked in the legislature, the Democrats turned to the courts. Bringing suit before the state Supreme Court against Judge A. J. Shaw of the Eighth Judicial Circuit, Attorney General James Conner asked the Court to invalidate the election of Shaw and five other judges chosen at the same time because, according to Conner, their election had not followed the procedures outlined in the state constitution. Judge Shaw's attorney countered that the state had no case because the General Assembly had followed the procedure prescribed by the constitution. The state Supreme Court disagreed. In a split decision, the Court voted along political lines and ruled that Shaw and his fellow judges must give up their positions.[17]

15. Charles H. Simonton to James Conner, November 1, 1877, and Francis Dawson to James Conner, November 28, 1877, both in the James Conner Papers, South Carolina Historical Society, cited hereafter as SCHS; News and Courier, December 6–7, 1877.

16. News and Courier, January 21–22, 1878.

17. Shaw v. State of South Carolina, 9 South Carolina 94 (1878). The two Democratic Associate Justices, Henry McIver and Alexander Haskell, decided in favor of the state; the Republican Chief Justice, Amiel Willard, dissented.

As soon as the state Supreme Court made its decision, the Democratic legislators caucused to name six new judges. They retained two Republicans: T. J. Mackey, who had supported Hampton in 1876, and A. J. Shaw, the defendant in the Democratic suit.[18] After this election the state courts had six Democratic and only two Republican judges, rather than six Republicans and only two Democrats.

III

Friendly relations with the Republican administration in Washington and with Northern public opinion in general became as necessary to Hampton's regime as the consolidation of Democratic control in South Carolina. To avert the return of troops, the Democrats made efforts to gain the trust and confidence of the North. Since the 1872 Liberal Republican movement, much of the respected opinion in the North advocated reconciliation with the South. Realizing that for Southerners any lasting reconciliation meant the return of responsible, native whites to political dominance, they demanded a Southern policy leading to that end. Echoing political groups, business and financial interests which felt that a growing economy could not reach its potential without the South also advocated the end of Radical rule in the section, because no investor wanted his capital in such an unstable region. By 1876, this combination of pressures rendered bankrupt any Southern policy requiring the support of Republican state governments with Federal troops.

Aware that their Southern program needed radical revision, the national Republican party had nominated Rutherford B. Hayes for the presidency. Hayes, who supported a moderate policy toward the South, deplored the passion generated by continuous appeals to memories of the war. He wanted to build a new Southern Republican party that would draw its leaders from moderate, conservative, and responsible men like himself. During his administration, Hayes hoped to see all sectional rancor buried forever; he tried to convince Southerners that they would be as safe with him in the White House as with his Democratic opponent, Samuel Tilden.[19]

18. *News and Courier*, February 14, 1878. Judge Shaw's election by acclamation reveals the political intent of the state's suit. On that point, see the remarks by the state Supreme Court reporter, a Republican. 9 South Carolina 94, n. 1.

19. Harry Barnard, *Rutherford B. Hayes and His America* (Indianapolis: The Bobbs-Merrill Company, Inc., 1954), p. 435; and Hayes's inaugural in James D. Richardson, *A Compilation of the Messages and Papers of the Presidents, 1789–1897* (Washington: U.S. Government Printing Office, 1898), VII, 442–47, esp. p. 444.

Governor Wade Hampton assiduously cultivated this rising Northern sympathy for the Southern white. He spoke often of his concern for justice, stable government, and Negro rights. Throughout the campaign of 1876 he admonished his followers to refrain from violence and intimidation. Although he by no means prevented all such practices, his efforts succeeded in limiting their extent. His moderating influence, even more apparent during the tense weeks between the state elections and the removal of Federal troops five months later, on at least one occasion prevented angry Democrats from assaulting Republicans in the state capitol.[20]

Hampton did more than work to maintain peace and order in his own state. Attempting to impress Hayes with his earnest wish for peace and good government, he told the Republican leader that South Carolina Democrats " condemn[ed] the exhibition of armed force " to right political wrongs. He assured President Hayes that removal of Federal troops from South Carolina would not result in chaos and violence but instead " would establish law, insure domestic tranquility, [and] revive our wasted industries." [21]

Hampton did not stop his endeavors on behalf of his regime and his state with letters defending his position. After a note of warmth had entered their relationship, Hampton told Hayes of the plans and plots of Hayes's Republican enemies.[22] When the President made his Southern tour in 1877 from Louisville through Atlanta to Virginia, Governor Hampton was a conspicuous member of his party. To enhance his image as a man of moderation not governed by partisan politics, Hampton appointed former Republican legislators to posts under the Democrats; he also forced his party to accept a Republican as Chief Justice of the Supreme Court.[23]

In turn, Hayes listened to Hampton's opinions on federal appointees in South Carolina. One disconsolate regular Republican complained, " It is understood in S. C. that no man [Republican] can get a place from this administration unless he gets the endorsement of the Democrats." [24] To fill the most sensitive federal position

20. Jarrell, *Hampton, passim*; Simkins and Woody, *Reconstruction*, chaps. xviii and xix.

21. Hampton to Hayes, December 28, 1876, and March 26, 1877, quoted in Jarrell, *Hampton*, pp. 170-171. All Hampton-Hayes correspondence, unless otherwise stated, comes from Jarrell, *Hampton*, Appendix C. Jarrell printed all of the letters between the two men held by the Hayes Memorial Library, Fremont, Ohio.

22. Hampton to Hayes, January 9, 1878, and Jarrell, *Hampton*, p. 133.

23. *Infra*, sec. II, chaps. ii and iii.

24. Statement of E. W. M. Mackey dated February 1, 1878, in the Lucius C.

in the state, U.S. District Attorney, Hayes appointed Lucius C. Northrop, a white native South Carolina Republican, who was acceptable to Hampton and other leading Democrats.[25] Regular Republicans in South Carolina resented the Northrop appointment and agreed with the *New York Times* in condemning the choice of Northrop as no more than a " gift " from Hayes to Hampton.[26]

Hampton's efforts to establish his administration firmly among Democrats and Republicans and his determination to present his state before the nation as a peaceful, law-abiding commonwealth led to a major political agreement with the Hayes administration. After the racial violence in South Carolina during the summer of 1876, the federal government decided to prosecute many of the whites, all Democrats, involved. This legal action, the Ellenton Cases, would adversely affect the image of a peaceful, moderate people Hampton had worked so hard to build. Moreover, if the government secured convictions, Hampton's regime might lose popular support. Cognizant of these unwanted possibilities, Hampton hoped to get Hayes to call off the prosecutions.

Because Conservative Democrats did not expect President Hayes to grant their request without recompense, they prepared to bargain with the Republican President. The 1876 Democratic campaign charges of venality in the Republican government resulted in appointment of a legislative committee to investigate the suspected Republican malfeasance. This commission, recommended by Governor Hampton and composed of both Democratic and Republican legislators, was directed to make a thorough investigation of governmental practices between 1868 and 1876 and to report to the legislature.[27] The committee's voluminous report, covering the four Republican state administrations, listed every conceivable excess, from expensive cuspidors for the legislators to rigged elections for the

Northrop Case (Sen. 45 B–A5), Nominations File, Records of the United States Senate, Record Group 46, National Archives, cited hereafter as NA.

25. Northrop to Hampton, November 15, 1877, Incoming Correspondence, Wade Hampton Papers, Executive File, South Carolina Archives, cited hereafter as SCA. Also, see Hampton to Hayes January 9, 1878. The prominent South Carolina Democrats who recommended Northrop included Lieutenant Governor Simpson, Attorney General Conner, Comptroller General Johnson Hagood, and Congressmen Michael P. O'Connor and John Evins. Lucius C. Northrop Case (Sen. 45 B–A5), Nominations File, Records of the United States Senate, Record Group 46, NA.

26. *New York Times*, October 12, 1877, and *supra*, n. 24.

27. *News and Courier*, April 27, 1877, and *Senate Journal* (Special Session, 1877), p. 10.

United States Senate.[28] Without doubt, a certain amount of fraud
and bribery existed in those eight years, but the Democrats had in
mind a more important purpose than listing Republican misdeeds.
"The moral evidence" of such a report, Attorney General James
Conner told Lieutenant Governor Simpson, "would politically
guillotine" the Republican party in South Carolina.[29] Both the
investigation and the report aimed mainly at political banishment
of South Carolina Republicans, but they also incriminated Republicans before the public opinion of state and nation.[30]

The threat of criminal prosecutions against Republicans indicted
because of the committee's findings gave the Hampton administration leverage to use for abandonment of the Ellenton Cases. Public
trials in state courts that exposed and magnified every wrong and
stupid act by Republicans might prove embarrassing to President
Hayes and his party on a national level. South Carolina Republicans
facing possible prosecution told the President that he could not
abandon them and pressed him to come to some agreement with the
Democrats.[31]

Governor Hampton broached to President Hayes on May 11,
1877, the suggestion that each side drop its case. Hampton informed
Hayes that the state Attorney General would *nolle prosequi* all
cases growing out of the Fraud Commission report, provided that
the President would invoke executive clemency " as the circumstances will warrant" for those Democrats being prosecuted.[32] On
the next day, Hayes wrote Hampton that the national government
intended to bring to trial " only three indictments in the Ellenton
Cases." As for " the parties in all other cases . . . they need not
prepare for trial." Although Hayes did not accept Hampton's
proposition in full, he did tell the Governor that " a general amnesty

28. *Reports and Resolutions of the General Assembly of the State of South
Carolina* (1877–78), pp. 629–94, 949–56, and 1013–1779.
29. James Conner to William Simpson, April 24, 1877, quoted in Joel Williamson,
After Slavery: The Negro in South Carolina during Reconstruction, 1861–1877 (Chapel
Hill: University of North Carolina Press, 1965), pp. 414–15.
30. *Ibid.*, and John S. Reynolds, *Reconstruction in South Carolina, 1865–1877*
(Columbia, S.C.: The State Co., Publishers, 1905), p. 463.
31. William E. Earle to Daniel T. Corbin [former Republican United States
Senator from South Carolina], March 9, 1878, and Northrop to Charles Devens,
April 11, 1879. Source Chronological File of the Justice Department, Record Group
60, NA.
32. Hampton to Hayes, May 11, 1877, and Hampton to Chief Justice Morrison
R. Waite, May 11, 1877, Morrison R. Waite Papers, Library of Congress cited
hereafter as LC; *Senate Journal* (Special Session, 1877), pp. 134–35.

should extend to all political offenses except those which are of the gravest character." [33]

Although they reached no final agreement in 1877, both sides proceeded cautiously until they reopened negotiations the following year. Armed with a new resolution from his legislature, Hampton wrote to Hayes in March, 1878, asking him to exercise " executive clemency in behalf of those who are charged with the violation of U.S. Laws " in return for the Democrats' halting their prosecution of Republicans.[34] This time the national administration showed even more interest, but Attorney General Charles Devens wanted first to learn the views of Chief Justice Morrison R. Waite who had presided over the trial of the Ellenton Cases in 1877,[35] on " the expediency of attempting to bring these cases again to trial." [36] Waite refused to express an opinion, " as the cases are still pending and may come before me again for trial." Undaunted, the Hayes administration tried again a few months later. Secretary of State William Evarts informed Waite that " the President would be very glad if you would find it not too inconvenient to be here [the White

33. Hayes to Hampton, May 12, 1877.
34. *Reports and Resolutions* (1877–78), pp. 1815–16, and Hampton to Hayes, March 25, 1878.
The only Democratic opposition to Governor Hampton's policy in this instance was headed by Martin Gary. But Gary convinced only three other Democratic senators to vote with him as the resolution passed the state Senate by 26 to 4 (all six Republican senators voted aye). *Senate Journal* (1877–78), p. 939. No division occurred in the House. *Journal of the House of Representatives of the General Assembly of the State of South Carolina* (1877–78), p. 751.
35. Chief Justice Waite traveled the Fourth Circuit, which included South Carolina. These cases had been first brought to trial in Charleston in May, 1877, with Chief Justice Waite presiding. Their trial ended in early June with a deadlocked jury. Negroes voted for conviction, whites voted for acquittal, and Waite declared a mistrial. C. Peter Magrath, *Morrison R. Waite: the Triumph of Character* (New York: The Macmillan Company, 1963), pp. 157–63, and the *News and Courier*, May 15–June 5, 1877.
36. Devens to Waite, March 11, 1878, Waite Papers, LC. By that date, another element undoubtedly influenced the Hayes administration. In the *Reese* and *Cruikshank* cases, the United States Supreme Court ruled that before any federal conviction could be obtained, the government had to prove that any disturbance, crime, or conspiracy had been motivated by racial considerations. For a discussion of the Court's action see Magrath, *Waite*, pp. 119–30. That requirement made it much more difficult for federal attorneys to obtain convictions; on April 23, 1879, Federal District Attorney Northrop wrote to his superior, Attorney General Charles Devens (in Source Chronological File of the Justice Department, Record Group 60, NA), a twenty-page letter outlining the problems *Reese* and *Cruikshank* had made for him. Also see Hugh L. Bond [a federal circuit judge who presided in South Carolina] to Waite, April 24, 1877, Waite Papers, LC.

House] for some little consideration of the prudent judicial hearing
of the questions arising in S. Carolina." In an effort to overcome
Waite's expressed unwillingness to comment on just those questions,
Evarts went on to say, "The shape in which this matter comes
up is little understood by the public, and the questions are (legally,
without reference to political or popular interests) delicate and
important." Apparently Waite declined this invitation, because later
President Hayes himself wrote the Chief Justice. Hayes must have
been convinced that Waite would not commit himself, for he asked
only for a copy of Waite's Ellenton charge, where the Chief Justice
had used the Supreme Court's reasoning in *Reese* and *Cruikshank*,
and told the jurors that to find the accused guilty "they had to
find an unlawful conspiracy to deprive Negroes of their federal
voting rights on account of race or color." [37]

After studying the charge, the administration prepared to come
to terms with Hampton. It asked the Democrats to give amnesty
to all Republicans indicted and to drop their prosecutions in turn
for continuance of the Ellenton Cases. The Democrats refused. [38]
Governor Hampton had told William Earle, a native white Republican, although he regretted that some of the state's criminal actions
had begun, he would pardon those already convicted and continue
the other cases if the federal government would continue the Ellenton Cases. [39] Finally in April, 1879, after Hampton, now a United
States Senator, had met with Hayes, they reached an agreement:
both the United States and South Carolina would continue all cases,
and the latter would pardon two important Republican leaders
already convicted. [40]

37. Waite to Devens, March 25, 1878; William Evarts to Waite, July 29, 1878;
Hayes to Waite, November 14, 1878, all in Waite Papers, LC; Magrath, *Waite*,
pp. 161–62.

38. Francis Dawson to Senator Matthew C. Butler, April 18, 1879, and Butler to
Dawson, April 20, 1879, both in Francis W. Dawson Papers, Duke.

39. Earle to Daniel Corbin, March 9, 1878, and Corbin to Devens, March 13,
1878, Source Chronological File of the Justice Department, Record Group 60, NA.
Also see Robert Aldrich [chairman of the judiciary committee of the South Carolina
House of Representatives] to Devens, April 24, 1878, *ibid.*, and Hampton to Hayes,
August 7, 1878, Hampton Letterbook 1877–78, Executive File, SCA.

40. The final terms are outlined in a memorandum dated April 17, 1879, in the
Dawson Papers at Duke. The final agreement was reached in a letter from James
Conner to Northrop, April 21, 1879, *ibid.*

For other pertinent evidence, see Michael P. O'Connor to Dawson, April 17, 1879,
ibid.; John C. Haskell [writing for Governor Simpson] to Hampton, April 17, 1879,
Simpson Letterbook I, Executive File, SCA; and Senator Butler to James Conner,
April 23, 1879, Conner Papers, SCHS.

IV

Hampton and the Conservative Democrats governed a state that had a constitution written and adopted by Republicans. Never during their thirteen years of power did the Conservative leadership seriously consider replacing that legacy of Reconstruction. In the basic political unit of the 1868 Constitution, the county,[41] voters elected most of their officers, such as sheriff, clerk of the Court of Common Pleas and General Sessions, and the probate judge, although certain other officials such as the treasurer and the trial justices received their appointments from the Governor.

Theoretically, those public servants governed their counties, but real power lay with the most important elected officials in the county —the legislative delegation. The county senator and the representatives controlled the appropriations allotted by the legislature for each county; moreover, the legislature practically never passed any law pertaining to the affairs of a county without the expressed approval of that county's delegation. In practice, in order to be considered, not to say passed, legislation affecting a county had to be introduced by one of the delegation.[42]

The legislature dominated the business of the state, just as its members directed affairs in their bailiwicks. All final decisions on appropriations were made by the General Assembly. The senators and representatives also had an influential voice in judicial affairs, for they chose both the Chief Justice and the two Associate Justices of the state Supreme Court, along with the circuit judges who presided over the lower state courts. The Governor did not have appointive powers for any members of the state bench, either in the circuit courts or in the Supreme Court.

The legislators had a check on the Governor's appointive powers. After 1882, the state Senate had to confirm the appointments of county treasurers and auditors; five years later, the senators gave themselves the same privilege with the office of trial justice.[43] In practice, their control over local appointments went farther than mere confirmation of a gubernatorial appointee. Governors from

41. The 1868 constitution (Art. 2, sec. 3) replaced the ante-bellum election districts with counties.
42. The 1868 Constitution gave each county one senator except for Charleston, which had two. South Carolina, *Constitution* (1868), Art. 2, sec. 8. For the general powers of the General Assembly, see *ibid.*, Art. 2.
43. South Carolina, *Statutes at Large*, XVII, 1007, and XIX, 818.

Hampton to John P. Richardson rarely appointed anyone who did not have the blessing of his county's delegation, especially of his senator. When problems arose with local appointments, the final arbiter was always the delegation. The Governor's office referred every applicant for a county position and every supporter of an application to the delegation. Governors hesitated to act contrary to the wishes of the county delegation, even at the expense of personal friendships and political considerations.[44]

Even so, the Governor of South Carolina occupied an important and prestigious position. Prior to 1865, men from the state's most prominent families sat in the Governor's chair.[45] When the Democrats triumphed with Wade Hampton in 1876, South Carolinians thought their state had returned to the polity of 1860, when the Governor often spoke for the state. The state's most prominent citizen, Wade Hampton, governor from 1876 to 1879, restored and even increased the reputation of that office. Although the legislature had more actual political power than the Governor, it rarely succeeded in speaking with one voice and never did an individual legislator have the prestige of the Governor. The governors of the Conservative era enjoyed more legal power than had their ante-bellum counterparts. The 1868 constitution gave the Governor the right of veto, which could only be overridden by a two-thirds vote of the legislature.[46] His message at the beginning of each legislative session often set the guidelines for the work of that body.

The Democratic party paralleled the state government in organization. Party structure rested in large part on the county level, although a statewide convention set general policy for the party. In one aspect, the existence of an important unit below the county level, party mechanics differed from those of the state government. The Democratic club, organized in each election precinct, brought

44. The Executive File in the SCA constitutes my major source for these generalizations on appointment policy and the relationship between legislators and the Governor's office. For specific examples, see Johnson Hagood to J. A. Sligh [Newberry county], and to J. Wilson [chairman, Newberry delegation], both on November 9, 1882, Hagood Letterbook D; Wade H. Manning [Governor Hampton's private secretary] to J. J. Hemphill [Chester county], October 4, 1877, Hampton Letterbook 1877–78; Hugh S. Thompson to W. A. Courtenay, December 13, 1882, Thompson Letterbook A; also see N. G. Gonzales to J. C. Hemphill, March 23, 1889, N. G. Gonzales Papers, South Caroliniana Library, University of South Carolina, cited hereafter as SCL.

45. Wallace, *South Carolina*, III, 495–500.

46. South Carolina, *Constitution* (1868), Art. 3, sec. 22.

the party into direct contact with the voter. On this local level, where everyone knew everyone else, membership in the party that—in their minds—had saved South Carolina in 1876 became mandatory for social acceptance. Every man knew whether his neighbor belonged to a club, and rolls of the several clubs in a county were published in the local newspaper.[47] No white man, who either occupied or desired to occupy a position of respectability in a community, wanted to create doubts of his enthusiasm for the Democrats, because party leaders were quick to brand anyone who even thought of leaving the Democratic party an enemy of the interests and honor of South Carolina. Republicans attempting to lure whites away from the Democrats testified to the success of the Conservative leadership in maintaining allegiance to their party. One Republican, writing to President Benjamin Harrison in 1889, commented on " the social ostracism that awaits [anyone] should they go into a movement against the Democratic Party." [48]

The major duties of the club included encouraging club members and other citizens to become active in the party and creating local interest in elections. The state party constitution required every club to have a committee on registration. Enrollment in a club normally included a public pledge to support all candidates and policies of the party; the club member was expected to support the financial needs of the party.[49] During an election canvass, the state constitution of the Democratic party required a club to meet frequently, and also suggested that an invited speaker address each meeting.[50]

Immediately above the club came the county convention, which directed the activities of the party in the county. This body was

47. The operations of a club can be observed in the Richland Democratic Club: Minutes and Scrapbook, 1876–80, SCL. Most local newspapers published club rolls, e.g., see the Newberry *Herald*, February and March, 1878.

48. J. H. Ostendorff to Benjamin Harrison, May 14, 1889; also Samuel Melton to E. W. Halford [in the White House] April 17, 1889, and L. Edwin Dudley to President Harrison, May 28, 1889, all in the Benjamin Harrison Papers, LC.

49. *Constitution of the Democratic Party of South Carolina* (1882), Art. 1. The pledge required of all joining a club in Georgetown county was typical: " I do hereby solemnly promise that as long as I shall remain a member of the ——— Club, I will vote for and support the regular Democratic nominees for County, State and Federal offices, and will do all in my power to promote the successful execution of all lawful measures proposed by said party." *Constitution of the Democratic Party of Georgetown County* (1886), Art. 2, in the Georgetown *Enquirer*, August 4, 1886; *Constitution of the Democratic Party of Spartanburg County* (1880), Art. 4, in the Spartanburg *Carolina Spartan*, June 2, 1880.

50. *Constitution of the Democratic Party of South Carolina* (1886), Art. 2.

composed of delegates elected by the clubs. Although the particulars
varied in different counties, most counties apportioned county convention delegates on the basis of the number of members in a club.
The state party constitution directed that county conventions " be
composed of delegates elected by the several local Clubs—one delegate for every Club, and an additional delegate for every twenty-five
(25) enrolled members," but the constitution allowed " the right
to each County Convention to enlarge or diminish the representation according to circumstances." [51] The constitution allowed the
counties wide discretion in their party matters. It empowered county
conventions to set their own rules of membership; a county convention could decide, through its credentials committee, on the legality
of a club where two or more groups contested for recognition. Each
county convention elected delegates to the state convention, discussed
the constitution of the county party, and elected an executive committee.[52]

This executive committee, usually made up of one member from
each club and headed by a chairman, spoke for the county Democratic
party between conventions.[53] The county convention was the supreme
body in a county; but because it met only in election years, the
executive committee really dominated party activities. The chairman,
the chief party officer in the county, was chosen by the committee
itself. Like the committee as a whole, the chairman served a two-
year term but could be re-elected and sometimes was; each convention chose a new executive committee. Responsible for the health
of the party in the county, the executive committee accomplished its
main work in preparing for each electoral campaign. In this effort
the county committee worked closely with the state Executive Com-

51. *Ibid.* (1877), Art. 5. County practices reveal a variety of rules. In Georgetown
county, each club was allotted one delegate outright, and others for each ten enrolled
members. *Constitution of the Democratic Party of Georgetown* (1886), Art. 3, in
Georgetown *Enquirer*, August 4, 1886. The Spartanburg county Democrats decided to
base club representation in the county convention " upon the Democratic voting
strength " exhibited by each club in the previous election. *Constitution of the Democratic Party of Spartanburg County* (1880), Art. 7, in Spartanburg *Carolina Spartan*,
June 2, 1880. Anderson county, however, followed exactly the provisions in the
state constitution. Anderson *Intelligencer*, May 30, 1878.

52. *Constitution of the Democratic Party of South Carolina* (1882), Arts. 4 and 5;
for county constitutions which detail county authority, see the constitutions of Spartanburg and Georgetown cited above.

53. See the Georgetown (Art. 10) and Spartanburg (Art. 2) constitutions cited
above.

mittee to ensure the harmony of the county with the plans of the state party.

The state Democratic convention, the supreme body in the party, met twice in each election year.[54] Delegates to the state convention came " from each county in the numerical proportion to which that county is entitled in both branches of the General Assembly." [55] The spring meeting made rules for the coming general election, and the summer convention nominated a ticket for the state officers. The state convention had three primary tasks: the nomination of state officers; the amending of the party constitution; [56] the election of a state executive committee.

Just as county executive committees spoke for the party in the counties, the state Executive Committee directed party affairs on the state level. The state party constitution directed that " the State Executive Committee shall be composed of three from each Congressional District." [57] Delegates from each district nominated the candidates from that district, who were then elected by the convention. Once elected, the Executive Committee selected its own chairman and other officers. The party constitution authorized the state Executive Committee " to call a Convention of the Democratic party of the State at such time and place as it may designate; and . . . charged [it] with the execution and direction of the policy of the party in tthe State." [58] Subject only to the state party constitution and an expressed wish of a state convention, the state Executive Committee directed party affairs.

Conventions, executive committees, and constitutions worked toward one goal, the election of loyal Democrats to all offices from the county level to Governor. Just as important as the election of

54. Two conventions—the judicial circuit and the Congressional district—did come between the county and state conventions, but they met only to nominate candidates for solicitor and for Congress. Delegates to both were elected by the county conventions.

55. *Constitution of the Democratic Party of South Carolina* (1886), Art. 7. Normally, each county received twice as many delegates as it had members in its legislative delegation.

56. At different times I have quoted from different party constitutions; although a new one was written every two years, each one tended to be an exact duplication of its predecessor.

57. *Constitution of the Democratic Party of South Carolina* (1882), Art. 9. In addition, the state representative on the Democratic National Committee automatically had a seat on the state Executive Committee.

58. *Ibid.*, Arts. 9–11.

Democrats was the method by which any Democrat became the party's candidate for any office, because nomination by the Democratic party meant, in most cases, election.

The state party constitution directed the county convention to regulate "the mode and manner of nominating candidates for county officers." [59] The counties used two different methods of choosing men to represent the party in the general election. The traditional, and initially most widespread, practice was for the county convention to choose the nominees. Most party leaders felt that a choice in a convention of party regulars ensured solidarity and a minimum of hostile feeling in the ranks. Any nomination made outside the party convention increased the possibility of independent candidacies and of desertions from the party.[60]

Quite early, however, appeared a new technique that later replaced the convention system. In 1876, Pickens county used the primary to choose Democratic candidates for county offices. By 1878, newspapers across the state cried for the primary.[61] State party leaders raised no objections. The state Executive Committee, "impressed with the importance of the system of Primary elections . . . as thereby tending to unify and harmonize the party throughout the State," recommended in April, 1878, to each county chairman that his county adopt the new system.[62] Counties tended to follow the advice of the state Executive Committee, and by 1880, twenty out of the thirty-three counties used the primary. By 1888, all but two of the state's thirty-four counties employed primary elections in local contests.[63] A dual system of choosing local officials had little effect on party policy or harmony. The party leadership had decided to leave the question with the counties, and there it remained. Prior to

59. *Constitution of the Democratic Party of South Carolina* (1886), Art. 6.
60. *Daily Register*, April 5, 1878; Anderson *Intelligencer*, May 2, 1878; Port Royal *Palmetto Post*, June 22, 1882.
61. Winnsboro *News and Herald*, May 15, 1878; Newberry *Herald*, May 1, 1878; Spartanburg *Herald*, April 17, 1878; *News and Courier*, May 2, 1878.
62. A copy of the state Executive Committee's circular is in the James A. Hoyt Papers, SCL.
63. For this information and for other general comments on the history of primaries in South Carolina, I am indebted to Mr. Frank E. Jordan, Jr., of Columbia, South Carolina. Mr. Jordan gave me access to his unpublished manuscript on the development of primaries.

Copies of primary regulations for different countries can be seen in the Kingstree *Williamsburg Herald*, August 31, 1882; the Sumter *Watchman*, September 5, 1878; the *Daily Register*, August 3, 1880.

1886, no individual or group attempted to make any kind of political issue on a statewide level over primaries.[64]

V

The Conservatives who redeemed South Carolina from the Republicans strove to restore the ante-bellum commonwealth that had nurtured them. Describing the state in 1880, Edward Hogan found " a pervading air of age about the towns . . . Decay seems to be hovering in the atmosphere. The true South Carolinian lives in the past." [65]

Most of the leaders of the Conservative Democratic party were older men, intimately tied to the South Carolina that had existed prior to the Civil War.[66] Born and raised either on plantations or in professional surroundings, they reached maturity before 1860 and imbibed the ebullient, heady confidence that then reigned in South Carolina and throughout the South.[67] Over 85 per cent of them attended college in their native state before 1860,[68] when the educational institutions imparted a pervasive and overpowering Southern nationalism. When the future Conservative leaders thought that they saw their civilization threatened, they took up arms and led the fight for its preservation.[69] For them, that effort remained sacred and inviolate; it became, in the words of Robert Penn Warren, " a city of the Soul." [70]

The bleak years following Appomattox offered them little. Consequently, they looked back and praised the glory and heritage of the past—their vision intensified and magnified by the bitter experiences of military defeat and Reconstruction. Their political thinking was " built upon the foundation of the old [pre-war South Carolina] and perpetuate[d] all that was fundamental and essential in the

---

64. *Infra*, chap. vi.

65. Edward Hogan, " South Carolina To-Day," *The International Review*, VIII (February, 1880), 117.

66. For the leaders and methods of selection, see Appendix A. The average Conservative leader (data on 100 per cent) in 1890 was 55.19 years old; in fact almost one-third—32.6 per cent—were at least 60 years of age. Only four were under 45. For a similar analysis of the leaders of the Tillman movement, see below chap. vi, sec. V.

67. Appendix A, Table I.

68. *Ibid.*, Table VI.

69. *Ibid.*, Table IV.

70. Robert Penn Warren, *The Legacy of the Civil War* (New York: Random House, 1961), p. 14.

old." [71] Few speeches or formal messages omitted a eulogy of the past.[72] Appeals to that past served both as a defense against critics and as a platform for political success.[73] Largely removed from first-hand acquaintance with agricultural depression, the major economic problem faced by the state in the 1880s,[74] the Conservatives attempted to re-create what they considered the foundations of ante-bellum South Carolina—an economy-minded government ruled by whites and buttressed by a state-supported institution of higher learning devoted to instilling the ideals of the past into the future generations.

South Carolina College, pride of ante-bellum South Carolina and of the Conservative Democrats, had a checkered history in the years following Appomattox.[75] The first Reconstruction government composed of native whites supported the College and attempted to keep the school open for whites. The Republican government at first maintained an uneasy truce with the College. In fact, the Republicans provided more liberal financial support than had the native regime; moreover, the Republican-controlled legislature allowed the College officials to conduct the teaching and administration with relatively little interference. Even so, attendance remained poor because the state's whites feared a Republican take-over or, to them even worse, the admission of Negro students. Those fears became reality in 1873 when the Republicans decided to assume total control of the school. They fired old teachers and admitted Negro students. For the next four years, the University of South Carolina represented everything its loyal native supporters detested. Yet they did not cast off their veneration for their school; rather, they determined to set it aright as soon as they regained control of the state.

71. Edward McCrady described the political philosophy of his father, the prominent Conservative legislator of the same name, to Yates Snowden, August 28, 1916, Yates Snowden Papers, SCL.

72. *Daily Register*, August 6, 1886, and *Address of Hon. M. C. Butler at the Laying of the Corner-Stone of the Confederate Monument at Orangeburg, S. C., on the 12th Day of April, 1892* (Orangeburg, S. C.: *Times and Democrat* Job Print, 1892).

73. *News and Courier*, December 2, 1882; *New York Times*, January 28, 1889; William Watts Ball, *The State that Forgot: South Carolina's Surrender to Democracy* (Indianapolis: Bobbs-Merrill Company: 1932), p. 170. Cf. William B. Hesseltine, *Confederate Leaders in the New South* (Baton Rouge: Louisiana State University Press, 1950), chaps. i and iii.

74. *Infra*, chap. iv; Appendix A, Table II.

75. The following historical sketch is based on Daniel Walker Hollis's excellent *College to University*, Vol. II: *University of South Carolina* (Columbia: University of South Carolina Press, 1951 and 1956), chaps. ii-iv.

Once the Democrats gained power, the University's partisans quickly acted to close down the Republican-dominated school. The entire Democratic party consented. In June, 1877, the General Assembly passed a joint resolution directing Governor Hampton to take charge of the University's property; at the same session, the legislature appropriated only $1,500 to the University for the fiscal year beginning November 1, 1876.[76] Thus, in the autumn of 1877, the school could not open.

Although the Radical University no longer existed, the efforts to reorganize the University and reopen it under white native control encountered fierce opposition. When a bill to provide for the organization of a state university came before the General Assembly, it exposed the extent and source of the opposition. Benjamin F. Perry, a trustee, informed Governor Hampton that he opposed reopening the University.[77] It would be cheaper, Perry argued, for the state to pay all expenses of would-be university students at schools outside the state rather than to re-establish the University of South Carolina on a proper foundation.

Although the state Senate granted far from unanimous support for reopening the University, the House witnessed the main legislative battle.[78] Led by R. R. Hemphill of Abbeville county, enemies of the University bill asserted that the existence of denominational colleges made a state institution unnecessary. Hemphill considered it unfair to tax denominational people for a college they had no intention of using. One of his associates adopted " the broad ground that a State has no right to tax its citizens for professional or higher education." The strength of the friends of Erskine College, Wofford College, and Furman University almost succeeded in preventing passage of the University bill.[79]

After hard fights in 1878 and 1879, the legislature passed the measure reorganizing the University of South Carolina.[80] The South

---

76. *Statutes at Large*, XVI, 314, and 256-57; *Senate Journal* (Special Session, 1877), p. 25.

77. *Daily Register*, January 25, 1878; Perry to Hampton, December 3, 1877, Benjamin F. Perry Papers, SCL.

78. *Senate Journal* (1877-78), pp. 574-75; *News and Courier*, January 30, 1878.

79. *Daily Register*, January 25, 1878; *News and Courier*, January 28, 1878; William Grier [President of Erskine College] to Hemphill, February 1, 1878, Hemphill Family Papers, Duke; Hollis, *College to University*, p. 86.

80. The University of South Carolina was reorganized with two branches: South Carolina College in Columbia for whites, and Claflin College in Orangeburg for

Carolina College of Agriculture and Mechanics, the branch for whites, opened its doors in Columbia on October 5, 1880. Initially, the College of Agriculture and Mechanics had an appropriation of only $2,100, but in that form, the College had a short life. By 1882, with an appropriation of $12,500, the trustees re-established what they had wanted all along—the old South Carolina College with a literary and classical curriculum.[81]

At the same time the General Assembly increased the University's appropriations it provided for a sister institution. The South Carolina Military Academy, the Citadel, like South Carolina College had ante-bellum origins. Founded in 1842 when talk of nullification and secession pervaded the state, it supplied officers for the South Carolina militia and the state arsenals.[82] The United States government occupied the Citadel from 1865 to 1881; when it returned the physical plant to the state, Governor Johnson Hagood, an alumnus, informed the legislature that it was " now practicable to re-open this school, and it should be done." The college needed Hagood's prestige and insistence, for the Citadel bill met opposition as determined as that faced earlier by the University. It passed the state Senate only with the vote of Lieutenant Governor John Kennedy, a graduate of South Carolina College.[83]

The enemies of South Carolina College and the Citadel did not vanish after 1882. Increased appropriations never got through the legislature with ease, but serious opposition to the institutions did not arise until the advent of Benjamin Tillman. Initially, Tillman called for the abolition of the Citadel and consistently spoke out against South Carolina College, which suffered when he gained

---

Negroes. Embracing both white and Negro colleges, the University retained the same name throughout the period. But the white branch in Columbia had three different names:

South Carolina Agricultural and Mechanical College—1880
South Carolina College—1882
University of South Carolina—1888.

81. Hollis argues that even in the Agricultural and Mechanical College " it does not appear that the chief interest of faculty and students was in the field of agriculture of mechanics." Hollis, *College to University*, p. 96.

82. When war did come in 1861, graduates of the Citadel filled the role envisioned for them. Of the 226 alumni living at the outbreak of the Civil War, more than 200 became officers in the Confederate States Army. South Carolina, State Board of Agriculture, *South Carolina, Resources and Population, Institutions and Industries*, ed. Harry Hammond (Charleston: Walker, Evans and Cogswell Printers, 1883), p. 509.

83. *Senate Journal* (1881), pp. 26-27; *News and Courier*, January 14, 16, 18, and 21, 1882.

power. Conscious of Tillman's intentions, dedicated College alumni allowed sentiments for their alma mater to influence even their political battles.[84]

The greatest contribution of South Carolina College between the years 1877 and 1890 lay in its influence on alumni. A roll call of Conservative leaders read like the roster of the University's alumni association. Vice-presidents of that group included W. D. Simpson and Henry McIver, members of the state Supreme Court, and Charles H. Simonton and Fitz-William McMaster, leaders of the legislature.[85] Another vice-president, General John Bratton, summed up the importance of the College to its alumni when he called it " the cornerstone of our *system*." [86] Charles H. Simonton, a Charleston attorney, member of the Board of Trustees, and architect of the policy that re-established the College, outlined the essentials of that system. In offering the presidency of the College (in 1877) to William Porcher Miles, a former South Carolina congressman, Simonton spoke of the necessity of getting a reorganized College that would impart " our . . . notions of personal honor and truth." The years that the College had been closed or had operated under alien direction disturbed Simonton. He went on to tell Miles that " the war and the events since the war have demoralized our people. A whole generation has grown up uneducated. The honor and name of the State are to them but a dream of their fathers." The College, according to Simonton, would resurrect that conception, and if it failed

84. *Infra*, chap. v.
85. Hollis, *College to University*, p. 99. Of the 34 different Democrats who held the following positions in the Conservative Democratic party, 58.2 per cent were alumni of South Carolina College. The addition of Citadel alumni brings the total to 67.6 per cent.
    Positions:
      United States Senator
      United States Congressman
      Governor
      Lieutenant Governor
      Speaker of the state House of Representatives
      President *pro tempore* of the state Senate
      Member of the state Supreme Court
      Federal District Judge for South Carolina
      Chairman, state Democratic Executive Committee
For a complete and detailed discussion of South Carolina College, see Daniel Walker Hollis's *South Carolina College,* Vol. 1: *University of South Carolina* (Columbia: University of South Carolina Press, 1951 and 1956), *passim*. My brief treatment of the ante-bellum institution is based on Professor Hollis's exemplary volume.
86. Bratton to J. L. Weber, April 11, 1891, Yates Snowden Papers, SCL.

the regime would fail with it. Understanding Simonton's fears, Miles wrote that he wanted to assist " in building up once more the old South Carolina College." [87]

The old South Carolina College had been a liberal arts school that taught its students more than classics, literature, and history. It developed a fierce pride in state and section, while it dwelt on the futility of man's attempting to tamper with society. It emphasized the honor of the State of South Carolina, and impressed upon its students their good fortune in living in that commonwealth. The College supported the aristocratic nature of ante-bellum South Carolina although it did not demand pedigrees or wealth as entrance requirements.[88] The true worth of the College to the ante-bellum planters, a truth Simonton recognized in 1877, was its ability to take a poor man with no family connections and inculcate in him the values and myths of the state's conservative leadership—whether in 1860 or 1880.

The leaders of the Conservative Democratic party believed, and with some reason, that without the College as the dominant force in education in the state, their system of honor and conservatism might succumb. Only their loyalty to ante-bellum South Carolina College and their hope for its continued service to their values can explain their fervent devotion to their alma mater.

87. Simonton to Miles, May 25, 1877, and Miles to Simonton, August 11, 1877, both in William Porcher Miles Papers, Southern Historical Collection, University of North Carolina.

88. This fact remained true in the Conservative College. The only cost prior to 1886, when a tuition fee of $40.00 per year was set, was a $10.00 per year student fee. Even after 1886, the College was allowed to remit fees to any deserving student who could not make the required payments. Hollis, *College to University*, pp. 106, 141.

The Citadel had a system of beneficiary cadets whereby the state paid the fees for two cadets from each county in each class. This policy remained in effect, with minor changes, from 1882 to 1890. *Ibid.*, p. 101, and *Statutes at Large*, XVIII, 728.

CHAPTER II

THE STRUGGLE FOR UNITY

I

While Conservatives struggled to eliminate Republican influence in the state government, a Republican policy evoked the first issue to endanger Democratic solidarity. Although the Democrats accused the Republican party of corruption and fraudulent actions designed to wreck the credit of the state, the Republicans themselves had recognized the dangerous condition of the state's credit and, three years prior to the campaign of 1876, the Republican state legislature had passed the Consolidation Act of 1873, which repudiated certain portions of the state debt and provided for the funding of the remaining valid portions.[1] This legislation, which supposedly settled the debt question in South Carolina, again in 1876 became an issue. Pledging to honor their commitments of 1873, the Republicans called their Democratic opponents "repudiators." To an apprehensive North, they predicted that the Democratic victors would declare all Reconstruction bonds null and void.

Keenly attuned to Northern opinion, the Democratic state Executive Committee announced in October that it "consider[ed] the adjustment [of 1873] as final, and pledge[d] the party to abide by it."[2] During the tense months of dual government, the Democrats sensed a need to reassure Northern financial interests that Democratic control in South Carolina would not make the bonds they held worthless. The Wallace House resolved: "That in order to correct understanding of our objects and purposes by all the people, it is proper that we should, and hereby do, reiterate, in good faith, our

1. South Carolina, *Statutes at Large*, XV, 518–23. Also, see Francis Butler Simkins and Robert Hilliard Woody, *South Carolina during Reconstruction* (Chapel Hill: University of North Carolina Press, 1932), pp. 165–67, and B. U. Ratchford, *American State Debts* (Durham: Duke University Press, 1941), pp. 185–86. The act declared the entire state bonded debt to be $15,851,625; it repudiated $5,965,000, and funded the remaining $9,886,625 at 50¢ on the dollar in new 6 per cent consolidated bonds.
2. Columbia *Daily Register*, May 17, 1877.

45

pledge to redeem, at the earliest practicable moment, the credit of the State, by the payment of the matured interest on the valid, legal and recognized bonded indebtedness of the State as now provided for by law." [3] At the same time, the newly elected Democratic United States Senator Matthew C. Butler, whose seat was being contested by Daniel T. Corbin (chosen by the Mackey House and the Republican senators), worked in New York City to assure Northern financiers that the Conservative Democrats would not repudiate the debt.[4]

Recognizing that the average South Carolinian had grave doubts about the state debt, even though the statements of the Executive Committee and the Wallace House seemingly placed the party on record, Governor Hampton asked the legislature in April, 1877, to study the debt question. The legislators then created a commission to investigate the debt because, according to the joint resolution, " of the great uncertainty that exists in the minds of the property owners and taxpaying portion of our people." [5]

The commission had little opposition,[6] but the divided feelings on the debt problem erupted on the question of meeting the summer interest payments. Led by Martin Gary of Edgefield county, state Senate advocates of repudiation argued that passage might set a precedent for accepting the Reconstruction debt without question; they eliminated from the supply bill passed by the House the section appropriating $270,000 to meet interest payments. Gary articulated the feeling of certain up countrymen that " the people of upper Carolina are bitterly hostile to any compromise on the debt question." Initially, conference committee attempts to compromise failed; finally, a second conference committee agreed that the summer interest would be paid only on that portion of the public debt found valid by the bond committee.[7]

Between the special legislative session that ended in June, 1877,

3. *Ibid.*

4. A memorandum dated September 21, 1877, and written by Francis Dawson in the Francis Dawson Papers in the Duke University Library (cited hereafter as Duke) notes Butler's work.

5. Charleston *News and Courier*, April 27, 1877; *Statutes at Large*, XVI, 318–20.

6. The House passed the resolution by more than three to one. *News and Courier*, May 19, 1877.

7. *Ibid.*, May 26, 28, 30, and 31 and June 1–2, 5–6, 1877. The quotation is taken from a letter written by R. R. Hemphill and J. C. Hemphill to Sen. [Richard G.] Howard (Marion county), July 23, 1877, Hemphill Family Papers, Duke.

and the opening of the regular session the following November, Hampton labored for an equitable settlement. In an interview in the *New York Herald*, he reassured the North that the Conservative Democrats would meet the state's obligation. Back in his own state, Governor Hampton told a Darlington audience, "You must remember that we have the honor of the State in our hands, and her just debts must be paid. *We mean to put the credit of the State where it was before the war.*" To the legislature due to receive the bond committee's report, he reiterated that the credit of the state must be " restored to, and maintained at, its ancient high character." To achieve that goal " under no circumstances [could] repudiation, direct or indirect be entertained," because " repudiation would bring inevitable disaster and entail indelible disgrace." [8]

Administration supporters joined the Governor's campaign. Leaving considerations of state honor to Hampton, the Charleston *Journal of Commerce* declared that if the North feared repudiation, it might decide " to cripple our newly won independence." Following suit, the Spartanburg *Herald* denied that the regime could afford to have " even the imputation of repudiation cast upon [it]." To the *News and Courier*, possible consequences of Democratic double-dealing were too grim to consider; to editor Francis Dawson, " the financial good faith of South Carolina " might spell the difference between the success or failure of the Democratic party.[9]

Submission of the bond committee's report in February, 1878, renewed the battle.[10] The committee, contrary to expectations, did not accept as valid all the bonds covered in the Consolidation Act of 1873. Prior to the committee's report, all who opposed outright repudiation had joined together to denounce the very few who advocated throwing out all the state debt, at least all contracted between 1868 and 1876. But when the committee recommended that the legislature declare $3,608,717 of the consolidation debt illegal and void, the alliance broke down. Speaking for those who advocated assumption of the entire debt under the act of 1873, the *News and Courier* found " no pretext for violating the Consolidation Act."

8. The *News and Courier* reprinted the interview on June 26, 1877; *ibid.*, November 5 and 29, 1877.

9. Charleston *Journal of Commerce*, January 10, 1878; Spartanburg *Herald*, September 19, 1877; *News and Courier*, February 12, 1878, and June 6, 1877.

10. *Reports and Resolutions of the General Assembly of the State of South Carolina* (1877–78), pp. 859–948.

Representative J. J. Hemphill of Chester county told the House that the Democratic party, which had agreed in 1876 to uphold the Consolidation Act, must uphold its "obligations and pledges." But James Callison of Edgefield countered that those actions in 1876 amounted to no more than expediency. The committee's supporters called the 1873 legislation "a cheat and a fraud." [11]

After weeks of debate, legislators realized that neither the committee's report nor the Consolidation Act could command majority support.[12] Probing for a compromise, certain legislators looked to a judicial solution.[13] Led by Charles H. Simonton of Charleston county, they proposed that the legislature create a special Bond Court, composed of three circuit judges, to "hear and determine any case or cases made up or brought to test the validity" of any item in the bond committee's report. Even so, this court did not stand as the final arbiter; Simonton's resolution provided for appeal to the state Supreme Court and on to the United States Supreme Court. To expedite the Bond Court's work, the Attorney General was authorized to draw test cases making the state the defendant.[14] Simonton's plan, satisfactory to most Democrats, passed the House by a comfortable margin; the Senate agreed without a division.[15]

When the legislators went home in March, 1878, they thought the vexing debt problem had been removed from politics; but

11. *Ibid.*, p. 867; *News and Courier*, February 9, 28 and March 1, 1878; Winnsboro *News and Herald*, January 23, 1878, and Edgefield *Advertiser*, February 21, 1878.

12. Martin Gary wrote a friend that "the vote on the bond question will be a close one." Gary felt that most Democrats opposed paying the debt just as he did, but that the remaining Democrats would join the Republicans and push acceptance through the legislature. Gary to Hugh Farley, February 28, 1878, Martin W. Gary Papers, South Caroliniana Library, University of South Carolina; cited hereafter as SCL.

Professor David D. Wallace in his *History of South Carolina* (New York: American Historical Society, Inc., 1934), III, 327, argued that Charleston interests and Republicans combined to prevent adoption of the committee's report. But a close study of both the state House and Senate journals failed to reveal any such combination. Charleston would have needed considerably more help than the few Republicans in the legislature could provide to defeat any measure desired by most Democrats.

13. *News and Courier*, February 28 and March 1, 2, 4, 6, 7, 9, 11, and 13, 1878.

14. *Ibid.*, March 13, 1878; *Journal of the House of Representatives of the General Assembly of the State of South Carolina* (1877–78), pp. 653–56; *Statutes at Large*, XVI, 669–73.

15. The House vote was 56 to 36; in the minority were 30 Republicans and only 6 Democrats, each one from a different county. *House Journal* (1877–78), p. 657, and *Journal of the Senate of the General Assembly of South Carolina* (1877–78), pp. 885 and 942; William Arthur Sheppard, *Red Shirts Remembered: Southern Brigadiers of the Reconstruction Period* (Atlanta: Ruralist Press, 1940), p. 271.

dissension reappeared. One final time at the opening of the legislature in November, 1878, the small group of outright repudiators attempted to throw out all the debt by repealing the Simonton resolution. Up to this point, these men led by Senator Gary had been relatively quiet. In the debates over the bond committee's report, they had concealed their real feelings by joining the substantial number of Democrats who supported the report. Now they stood alone and in the open.[16] Senator Gary attacked Governor Hampton and the *News and Courier* for favoring " the bloated bond holders." Accusing Hampton of using threats to silence all opposition to the settlement of the previous March, Gary proceeded to " open the vials of his wrath " upon everyone from senators and governors to legislators who favored paying the debt.[17] The vote on Gary's motion to reopen the entire debt question revealed the real weakness of the outright repudiators, for only five other Democrats joined Gary.[18]

After Gary's failure in December, 1878, no one else attempted to interrupt the judicial proceedings on the public debt. Declaring certain bonds in the 1873 settlement void because of improper issue, a divided Bond Court followed the general outlines of the bond committee's report in its decisions.[19] Immediately, the appellants appealed to the state Supreme Court. That Court's decision in September, 1879 upheld the opinion of the Bond Court.[20] The

16. The state House Ways and Means committee reported unfavorably a resolution to reopen the question by repealing the Simonton resolution. *News and Courier*, December 5, 1878.

17. *Ibid.*, December 7, 1878. Gary consistently opposed accepting the debt, but there is evidence in his papers in the SCL that, at the same time, he was involved in transactions involving state bonds. See esp. Philip L. Cohen [of John J. Cohen and Sons, Brokers, in Augusta, Georgia] to Gary, December 7, 1878, Gary Papers, SCL. He had also urged (back in 1871 at the Taxpayers' Convention) that the debt be declared valid. Joel Williamson, *After Slavery: The Negro in South Carolina during Reconstruction, 1861–1877.* (Chapel Hill: University of North Carolina Press, 1965), p. 384.

My research has uncovered no evidence to support the broad generalization made by Williamson in his *After Slavery*, p. 384, that a bond ring " was eminently successful " in 1877 and 1878; Williamson himself cites no evidence for his statement. Of course, I assume that in using the term " bond ring " Williamson is referring to corrupt, underhand dealings rather than merely the people who favored validating the debt.

18. *Senate Journal* (1878), p. 6. The vote was 19 to 10; the four Republican senators joined Gary.

19. *House Journal* (1877–78), p. 781. For the Bond Court's decision in December, 1878, see 12 South Carolina 212.

20. For the Supreme Court's decision, see 12 South Carolina 263 (1879). Chief Justice Willard supported McIver's opinion, but Associate Justice Alexander Haskell dissented.

opinion of the Supreme Court written by Associate Justice Henry McIver declared consolidated bonds invalid if they represented bonds that were in any way illegal or unconstitutional prior to the Consolidation Act of 1873. The Court further directed the legislature to create a commission that would examine every consolidated bond to determine the extent of its illegality, if any. After the commission had performed its task, bondholders were required to exchange their consolidated bonds for new ones; the new bonds excluded that portion of the debt—$1,126,173—declared void by the commission using the guidelines set by the state Supreme Court.[21]

The Supreme Court's decision satisfied all parties. Praising Justice McIver's opinion, the Columbia *Daily Register* pronounced the death of the debt controversy. Even Gary, the chief spokesman for repudiation, decided to hold his peace; he told a political friend, " I have made up my mind not to agitate the debt issue any further." Recounting the bitterness and hostility caused among Democrats by the bond question, the *News and Courier* rejoiced at the general acquiescence in the Court's solution to " an agitating discussion." [22]

II

The death—in March, 1877—of Franklin J. Moses, Sr., Chief Justice of the South Carolina Supreme Court, offered Hampton another opportunity to increase the good feelings between Columbia and Washington. Hampton preferred for the post the Court's senior Associate Justice, Amiel J. Willard, a white Republican.[23] Willard, a New Yorker, had come to South Carolina as an officer in a Negro regiment. Remaining after the war, he joined the Republican party and in 1868 was placed on the supreme bench. Even though a Republican, Willard in 1876 had stanchly supported the Democratic claims that they, not the Republicans, represented the legitimate government.[24]

Although Willard's performance had pleased the Democratic party, most South Carolina Democrats wanted in the state's highest judicial post one of their own, not a carpetbagger.[25] An Abbeville

21. *Statutes at Large*, XVII, 104–7; Ratchford, *State Debts*, p. 186.
22. *Daily Register*, September 30, 1879; Gary to Blake L. White, April 3, 1880, Gary Papers, SCL; *News and Courier*, January 5, 1880.
23. *Daily Register*, May 16, 1877.
24. *Ex Parte Norris*, 8 South Carolina 408 (1876).
25. Cf. Anderson *Intelligencer*, April 19, 1877.

county official wrote a member of his legislative delegation that "the people don't want Willard at any price—they prefer McGowan, or someone else who is a Democrat."[26] Samuel McGowan, a former Confederate brigadier, had been first proposed for the position by the Spartanburg *Herald*; other papers quickly rallied behind him. An exception, Francis Dawson's *News and Courier*, supported William D. Porter of Charleston.[27]

While the Democrats divided over who should be chosen Chief Justice, most endorsed nomination by caucus. According to the Edgefield *Advertiser*, an important Gary newspaper, the Democratic party "must caucus for nominations." The *News and Courier* admonished every Democrat to "stand to his colors" and support the decision of the party caucus.[28] Fearing disunity before Democratic control had become entrenched, the Greenville *Enterprise and Mountaineer* cautioned the Democrats of dangers in a "split on any question."

"We are authorized to state," reported the Columbia *Daily Register* on May 3, two weeks prior to the Democratic caucus scheduled to select Chief Justice Moses's successor, "that Governor Hampton desires it to be known that he favors the election of Mr. Willard as the Chief Justice." "Political wisdom" dictated the choice of Willard, Hampton told his constituents; besides, he added, "There ought to be no hesitation in acting with magnanimity and justice toward a gentleman whose acts have been in striking accord with a sense of duty and the promotion of good government."[29]

Hampton's plea to elect Willard brought results. Noting the article in the *Daily Register*, the Charleston *Journal of Commerce* announced its support of Justice Willard. The *Hampton Herald* perceived the only honorable course for Democratic legislators in the "unqualified endorsement" of Governor Hampton's candidate. The Lancaster *Ledger* asserted that the legislature must stand with Governor Hampton, "especially at this critical juncture of our affairs." Similarly, the *Daily Register* declared that state representa-

26. J. T. Lyon to R. R. Hemphill, May 7, 1877, Hemphill Family Papers, Duke.

27. Sheppard, *Red Shirts Remembered*, quotes the *Herald* and others on p. 198; *News and Courier*, April 11, 1877.

28. *News and Courier*, April 21, 1877; other newspaper references in this paragraph come from that issue of the *News and Courier*, which published a compendium of opinions on the caucus question.

29. *Daily Register*, May 3, 1877.

tives in the General Assembly must " sustain the administration in its preference." [30]

Still, a segment of the South Carolina Democratic party refused to follow Hampton's lead. Calling the Governor's support of Willard " a political monstrosity," A. M. Speights of the *Greenville News* said he could not " consent to the bulldozing of the legislature of South Carolina by Governor Hampton into voting for Willard, a Carpet-bagger, for Chief Justice." Assuming direction of the anti-Hampton Democrats, Gary decided that only a Straightout South Carolina Democrat should be elected.[31]

In a speech to the Abbeville county Democratic convention, Gary's nephew, Eugene Blackburn Gary, accused Hampton of having made a deal with Willard: In turn for Willard's judicial support in 1876, Hampton had promised him the chief justiceship. Echoing editor Speights, young Gary doubted " that Republicanism ha[d] been so enhanced in value as that a [carpetbagger] of that persuasion should be preferred to a native-born Carolinian of the highest type of intellect and moral worth." [32]

With battle lines drawn, the Democratic legislators went into caucus at 8 P.M. on May 14 to choose the Chief Justice of the South Carolina Supreme Court. On the first ballot, Willard received thirty-eight of the forty-one votes necessary for election.[33] Samuel McGowan, supported by Gary and the Abbeville county delegation, trailed with twenty-three. Ten other votes were scattered. By midnight McGowan had picked up three more votes, but the Willard forces stood firm. Finally, at 3 A.M. those legislators opposed to Governor Hampton's wishes surrendered; Amiel J. Willard became the choice of the Democratic caucus for Chief Justice.

A decision by the caucus supposedly bound all Democrats, but an angry Gary refused to be bound. Immediately he began to search for a man who would go before the General Assembly as Willard's opponent. If some South Carolina Democrats shared General Gary's

30. Charleston *Journal of Commerce*, May 7, 1877; quoted in the *News and Courier*, May 15, 1877; *Daily Register*, May 4, 1877.
31. Quoted in Sheppard, *Red Shirts Remembered*, p. 208; Hampton M. Jarrell, *Wade Hampton and the Negro: the Road Not Taken* (Columbia: University of South Carolina Press, 1950), p. 125.
32. Sheppard, *Red Shirts Remembered*, pp. 205–7.
33. Nomination required a simple majority of all 81 Democratic legislators. Even though only 71 were voting for the Chief Justice, a total of 41 votes was required for nomination. *Ibid.*, pp. 209–10; *Daily Register*, May 31, 1877.

chagrin over the imminent election of Willard, none wished to oppose actively both Governor Hampton and a caucus decision. Gary's search ended in failure. When the General Assembly officially elected Willard Chief Justice, only one obscure Democratic representative joined Gary in voting against the decision of the caucus.[34]

III

Gary, an Edgefield county lawyer in his mid-forties, became the only important opponent faced by the Hampton administration. As a student he had been dismissed from South Carolina College for disciplinary reasons; he then entered Harvard and graduated in 1854. During the Civil War he rose to the rank of brigadier general, but the campaign of 1876 made him famous in South Carolina. The originator of the Straightout movement, the policy of the Democratic party of South Carolina in 1876 not to attempt any alliance or fusion with any segment of the Republican party, Gary helped convince Hampton to run for Governor and served as one of the chief Democratic managers during that campaign. In fact, he believed the Democratic triumph in 1876 due largely to his efforts and ideas. Even so, Hampton became Governor, and Gary's Edgefield colleague, Matthew C. Butler, became United States Senator, while Gary remained no more than a member of the state Senate from Edgefield county.

An ambitious man, Gary determined that he should receive a reward commensurate with his services in 1876. Confessing to a close friend that he was " somewhat like Byron after the publication of *Childe Harold*," Gary wrote that the fame that had come to him had changed him in "habit, thought and deportment." Butler's overwhelming election to the United States Senate in 1876 bitterly disappointed Gary, who had coveted that position for himself. Senator Butler predicted that Gary's ambition might lead the Edgefield senator "to antagonize [Hampton's] administration." [35] Gary had certainly charted his course for a point beyond the state legislature; to reach that destination he felt it essential to draw some of Governor Hampton's public support to his side.

To create a following that regarded him as a Democratic leader

34. Sheppard, *Red Shirts Remembered*, p. 210; *News and Courier*, May 16, 1877.

35. Gary to Hugh Farley, May 8, 1878, Gary Papers, SCL; Matthew Butler to James Chesnut, April 29, 1877, Williams-Chesnut-Manning Papers, *ibid.*

equal, if not superior, to Hampton, he countered most of the major
political and legislative aims of the Hampton administration. Bitterly
opposed to the regime's official policy of courting the Negro, he
argued against a two-mill tax for public education because, he contended, white taxpayers would be supporting Negro schools. His
basic difference with Hampton on racial policy stirred his major
opposition to the Hampton regime.[36] He also fought Hampton's
plan to honor the bonded debt incurred during Reconstruction; he
opposed both Willard's election as Chief Justice and Governor
Hampton's cessation of Republican prosecutions in return for the
federal government's abandonment of Democratic prosecutions.

Gary's efforts—during the special legislative session of 1877, the
regular session of that year, and the session of 1878—failed. His
attempt to become the guardian of the Democratic party, the pro-
tector of the white race from race mixing, and the defender of the
taxpayer from the greedy Hampton administration convinced few
legislators. Usually, no more than four or five Democratic senators
joined their colleague from Edgefield in his opposition to Hampton's
program. In fact, he threatened to succeed against Hampton only
when senators supporting the claims of the denominational colleges
joined with him to try to prevent the reopening of the University
of South Carolina.[37]

Gary carried his campaign beyond the legislature. He devoted
considerable time and energy to political strategy that would put
him in the United States Senate in 1878. Although Hampton would
be unbeatable in the gubernatorial contest of 1878, Gary knew the
1878 legislature would choose a Democrat to replace Republican
Senator John J. Patterson.

Even though Gary had no intention of making the race for
Governor, he still hoped to weaken Hampton by putting new men
on the ticket with him. As early as April, 1878, Gary told his closest

36. *Infra*, chap. iii.
37. A glance at votes in the state Senate shows Gary's failure. In his attempt to
defeat the *nolle prosequi* resolution in March, 1878, he commanded only three Democratic supporters and lost, 26 to 4. *Senate Journal* (1877–79), p. 939. In his effort
to defeat the constitutional amendment for financing public schools, he again commanded only three Democratic allies and lost, 24 to 4. *Ibid.*, (Special Session, 1877),
pp. 127–28. For his failure in the debt, see *supra*, sec. I; for race, see *infra*, chap. iii.
On a key vote during the fight to reorganize the University of South Carolina, Gary
was in the minority which lost, 15 to 11. *Senate Journal* (1877–78), pp. 574-75.

political confidant, editor Hugh Farley of the Spartanburg *Carolina Spartan*, that he would support the Governor, " but we must surround him with better advisers; " with failure to " surround Hampton with good advisers we are gone." [38] As he suggested names for the various state offices, Gary told Farley that " the way to get up a political furor is to cater to the ambitions of men all over the state." To make dissatisfaction with the status quo appear widespread, Gary did not plan " a personal fight against the present State ticket, except under cover of correspondents." [39]

Gary's attempt to create a furor succeeded, but he did not produce the kind of furor he had hoped. The Barnwell *People* voiced general state opinion on the suggested ticket changes: " It would be better for the wire-pullers of this programme, and the State at large," observed the *People*, " if a millstone were hanged around their necks and they drowned in the middle of the Atlantic." The Batesburg *Monitor* detected the machinations of " ambitious office seekers " in the effort to hurt Hampton. Denouncing all attempts to change the ticket, the Spartanburg *Herald* asserted that " public interest call[ed] for experienced helmsmen." The York county Democratic convention did not act alone when it adopted unanimously a resolution praising all the state officers and calling for their re-election along with that of Governor Hampton.[40]

When the state convention for nominating party candidates met on August 1, 1878, it exposed Gary's overconfidence. The convention, securely in the hands of Hampton men, ran smoothly—for them.[41] General John D. Kennedy, chairman of the state Executive Committee, nominated Colonel James S. Cothran for temporary president; Cothran, chosen unanimously, in turn suggested Kennedy for permanent president. Kennedy also received unanimous endorsement. Finally, A. C. Garlington of Greenville proposed that the convention, " having full confidence in the ability, honesty and

38. Gary to Hugh Farley, April 6 and 8, 1878, both in Gary Papers, SCL. See also Johnson Hagood to James Conner, April 27, [n.d. but it must have been 1878], James Conner Papers, South Carolina Historical Society; cited hereafter as SCHS.

39. Gary to Hugh Farley, April 6 and 13, and May 20, 1878, Gary Papers, SCL.

40. Barnwell *People*, July 25, 1878; Batesburg *Monitor* quoted in Sumter *Watchman*, March 7, 1878; Spartanburg *Herald*, March 27, 1878; Yorkville *Enquirer*, June 27 and July 4, 1878. My research has discovered no counties except Edgefield doing otherwise.

41. Gary to Hugh Farley, July 17, 1878, Gary Papers, SCL; *Daily Register*, August 2, 1878.

fidelity " of the entire state ticket, renominate them all. Garlington's motion carried without dissent.

Undaunted by the administration's triumph in the state convention, Gary pushed ahead his campaign plans for election to the United States Senate in December. Since the summer of 1877, friends who praised him in newspaper articles and quietly worked for him in their bailiwicks had kept his name before the public.[42] From different sections of the state, Gary's friends sent him reports of their activities in his behalf during late summer and early fall of 1878 and estimated his standing in their communities. From Abbeville county, Ellis G. Graydon wrote Gary, "Your stock is rising considerably in this county," Graydon confidently assured Gary he could "beat any man in the State for the U.S. Senate if left to vote of Abbeville." Telling Gary that he had "a great many friends and admirers in this county," Samuel Maurice of Williamsburg invited the Senate hopeful to speak in his county, where Gary's name would "bring out as many as Hampton's." R. K. Charles in Darlington promised to make every effort for Gary and wanted to publish Gary's "course" in the local paper. From Marlboro county, Joshua H. Hudson reported that Gary's cause was flourishing. These messages turned Gary's enthusiasm into the confidence he expressed to Hugh Farley: "I am greatly flattered on my chances of election—have a network of friends for me all over the State." [43]

While becoming more confident, Gary had one great worry. Should Hampton, though renominated for Governor, choose to be a candidate for the U.S. Senate, he would probably destroy Gary's hopes. Hampton had promised to serve out his second term as Governor, but Gary wanted to make sure he stayed in South Carolina. In late August, he told his friend Hugh Farley, "I wish you to show that he [Hampton] is the only man that can keep the blacks and whites harmonized for the next two years." [44]

A letter signed "Cato" in the Columbia *Daily Register* on

42. For example, see Y. St. Julien Yates to Gary, July 4, 1877, Gary Papers, SCL. As early as January, 1877, the Spartanburg *Carolina Spartan* had proposed Gary for the United States Senate. See also the Anderson *Intelligencer*, January 24, 1877.

43. Ellis G. Graydon to Gary, August 19, 1878; Samuel Maurice to Gary, October 24, 1878; R. K. Charles to Gary, August 15, 1878; Joshua H. Hudson to Gary, September 9, 1878; Gary to Hugh Farley, September 8, 1878, all in the Gary Papers, SCL.

44. Gary to Hugh Farley, June 7 and August 25, 1878, *ibid.*

November 21, 1878, argued that "*South Carolina* cannot, dare not, lose his [Hampton's] invaluable services." Four more epistles from Cato followed within two weeks.[45] Each of them discussed, with turgidity and verbosity, the magnificence of Hampton who was declared the equal of George Washington and Robert E. Lee. Calling Hampton "our blameless leader," Cato asserted that "as United States Senator his power for good in this State would be almost destroyed." In a final letter, the day before the legislature selected a new senator, Cato begged that the Governor might be spared for the state. Hampton was "the only pilot who [could] guide the ship of State through tempestuous waves which threaten to engulf her; over the jagged rocks and dangerous shoals which lie concealed below."

Gary failed to convince the South Carolina Democrats that their survival depended on Governor Hampton. Declaring that South Carolina need fear Radicalism no longer, the Newberry *Herald* demanded that Hampton, the ablest man in the state, be elected to the Senate. Echoing the *Herald*'s cry, the Marion *Merchant and Farmer* urged its readers to "send Hampton to the Senate" because "the State government . . . [was] purged of Radicalism." From Charleston, the *News and Courier* had "had no doubt, from the beginning, that Hampton was the man for the time." Both the Winnsboro *News and Herald* and the Yorkville *Enquirer* agreed that Hampton would be elected if he were "willing to accept." [46]

Whether or not Hampton sincerely intended to complete his term as Governor, his appearance in every corner of the state during the canvass prior to the election in November, 1878, did not lessen his eminence among political figures in the South Carolina Democratic

45. *Daily Register*, November 21, 1878. The letters appeared on November 23, 28, 30, and December 10, 1878. All of the quotations come from the letters. See also the *Laurensville Herald*, November 29, 1878. I cannot prove that "Cato" was either Gary or a Gary supporter, but the timing of the articles and their content, which developed themes Gary discussed with Hugh Farley, suggest they came from the Gary camp. Moreover Henry Farley, Hugh's brother, told Gary a month before the Cato letters appeared that he had seen articles written by Eugene Gary [Martin's nephew] on the necessity of keeping Hampton in the state. Henry Farley to Gary, October 11, 1878, Gary Papers, SCL. My research uncovered no other articles that might have been the ones mentioned by Henry Farley.

46. Newberry *Herald*, December 4, 1878; Marion *Merchant and Farmer* quoted in the *Daily Register*, December 1, 1878; *News and Courier*, December 2, 1878; Winnsboro *News and Herald*, November 27, 1878; Yorkville *Enquirer*, November 28, 1878.

party, and his resounding triumph in that election added to his prestige.[47] He could have the senatorship if he wanted.

When the legislature prepared to elect a new United States Senator, Governor Hampton was bedridden. In the month prior to the voting, he was critically ill from a hunting accident suffered on the day after his November 6 victory. He had fallen from a mule and broken a leg; complications threatened his life and finally resulted in the amputation of his right leg. On November 18, in the midst of this illness, Hampton issued a proclamation directing Lieutenant Governor Simpson to assume his official duties.[48] Aware that he had been spoken of as Patterson's replacement, the Governor sent a letter to the legislators announcing, " I must not be considered a candidate for the office." But in the same letter, Hampton said he would follow any course the state set; he would go to Washington or just as " cheerfully " remain in Columbia.[49]

The legislature wasted little time in deciding Hampton's future. Representative Samuel McGowan of Abbeville county, whom Gary had supported against Willard and Hampton during the chief justice fight in May, 1877, rose in the House to perform a task he considered " a duty." After a brief speech of praise, he told the House that his nominee represented " in the truest sense the embodiment of the brave, just, conservative Democracy of the State." Believing that " no one can mistake to whom I allude," McGowan informed the House that the people of South Carolina wanted Wade Hampton elected to the United States Senate.[50] Even after months of preparation, no one nominated Martin Gary. Unable to do anything for himself, Gary, along with all but two other legislators, cast his ballot for Wade Hampton.[51]

Gary's struggle for the Senate, a complete failure, had confronted

47. *News and Courier*, September 20 and October 3, 14, 1878. Hampton received all but 213 votes out of 119,763 cast. *Reports and Resolutions* (1878), p. 463.

48. Manly Wade Wellman, *Giant in Gray: Wade Hampton of South Carolina* (New York: Charles Scribner's Sons, 1949), p. 303.

49. *House Journal* (1878), p. 166. Of course Hampton's letter might have been political double talk, but I have found no evidence of any campaign conducted by Hampton to get himself elected to the U. S. Senate. It must be remembered, however, that between 1877 and 1880, the white citizens of South Carolina looked upon Hampton as the savior of their state; just by being alive in 1878 he was assured the Senate seat, unless he firmly and publicly denied any interest in it.

50. Sheppard, *Red Shirts Remembered*, pp. 274–75.

51. Two Republicans voted for another man. *House Journal* (1878), pp. 166–67; *Senate Journal* (1878), pp. 113–14.

tremendous obstacles. In face of these handicaps, his optimism and confidence seem inexplicable.[52] Gary had a small base from which to attack a man who had become a public saint. Having routed the Hampton forces led by former Governor Milledge Luke Bonham, Gary controlled Edgefield, but Edgefield was only one county.[53] Failing to obtain support from any of the larger newspapers in the state, Gary had to be content with local sheets, although few turned against Governor Hampton.[54] General Gary's circle of advisers and friends throughout the state encouraged him but did not support him publicly. Joshua Hudson spoke for those friends when he asked Gary to keep silent about their political friendship " for prudential reasons." [55] No politician wanted to risk Hampton's displeasure by publicly backing Martin Gary against the dominant faction in the party.[56]

The displeasure of Hampton could hinder the political aspirations

52. Throughout the spring, summer, and fall of 1878, Gary made statements to Hugh Farley similar to the remark he made on May 20 " I think I am gradually gaining ground." See also letters to Hugh Farley on May 9, July 17, and September 8, all in the Gary Papers, SCL.

53. Gary to R. R. Hemphill, September 25, 1878, Hemphill Family Papers, Duke; see also Lark O'Neall (who accused Gary of counting out his opponents), to Bonham, September 9, 1878; Robert Aldrich to Bonham, September 11, 1878; George Johnstone to Bonham, October 20, 1878, Milledge Luke Bonham Papers, SCL.

54. Gary's closest political adviser, Hugh Farley, edited the Spartanburg *Carolina Spartan* in 1877 and 1878; Hugh's brother Henry edited the Columbia *Straightout*. The *Carolina Spartan* was pro-Gary only during Farley's two-year tenure and I have been unable to find any files of that newspaper for those two years. Not even fragments of the *Straightout* remain. Only fragments of the other important Gary paper, the Edgefield *Advertiser*, exist for the years 1877–80. Other small newspapers probably supported Gary, but I found none.

In an attempt to overcome his newspaper problem, Gary tried to get the state's largest newspaper, the *News and Courier*, to publish without critical editorial comment items written by his friends and favorable to his cause. He was willing to pay to have such items printed. The *News and Courier* agreed to publish, without charge, letters supporting Gary but reserved the right to say what it wanted about them. A letter from W. T. Gary to Martin Gary, September 21, 1878, Gary Papers, SCL, outlines the negotiations betwen the Gary men and Dawson.

55. Hudson to Gary, January 14, 1878, and Henry Buist of Charleston to Gary, December 10, 1878, Gary Papers, SCL.

56. Of course no one in a one-party state like South Carolina wanted to be publicly identified as the man who wanted to break up the Democratic party. Gary, a loyal Democrat, had no desire to do that; his opposition to Hampton and the dominant faction in the Democratic party has to be understood in the terms of factionalism discussed by Maurice Duverger in his *Political Parties: Their Organization and Activity in the Modern State* (New York: John Wiley and Sons, Inc., 1955), pp. 120–21, 255–80.

of anyone in South Carolina; it did not help Gary's. Hoping to make himself better known, Gary had planned to use the canvass of 1878 as an opportunity for speaking in many South Carolina communities. He never got that chance because in September Hampton informed John Kennedy, chairman of the state Executive Committee, that " he would not attend where [Gary] was invited to speak." The Executive Committee, which assigned Democratic speakers, acceded to the Governor's demand, and Gary received no assignments after late September.[57]

Hampton's hobbling of Gary represented more than the efforts of one politician to thwart the ambitions of another. Political antagonism and personal bitterness merged. At first, Gary rarely spoke against Hampton personally but instead attacked his advisers and the regime's policies.[58] At the same time, his goal never changed; he wanted to remove Hampton from any position of power and prestige within the party and the state. Hampton knew what Gary was about. He told Bonham that he resented Gary's tactics: " He [Gary] has been praising me in public and trying to fly-blow me in private so I have grown tired of this proceeding." [59] In addition to using the state Executive Committee to wreck his opponent's political plans, Hampton spoke from the platform to counter Gary's moves. Warning his listeners against heeding " false Gods," he declared Gary " not authorized to speak for the party and gave his most emphatic dissent to General Gary's views," which were " inconsistent " with the policies of the Conservative Democrats.[60]

With Butler and Hampton entrenched in the United States Senate, Gary turned his attention to the governorship. As early as the autumn of 1879, certain local newspapers mentioned him as the best possible choice the Democrats could make.[61] Troubled by Gary's decision to

57. Gary to Hugh Farley, October 4, 1878, Gary Papers, SCL and Gary to R. R. Hemphill, October 4, 1878, Hemphill Family Papers, Duke.

58. Gary to Hugh Farley, May 9, 1878, and Henry Farley to Gary, October 12, 1878, both in the Gary Papers, SCL.

59. Hampton to Bonham, September 28, 1878, Bonham Papers, *ibid.* William Wallace told Gary on September 21, 1878 [Gary Papers, *ibid.*], that Hampton was " brooding" over the " vituperative language " Gary had used against him.

60. *News and Courier*, September 20, 1878.

61. Sheppard, *Red Shirts Remembered*, p. 278. Also consult Robert Aldrich to R. R. Hemphill, June 1, 1879, Hemphill Family Papers, Duke, and Benjamin Perry to Gary, December 4, 1879, Gary Papers, SCL; *Laurensville Herald*, December 5, 1879 and the Marion *Star* quoted in the *Daily Register*, October 22, 1879.

begin his campaign long before the nominating convention, William Wallace, former Speaker of the state House and now a circuit judge, cautioned him not " to take a running start which might be construed into a consciousness of weakness." Wallace also pointed out that Governor Simpson, who was "very popular," had not made his decision about 1880; Wallace felt that Gary should hold back until Simpson made up his mind, for if he refused, " it would be construed into opposition " to Simpson and alienate the Governor's friends.[62]

Besides Simpson, the problem of a campaign platform worried Judge Wallace. None of Gary's old issues like the debt question had any relevancy after the legislative session of 1878. He warned Gary that an attempt to present himself as the only true Democrat would be useless. Finally, Wallace admonished Gary to wait until after the legislative session of 1879 before committing himself. In that way, he might find some issue to take to the people.[63]

The Conservative regime did not share Wallace's concern with issues; neither did it have difficulty finding a candidate. Aware that Gary would again challenge them, the Conservatives decided to rest their case on his opposition to Hampton.[64] That he had accused Hampton of bargaining with the Republicans during the 1876 campaign made their defense much easier. Governor Simpson, after the 1879 legislature elected him Chief Justice of the South Carolina Supreme Court, promised to do all in his power to secure the nomination for Johnson Hagood of Barnwell county, a former Confederate brigadier, and since 1876 comptroller general.[65] Determined that Gary should never win, Hampton joined Hagood's forces and volunteered to come from Washington, if necessary, to stop Gary.[66]

Although the state press suggested other candidates, the contest quickly became a duel.[67] Hagood ran as the candidate of Hampton and the faction in the Democratic party that had controlled the state since 1877. Warning a friend in Beaufort county against Gary's efforts, Hagood confessed he was relying upon " Hampton's friends "

62. Wallace to Gary, September 18, 1879, Gary Papers, SCL.
63. *Ibid.*
64. Even the Gary camp realized this fact. On January 25, 1880, Henry Farley wrote Gary that the regime's biggest weapon was his " opposition to Hampton." *Ibid.*
65. Joseph W. Barnwell, " Life and Recollections of Joseph W. Barnwell," unpublished autobiography (MSS dated 1929), pp. 452–53, SCHS.
66. Sheppard, *Red Shirts Remembered*, p. 279; Anderson *Intelligencer*, quoted by the *News and Courier*, November 27, 1879; *New York Times*, December 26, 1879.
67. *Daily Register*, August 29, 1879.

to stop Gary. The regime's chief newspaper supporter, the *News and Courier*, unalterably opposed the nomination of Gary for Governor.[68]

Of the success of Hampton in blunting Gary's political offensive and in shifting to him the odium of public opinion, the Edgefield senator wrote: " I do not propose to surrender without a desperate struggle." [69] Embittered and frustrated, Gary publicly assailed Hampton's integrity in a final attempt to defame the man who, in Gary's mind, had denied him his rightful rewards. To a *New York Herald* reporter in December, 1879, Gary recounted how Hampton had sold out the national Democratic ticket in 1876. According to Gary, Hampton had agreed with the state Republican party to ensure that Hayes got the state's electoral vote in return for Republican assurance that Republican leaders would support Hampton for Governor.[70] Upon publication of this interview, Hampton called Gary's accusations " slanders " and " pronounce[d] them utterly and absolutely false." [71] The bitterness resulting from the charges and counter charges worked against Gary. Opinion in the state agreed with the Spartanburg *Carolina Spartan* that " Hampton's character [had] lost nothing in the controversy." The *News and Courier* had no doubt that Gary " damage[d] his prospects [for the governorship] " by " mak[ing] attacks on Senator Hampton and railing at him." [72]

After Gary's outburst in the *New York Herald*, the campaign proceeded quietly. In distinct contrast to his performance in 1877

---

68. Hagood to Benjamin Stuart Williams, March 23, 1880, Benjamin Stuart Williams Papers, SCL; *News and Courier*, May 21, 1880.

69. Gary to Hugh Farley, October 26, 1878, Gary Papers, SCL.

70. There were really two interviews; the *News and Courier* reprinted them on December 15 and 20, 1879.

71. Hampton's reply published in the *New York Herald* is quoted in D. D. Wallace, " The Question of the Withdrawal of the Democratic Presidential Electors in South Carolina in 1876," *Journal of Southern History*, VIII (August, 1942), 381.

In this instance Gary accused Hampton wrongly and must have known it. His champion William Sheppard in *Red Shirts Remembered*, pp. 279 ff., repeats Gary's accusations as facts but Wallace's article proves Hampton's innocence beyond any doubt. An article in the James A. Hoyt Papers, SCL, unavailable to Wallace, provides more evidence of Hampton's innocence. The four-page article entitled " Gary and Hampton" written in 1880 by Hoyt, secretary of the state Executive Committee in 1876, completely absolves Hampton of any connection with such a scheme. Both Wallace and Hoyt agree that an offer was made by state Republican leaders to the Democratic Executive Committee, but that Hampton and the Executive Committee promptly rejected it.

72. Spartanburg *Carolina Spartan*, February 11, 1880; *News and Courier*, December 17, 1879; *Greenville Weekly News*, December 20, 1879.

and in 1878, he had little to say in the legislature. Hagood, apart from condemnations of Gary, voiced few positive ideas on anything.

Into this calm, the regime unknowingly dropped a small explosive. When on March 10, 1880 the state Executive Committee issued a call for a state convention to be held on June 1,[73] at first no excitement arose, for such calls were routine Executive Committee business. But this call stated that the June convention would " nominate candidates for State officers " as well as discuss party rules and the upcoming election. Previously, a second convention in August had made nominations. Arguing that the time between June and November gave the Republicans too much time to prepare against the Democratic ticket, certain newspapers wanted nominations postponed until late summer. Other papers saw no problem; they either discounted the Republican threat or asserted that Democrats in some sections of the state needed as much time as possible to make ready for the November elections.[74]

Unfortunately for Gary, opposition to nominations did not mean support for his cause, which by late spring was faring badly.[75] Certain estimates of his strength can only be termed visionary in view of the results of county conventions.[76] One of his closest advisers, Circuit Judge Joshua Hudson, viewed the political front with more detachment. He delayed writing Gary in hope of seeing " some favorable turn in the tide of popular sentiment in your favor," but, ten days before the convention, he had to say, " It grieves me, however, to see that tide setting strongly in favor of your chief opponent." [77]

73. *News and Courier*, March 12, 1880.

74. Winnsboro *News and Herald*, March 24, 1880, and Spartanburg *Carolina Spartan*, March 17, 1880; Anderson *Intelligencer*, March 25, 1880, and *News and Courier*, March 26 and May 29, 1880. See also Hampton to James Conner, May 18 and 30, 1880, Conner Papers, SCHS.

75. *Daily Register*, June 2, 1880, and Winnsboro *News and Herald*, March 24, 1880.

76. On March 31, 1880, Blake L. White wrote Gary that he felt Charleston county would "send a solid Gary delegation to Columbia." A letter from Tilman R. Gaines on March 22, 1880 told Gary that after talking to Democrats all over the state he was confident that Gary would receive the nomination from the June convention. Both letters are in the Gary Papers, SCL.

At the same time, however, county conventions were acting and not in Gary's favor. *News and Courier*, May 21, 1880; *Daily Register*, May 16, 1880; *New York Times*, May 23, 1880. See also W. W. Ball to Professor D. D. Wallace, October 18, 1926, W. W. Ball Papers, Duke.

Even so, Gary retained control of Edgefield county. Winnsboro *News and Herald*, May 12, 1880.

77. Hudson to Gary, May 20, 1880, Gary Papers, SCL.

When the convention opened, many delegates still opposed nominations, but few opposed Johnson Hagood.[78] The only drama appeared in the dispute over nominations. As soon as the convention had been organized, William Munro of Union county moved that the convention proceed directly to the nomination of state officers. Hoping to win over the forces opposed to nominations, Munro wished also to prohibit the Executive Committee from opening the campaign earlier than the first week in September. This concession did not suffice, and a floor fight ensued. Leading the men opposed to nominations, John C. Sheppard of Edgefield, Speaker of the House and a strong Gary supporter, failed; Munro's motion carried by 84 to 63. With that question decided, the convention turned to nominations. Gary, evidently aware of the paucity of his support, refused to allow his name to go before the convention, and Hagood won nomination by acclamation instead of by an overwhelming majority.[79]

Once again the Hampton forces had crushed the political hopes of Gary, who left Columbia a broken man and renounced politics in his ten remaining months of life. Since 1877, he had led the opposition to the policies and the candidates of the Conservative Democrats dominated by Wade Hampton. His opposition, though bitter, had been vocal; he had never managed to construct a political organization to further his cause. After 1880, the Conservatives believed their new Governor when he said, "I think everything will go smoothly now." [80]

IV

After the political destruction of Martin Gary, harmony commanded the camp of the Conservative Democrats. The bitter intraparty fighting prevalent since the establishment of the regime in April, 1877, ended when the state Democratic convention of 1880 crushed Gary's political ambitions. With no other leader of Gary's prominence to oppose Senator Hampton and his associates or their program, political unity seemed assured. The prospect of harmony appeared even more likely when in April, 1881, Martin Gary died.

78. *News and Courier*, June 1, 1880, and *Daily Register*, June 2, 1880.
79. The Anderson *Intelligencer* reported on June 10, 1880, that Hagood had been the first choice of 130 of the 158 delegates. With a choice between Hagood and Gary, Hagood was the choice of 147. Thus, outside of Edgefield county's six delegates, Gary had only five supporters.
80. Hagood to William A. Courtenay, June 4, 1880, William A. Courtenay Papers, SCL.

To preserve the new-found political peace, Governor Hagood did nothing that might anger any of the Conservative chieftains. A leader in war and in 1876, a faithful servant of Hampton through the years of the Gary feud, Hagood held the allegiance of the Conservative leaders. He attempted to maintain his position, not by vigorous control of the party but by quiet, unobtrusive conduct that would bring honor and prestige to his office and sustain the loyalty that assured, in 1880, that he would be Hampton's chosen successor.[81] His decision not to seek re-election in 1882 indicated he had no wish to dominate a party which he believed—as he declared in his first inaugural—to be faring so well.[82]

Yet, Hagood's determination not to seek a second term threatened to destroy the post-Gary unity in the Conservative Democratic camp. Two men quickly emerged as the leading contenders for the party's gubernatorial nomination in 1882. The records of both Lieutenant Governor John Kennedy and Comptroller General John Bratton entitled them to the support of the Conservative leadership. Both had been general officers in the Confederate Army; both stood with Hampton in 1876; both had served the party faithfully, and in high office, since 1877. Bratton had been chairman of the state Executive Committee and comptroller general; Kennedy had been a state senator, chairman of the state Executive Committee, and Lieutenant Governor. Neither could be labelled a political associate or descendant of Martin Gary; neither could be branded as an apostate. To make their contest even tighter, Senator Hampton endorsed neither Kennedy nor Bratton. And thus, Conservatives could support without restraint the claims of either contestant.

The spring of 1882 ended the Bratton and Kennedy monopoly of the candidacy for the gubernatorial nomination. Their close ties to the Conservative leadership caused dissatisfaction among certain groups. This opposition originated in May when the *Greenville News*, crying for an end to the closed circle of political advancement and demanding a new face to lead the Democrats, suggested George D. Tillman of Edgefield, congressman from the Second District.[83]

---

81. On Hagood's personality, see N. G. Gonzales to Miss Emily Elliott, December 12, 1880, and January 9, 1881, Elliott–Gonzales Papers, Southern Historical Collection, University of North Carolina; cited hereafter as SHC.

82. *News and Courier*, December 1, 1880.

83. The dissatisfaction seemed to center in the up country, even though General Bratton's Fairfield county belonged to that section. The *Greenville News* (quoted by

Although the first call for Congressman Tillman came from the up country, his candidacy quickly gained adherents across the state. In early June, the Georgetown *Enquirer* placed " Tillman for Governor" on its masthead. Supporting a native son, the Edgefield *Chronicle* declared, " It is very clear that if this question is left with the people that Geo. D. Tillman will be the Governor." [84] By the end of June at least a dozen newspapers backed Tillman, who seemingly had emerged as a real challenger to Bratton and Kennedy.

While Bratton and Kennedy competed for the support of party leaders across the state and a strong segment of public opinion advocated a third candidate, many thoughtful Democrats feared for the safety of the party. Because disintegration of the Democratic party into factions could destroy the victory of 1876 and open the way for renewed Republican control of their state, they saw surety only in the return of Senator Hampton as Governor. If they could convince the Senator to come back to South Carolina and enter the race, the other candidates would defer to their chief and step aside. Party harmony would return. To Hampton went entreaties that only he could save the party and prevent possible disaster in November. Talk of Hampton's candidacy ended when, in a public letter to the *News and Courier*, he eliminated any possibility of running for Governor in 1882. Praising all the candidates, Hampton appealed for unity behind whichever contender the convention should choose.[85]

A month after Hampton's withdrawal Tillman's decision to retain the security of his seat in Congress returned the political contest on the eve of the state convention to its original position.[86] Bratton and Kennedy remained the only two active candidates, and neither had tempered his claim to be the candidate deserving loyal party support. Hampton's expression of confidence in the aspirants and his plea for a united party behind the man nominated quieted, but did not dispel, fears of the party's splitting into factions. As the

---

the Fairfield *News and Herald*, May 31, 1882) saw a ring that promoted loyal servants to higher office. Answering this charge, the *News and Herald, ibid.*, asked why there were two promotions for the same office at the same time. I found no evidence, supporting the accusations of the *News*, of an official promotion. In fact, the *New York Times* of January 2, 1882 declared that Senator Hampton's ring wanted Theodore G. Barker of Charleston for Governor.

84. Georgetown *Enquirer*, June 7 and 14, 1882; Edgefield *Chronicle*, June 12, 1882.
85. *News and Courier*, June 20, 1882.
86. Georgetown *Enquirer*, July 26, 1882.

convention approached, neither man held a definite margin, but friends of each were " equally confident" that their man would triumph. Few predicted which of the two contestants would receive the nomination, but all concurred in the opinion of the *News and Courier* that no dark-horse candidate would steal the prize from the two old soldiers.[87]

In spite of a general feeling that either Kennedy or Bratton would win the gubernatorial nomination, many delegates gathering in Columbia for the convention on August 1 favored neither candidate. The Greenville forces that had proposed George Tillman did not rush to one of the favorites when their man declined to make the race. Several other piedmont delegations and certain delegates from the Pee Dee area shared Greenville's disconcertion over the prospects of a ticket headed by either Bratton or Kennedy. Finally, on the morning of the convention these dissidents decided to throw their strength behind Hugh Smith Thompson and press for his nomination, even though Thompson himself had not met with them.[88]

Though a last-minute candidate, Hugh Thompson was no stranger to South Carolinians or to politics. A member of a well-known antebellum family, he had no impressive combat record with the Confederate Army—during the war he had served as an instructor at his alma mater the Citadel. When the Citadel was closed after the war, he organized an academy in Columbia. After the Democratic triumph in 1876, Thompson became state Superintendent of Education, a post to which he had been re-elected without opposition in 1878 and in 1880. Mentioned as a gubernatorial possibility in the spring of 1882, he removed his name from contention as soon as it was brought forward.[89] In fact, his ambitions lay in another direction entirely. During June and July he had been negotiating with the Board of Trustees of South Carolina College for the presidency of that institution.[90] When, on the Saturday before the con-

---

87. Fairfield *News and Herald*, August 9, 1882; *News and Courier*, August 1, 1882.

88. Fairfield *News and Herald*, August 9, 1882, and Anderson *Intelligencer*, August 10, 1882.

89. J. C. Sheppard to Thompson, March 2, 1882 and Thompson to J. C. Sheppard, March 7, 1882, Hugh Smith Thompson Papers, SCL.

90. See correspondence in June and July, 1882, between Thompson and college officials in the Thompson Papers, SCL; also Daniel Walker Hollis, *College to University*, Vol. II: *University of South Carolina* (Columbia: University of South Carolina Press, 1951, 1956), p. 104.

vention, Thompson withdrew his candidacy for re-election as Superintendent of Education, many assumed he had accepted the offer of
the College.[91]

When the convention opened, Thompson's supporters added their
candidate's name to those of Bratton and Kennedy.[92] The speech by
William L. Mauldin of Greenville nominating Thompson evoked
" spontaneous and heartfelt" cheering. In fact, one commentator
felt that the mention of Thompson's name brought about " the first
sign of political electricity " the convention had witnessed. Thompson led on the first ballot, even though his personal emissary had
informed the convention that Thompson was not a candidate and
" did not wish to be regarded so." The third ballot ended the contest
—Hugh Thompson would represent the Democrats in the November
general elections.[93]

Thompson attained a non-political political triumph. Consistently
disavowing interest in the governorship and refusing political consideration of his name, he did not in private contradict his public
utterances; he spoke truthfully when he claimed that he was " in
no way responsible for what has been done." [94] Those who decided
on the morning of August 1, 1882, that Hugh Thompson should be
Governor denied that any Thompson conspiracy had been planned
prior to the convention.[95] The disaffected Democrats garnered allies
from among those who feared for the solidity of the party, whether
under Bratton or Kennedy, and put Thompson across.

91. *News and Courier*, August 2, 1882.
92. *Ibid.*, and William Watts Ball, *The State that Forgot: South Carolina's Surrender to Democracy* (Indianapolis: The Bobbs-Merrill Company, 1932), pp. 180–81.
93. The voting went as follows (157 votes were needed for nomination):

	First Ballot	Second Ballot
Bratton	95	75
Kennedy	107	90
Thompson	112	147

After the second ballot, both Bratton and Kennedy withdrew from the race; thereupon, Thompson received the unanimous nomination of the convention. *Daily Register*,
August 2, 1882.
94. Thompson to William A. Courtenay, n.d. [sometime after the convention],
Courtenay Papers, SCL, and a wire from Courtenay to Thompson, August 1, 1882,
Thompson Papers, *ibid.*
Thompson's non-involvement was true, but at one point he seems to have regretted
his ardent denials of interest. Thompson to J. C. Sheppard, March 7, 1882, *ibid.*
95. William L. Mauldin Diary, entry of August 6, 1882, SHC; John D. Kennedy
to Thompson, August 7, 1882, Thompson Papers, SCL.

The party closed ranks to give its enthusiastic and united support to Thompson and John C. Sheppard, the nominee for Lieutenant Governor, even though their triumph constituted a major political change within the Conservative Democratic party. Neither Thompson nor Sheppard had been a Confederate officer. Prior to their nomination two governors, the two senators, and one of the two lieutenant governors had been general officers in the Confederate Army. Opinion across the state chorused with the Edgefield *Chronicle* that the nominees were " the very strongest that could have been named." The Greenville *Enterprise and Mountaineer* reported that the up country " rejoice[d] over the nominations." Party leaders from Senators Butler and Hampton to defeated candidate Kennedy expressed their congratulations to Thompson and pledged their support and loyalty.[96]

With intra-party discord settled, the Conservative Democrats looked to November and the general elections, where, party publicity notwithstanding, they faced in 1882 the most serious threat to their continued hegemony between 1880 and 1890. The Greenback-Labor party, supported by the state Republican organization, had nominated a full slate of state officers and congressional candidates to contest Democratic rule. First organized in South Carolina in 1880, the Greenback-Labor party had held, in September of that year, a convention at Chester and decided to put a state ticket in the field. Commanding only forty-five delegates from eight counties, the convention of this new party revealed its weakness in the state. The Greenbackers failed to achieve any fusion with the Republicans, except in a few local instances, and met with complete disaster in the election.[97] Against the Democratic ticket headed by Johnson Hagood, the Greenback party could deliver a mere 3.5 per cent of the vote.[98]

96. Edgefield *Chronicle*, August 9, 1882; Greenville *Enterprise and Mountaineer*, August 9, 1882. For other examples, see the Yorkville *Enquirer*, August 10, 1882. Numerous congratulatory messages with professions of support are in the Thompson Papers, SCL.

97. *News and Courier*, September 29, 1880, and *New York Times*, October 2, 1880; James Welch Patton, " The Republican Party in South Carolina, 1876–1895," in *Essays in Southern History*, ed. Fletcher Melvin Green in the *James Sprunt Studies in History and Political Science*, XXI (Chapel Hill: University of North Carolina Press, 1949), 93, and *News and Courier*, October 11, 1880.

98. Democrat Johnson Hagood received 177,432 votes while the Greenback candidate won but 4,277. *Tribune Almanac* (1883), pp. 71–72.

Only the assurance of Republican support could rescue the party from such a debacle and encourage its leaders in 1882 to try again. Besides giving hope to Greenback leaders, Republican strength could build the Greenback party into a formidable opponent to the Democrats in certain sections of the state. In Columbia in January, 1882, Thomas E. Miller, a prominent Negro Republican, and several Greenbackers including the party's state leader, J. Hendrix McLane, held a secret meeting. Subsequently, the Repubican party announced its endorsement of the Greenback ticket.[99]

McLane anticipated a bright future for his party. In an interview published in the *News and Courier* in January, he reported that the Greenbackers had " all kinds of encouragement from all sections of the State." He labeled the Democrats " fossilized," and urged " the Progressive element" to turn to his party. Calling victory for his party a foregone conclusion, he asserted that the Greenbackers might obtain 150,000 votes across the state. He predicted the triumph of the entire Greenback state ticket along with several congressional candidates.[100]

Any encouragement McLane might have received from Republicans multiplied at the Greenback-Labor party's state convention of 1882. Completely unlike its predecessor of 1880, the convention in Columbia included a Democratic state senator, as well as more than one hundred delegates from twenty-two counties. This convention named a state ticket head by McLane as gubernatorial candidate and chose nominees for six of the state's seven Congressional districts.[101]

Not even this improved convention could conceal the serious political problems faced by the Greenbackers. McLane claimed 30,000 white voters enrolled in Greenback organizations, but his Republican compatriots failed to discover them. Perhaps more important, Greenback leaders were " almost wholly unknown to the public," even locally.[102] Recognizing this problem they attempted to woo for their party Democrats such as John S. Richardson of

99. *News and Courier*, January 23, 1882; Patton, " Republicans," p. 93.

100. *News and Courier*, November 6 and January 14, 1882.

101. *Ibid.*, September 6, 1882. They failed to nominate a candidate for the Black District, the Republican stronghold, leaving it to their allies.

102. *New York Times*, November 5, 1882; also Samuel Melton to Benjamin Brewster, November 9, 1882, Source Chronological File of the Justice Department, Record Group 60, National Archives; Patton, " Republicans," p. 93, and Mauldin Diary, entry September 30, 1882, SHC.

Sumter, a former Democratic congressman who lost his seat in the 1882 redistricting of the state. Their failure contributed to their predicament. Lack of influence at the state capital stifled their attempt to obtain the appointment of at least one Greenbacker on every county election commission and compounded their difficulties.[103]

South Carolina Greenbackers also stumbled on issues. Their platform, which contained the usual Greenback money planks calling for Congress to issue legal tender greenbacks and condemning government bonds, denounced the lien law, the stock law, and the election law. Farmers in South Carolina had shared the difficulties of farmers across the land, but the public had no real interest in national financial questions.[104] Opposition to the censured state laws might have tempted sympathetic Democrats to break with their party, but the alliance between Greenbackers and Republicans restrained most Democrats from a shift to the new party.

Conservative spokesmen emphasized the gravity of such a choice by defining any independent or non-Democrat as a Radical—and for South Carolinians that sobriquet had an inescapable connotation. Senator Hampton gave public notice that anyone " not with us, with the Democratic party, is a traitor to his State." Following suit, Senator Matthew Butler declared, "An independent has no beginning, no end. He must be a Radical. There is no half-way ground." [105] Newspapers, both large and small, repeated the tenor of the leaders' warnings. The *News and Courier* called the Greenbackers " the Negro Party," while the Anderson *Intelligencer* designated Greenbackers really nothing more (or nothing less) than radical Republicans. A similar opinion came from the state Executive Committee chairman, James F. Izlar, who said the committee planned to conduct the canvass on that issue.[106]

103. John S. Richardson to Charles A Buckheit [secretary, Greenback–Labor party], September 1, 1882, John S. Richardson Papers, SCL.

The Greenback request is in the Johnson Hagood Papers, Incoming Correspondence, Executive File, South Carolina Archives; cited hereafter as SCA. The *News and Courier* printed the Governor's reply on October 9, 1882.

The county election commission collected the ballot boxes from the several polling places in the county, verified the ballots in the boxes, and forwarded the official results of the county's vote to the state commission in Columbia.

104. *News and Courier*, September 6, 1882; *New York Times*, October 13, 1882.

105. In an editorial on the Greenback–Labor party in South Carolina on October 30, 1882, the *News and Courier* printed the statements of both senators.

106. *Ibid.*, October 2, 1882; Anderson *Intelligencer*, September 7, 1882, and *Daily Register*, October 11, 1882; *News and Courier*, August 14, 1882.

When the votes had been counted, McLane's predictions for his party seemed visionary. The Greenback party won no local contests and failed by tremendous margins to elect any of their congressional candidates. The state ticket feared little better; though it improved on its 1880 showing, the increase came largely from Republican votes.[107]

The resounding triumph heralded for the Conservative Democrats an "Era of Good Feelings." Neither Governor Thompson, enthusiastically supported by all segments of the party, nor his administration made political enemies. As the 1884 election approached, no opponents to Thompson's nomination appeared. Everyone, the press believed, wanted Thompson for another term. In the state Democratic convention in June, 1884, a motion to renominate the entire state ticket by acclamation was carried "without a dissenting voice amidst a storm of applause." [108]

In November, Democratic victory was complete. The Greenback party had not revived from its disastrous defeat of 1882; the Republican party held to its program of not nominating a state ticket, and the national Republican party decided to cease prosecution in the trials growing out of Democratic activities against Republicans. More important, chances of renewal of such trials diminished considerably when the Democratic party won the national election. The Conservative Democrats of South Carolina rejoiced that friendly power controlled the national government once again.[109]

107. McLane received 20.9 per cent of the total vote, one-third of which came from Black District counties with the rest scattered. Of the five counties that gave him as much as one-third of their vote, three—Beaufort, Berkeley, and Georgetown—comprised the strongest Republican counties in the state. In Beaufort he got almost 80 per cent of the vote, the margin of victory for Republican candidates. The other counties that gave McLane at least one-third of their total vote were Chesterfield in the midlands and Oconee in the extreme northwestern part of the state. The Greenbackers failed to make any serious inroads into Democratic strength. The *Tribune Almanac* (1883), pp. 71–72, contains the figures; for the Beaufort county situation, see the Port Royal *Palmetto Post*, November 16, 1882.

108. Edgefield *Chronicle*, February 20, 1884, *News and Courier*, June 27–July 3, 1884, and *Daily Register*, June 26, 1884.

109. Although a group composed of "the old hulks of the Greenback Party" met in September of 1884, it could generate no serious political activity. *New York Times*, September 5, 1884; Patton, "Republicans," p. 93, n. 5; Ellison Keith, January 21, 1885, and Mrs. T. H. Diseher, March 3, 1885, to Grover Cleveland, Grover Cleveland Papers, Library of Congress (cited hereafter as LC), and the *News and Courier*, November 5–6, 1884.

V

A year after the unanimous renomination of Governor Thompson and his state ticket, the three-year-old political concord ended. No new party arose as the Greenbackers had in 1882; the dissent came from within the Democratic party itself. Although this disaffection within the party did not carry the force or power of Tillmanism, which came later, it did unsettle the regime. The distinctly sectional aspects of this new political unrest coupled with the initial vagueness of its protest against the status quo suggests that this agitation, beginning in the summer of 1885, had its antecedents in the sectional struggle existing in South Carolina since colonial times.

Men dissatisfied with political conditions first called for a new deal. Erupting without warning during the late summer of 1885 and led by the *Greenville News*, this campaign insisted on " the transfusion of new blood fresh from the people into every artery and vein of our political system." [110] Other papers picked up this argument from the *News* and broadened its scope. The Columbia *Daily Register* demanded that the " ring controlling state politics" be exposed and destroyed. From the Abbeville *Medium* came the cry that those who held office " should voluntarily give place to others equally as capable."

Francis Dawson led the Conservative regime's forces on the main battleground, the newspaper column. Dawson asked the new dealers to name the ring that dominated the State, to name those who had been in office too long, to indicate where corruption existed. No answers came. The *Greenville News* hedged that it never claimed a ring actually existed but, rather, had said there was " every element of a Ring." Neither did other critical newspaper editors name names or make specific recommendations.

After a month of accusation and recrimination, the agitators halted their campaign just as suddenly as they had begun. The Edgefield *Chronicle* declared that the new deal failed " for want of something

110. This quotation and all others, unless otherwise specified, are taken from the September 9, 1885 issue of the *News and Courier*, which had a complete discussion of the issue with numerous opinions of other newspapers, although discussion had begun a month earlier. *Ibid.*, August 20 and 22, 1885.

Contemporary editors used the phrase " new deal," and I have retained their terminology.

See also Associate Justice Henry McIver to Chief Justice William D. Simpson, September 24, 1885, William D. Simpson Papers, SCL.

substantial to support it." [111] Undoubtedly the collapse of the insurgents hinged largely on their unwillingness or inability to talk in precise terms.

One year after dropping their call for a new deal in state politics, Greenville forces initiated another assault on the Conservative Democrats. This time the attack centered on a single part of the party machinery. The *News* demanded a change in the method of calculating representation in the state Democratic convention.[112] The old system allotted delegates to each county " in the numerical proportion to which that County is entitled in both branches of the General Assembly." This procedure antagonized certain up-country counties that believed it silenced their rightful voice in party deliberations. The *News* advocated basing representation on the Democratic vote in a particular county.

The Greenville county Democratic convention meeting on July 17, 1886, endorsed the idea proposed by the *News*. A resolution instructed its delegates to the state convention to advocate changing the party's constitution so " as to provide for a more equitable and truer expression of the Democracy in said conventions; that is, upon the basis of the Democratic voting strength of the several counties." This true expression would come from an apportionment that allowed every county one delegate for each one hundred Democratic votes cast in the previous election.[113]

Dawson again led the Conservative defense. He called the Greenville plan " both unjust and inequitable." He argued that the numbers involved would make the state convention an unwieldy body—in 1880 there would have been 1,123 delegates. Moreover, the Greenville idea created " a fluctuating representation for an unchanging constituency." It would punish faithful Democrats " for the fault of the unfaithful " who had failed to vote in the last election. The apportioning of delegates for one year on the results of a previous election year also disturbed Dawson because he thought important contemporary political issues should not be decided on previous events.[114] Using county voting totals from 1884, Dawson attempted to ridicule the inequity of the proposal. The Democratic

111. Edgefield *Chronicle*, September 16, 1885.
112. *Greenville Weekly News*, July 6, 1886.
113. *News and Courier*, July 21, 1886.
114. *Ibid.*

vote in that year would have allowed Abbeville county to send thirty-six delegates to the state convention but permit Richland only seventeen and Berkeley but twelve. Yet all three of those counties had the same number of men in their legislative delegations. According to Dawson, such a system was patently unfair.[115]

The *Daily Register* based its opposition to the Greenville idea on a quite different issue. Initially supporting the new plan, the paper quickly reconsidered when it found Edgefield, " paying twenty-three million [dollars] into the State Treasury, would have a larger delegation than Charleston, paying one hundred-and-forty-two million [dollars]." The *Register* thought it absolutely essential that some arrangement be made to award wealth its proper place in the party's councils. Condemning manhood suffrage as " a Yankee idea," the *Register* praised South Carolina's ante-bellum constitution, which " allowed a representation to population and wealth evenly." The paper called for a renewal of that arrangement, though it was willing to give two-thirds of the representation to population, and only one-third to wealth.[116]

The Greenville idea came before the state Democratic convention on August 5, 1886. James L. Orr, Jr., son of the prominent ante-bellum unionist, led the forces that wanted the changes. Augustus Smythe, state senator from Charleston county, and Edward Croft, of Aiken, spoke for regime. They denounced the plan as unfair to large sections of the state. Croft " thought it useless to waste time in discussing it," for it would practically eliminate Beaufort and the other Black District counties from the party. The demonstration that followed Croft's short speech clearly revealed the temper of the convention. Then, after a brief discussion, on a viva-voce vote " the Greenville idea was buried under a tremendous majority amid great cheering." [117]

The Greenville idea was never resurrected, but its motivating forces remained very much alive. Doubtlessly, strong up-country interests

---

115. *Ibid.*, July 21 and 30, 1886. Cf. Spartanburg *Carolina Spartan*, August 4, 1886. The proposed change found at least one supporter outside of the piedmont. *Manning Times*, September 8, 1885.

116. *Daily Register*, August 3, 1886.

117. *Ibid.*, August 6, 1886, and the *News and Courier*, August 7, 1886. The newspapers did not give a breakdown of the voting, but the *News and Courier* reported that the Greenville forces found few allies and managed to obtain only 10 per cent of the vote.

felt denied the power they should have in the party; moreover, they felt this denial to be a conscious act on the part of the regime. The very partisanship that originated the Greenville idea enabled the Conservatives to defeat it with a cry, so effectively made by Croft, that its adoption would mean disaster for Democrats in the counties containing a substantial Negro majority.

Reapportionment of the General Assembly also chafed the dissident up countrymen. The state constitution of 1868 gave each county one senator; no factors such as wealth or population had any bearing on the membership of the state Senate. The House of Representatives consisted of 124 members apportioned among the several counties on the basis of total population alone. The constitution had directed the apportionment of the House to be decided after a state census taken in 1869, in 1875, and in every tenth year thereafter. The seats in the House had last been reapportioned in the spring of 1876 by the Republican-controlled legislature.[118]

As the date for the next census approached, the state Senate seemed reluctant to upset the existing apportionment system. In his message in 1884, Governor Thompson informed the legislature the constitution required a state census in 1885, and he asked the lawmakers to enact the appropriate legislation.[119] The legislators took no action on the Governor's request until the very end of the session. Then the House passed a census bill; but, because the bill failed to make an appropriation to finance the taking of the census, the Senate killed the proposal. The senators argued that all appropriations measures must arise in the House, and they did not think it properly their duty to ask for the $60,000 appropriation for the census, especially since the House alone would be affected by the census returns.[120]

The arrival of 1885, the year designated for the state census, brought little change. Thompson, knowing it to be the Governor's constitutional duty to have the census taken, asked for a ruling from the Attorney General, who replied that under existing law the Governor could not order a census without a specific appropriation

118. South Carolina, *Constitution* (1868), Art. 2, secs. 4, 5, 6, 8. For the result of the 1876 reapportionment, see *Statutes at Large*, XVI, 88.

119. *News and Courier*, November 27, 1884. Also, see Governor Thompson to C. R. Miles, May 2, 1885, Thompson Letterbook E, Executive File, SCA.

120. *News and Courier*, December 25, 1884. Also, consult the letter from state Senators Smythe and Buist in that paper on June 23, 1890.

from the legislature for that purpose. In his message to the legislature of 1885, Governor Thompson renewed his request for money for a census. Again the House passed a census bill, this time with an appropriation to implement it. Even so, the bill failed to get by the Senate because that body had decided on a new course. Still fearful of the expense and concerned about the feasibility of taking the census and reapportioning the House prior to the 1886 elections, the Senate passed a resolution that would amend the state constitution.[121] In place of a state census in the middle of each decade, the Senate's resolution called for a census in 1891 and in every tenth year thereafter. But its most important feature allowed the legislature at any time " in its discretion " to adopt " the immediately preceding United States census as a true and correct estimation of the inhabitants " of the state. That clause, thought the Senate, would save the state over $50,000 each census year.[122] The voters approved the resolution by a three-to-one majority, and the legislature ratified it in the 1886 session. With the signature of Governor John P. Richardson on December 22, it became part of the constitution.[123] Still dissatisfaction remained, for no census had been taken, and therefore no reapportionment of the House could ensue.

During two years of legislative wrangling and amending of the constitution, the up country was " open-mouthed " about the failure to reapportion.[124] Up countrymen accused the Senate of dragging its feet and subverting the will of the people. The *Greenville News*, the constant spokesman of piedmont disaffection, discounted the opinion of the state Attorney General and charged that Governor Thompson had shirked his constitutional duty in not ordering a census on his own. Supposedly, unscrupulous politicians from the low country, especially from Charleston, had the dubious honor of carrying on this illegitimate campaign against the right of the people. These politicians hoped to stave off reapportionment in order to maintain their hegemony in the legislature and the party. Of course

121. *Daily Register*, January 7, 1886, and Thompson to Miles, *supra*, n. 119; *House Journal* (1885), p. 29; *News and Courier*, December 6 and 17, 1885.

122. *Statutes at Large*, XIX, 452–53. To amend the state constitution required a two-thirds majority on the proposed amendment in the legislature, then a simple majority of the popular vote at the next election followed by another two-thirds vote in the newly chosen legislature.

123. *News and Courier*, December 2, 1886; *Statutes at Large*, XIX, 499–500.

124. *Daily Register*, December 30, 1885 (the quotation is from this issue) and January 7, 1886; the *News and Courier*, December 2, 1886; Governor Thompson to

the dissident up-country forces maintained that reapportionment would strengthen their section at the expense of the low country.[125]

The contest reached a climax in the legislative session of 1887. In both the House and Senate, supporters of reapportionment opened their assault on a new front. Claiming that the constitutional amendment adopted the previous year permitted immediate reapportionment with the federal census of 1880 for a guide, they submitted reapportionment plans in both houses. After a struggle, the House voted along sectional lines and passed a bill to reapportion itself.[126]

But the main conflict, for contemporaries and for the future, took place in the Senate. There James F. Izlar of Orangeburg county led the regime's defense. Basing his case on the invalidity of the very constitutional point that his opponents used, Senator Izlar argued that the amendment denied the use of any federal census prior to that of 1890.[127] Moreover, according to Izlar and Senator E. B. Murray of Anderson county, to use a census taken in 1880 for reapportionment in 1887 made little sense, especially when an accurate enumeration of the state's population would be available by 1890. After bitter arguments the Senate, voting along sectional lines, killed by a nineteen to fifteen margin any reapportionment scheme.[128]

Francis Dawson, December 30, 1885, and to Charles Simonton, January 9, 1886, both in Thompson Letterbook E, Executive File, SCA.

125. Of course the up country's concern was for under-represented white Democrats, because by 1885 and 1886 few Negroes voted outside the Black District. In actuality, as the following table shows, the apportionment of the House was fairly equitable, but only if total population is counted.

	Total Representatives (per cent)	Total population (per cent)	White population (per cent)
Low Country	31.5	26.2	19.8
Midlands	34.6	35.3	33.4
Up Country	33.9	38.5	46.8

Population figures are taken from U.S. Bureau of the Census, *Compendium of the Eleventh Census: 1890, Part 1, Population*, p. 505. In fact, in a reapportionment plan drafted by up-country forces in 1887, the low country would lose only four seats while the up country would gain that number; a few others changed within midlands counties. *News and Courier*, December 9, 1887. Thus, reapportionment would not give the piedmont much more strength than it already possessed. Based on the 1880 U.S. Census, this reapportionment plan really would not have been altered much had a state census been taken in 1885.

126. *News and Courier*, December 9, 1887, and the *House Journal* (1887), p. 177.

127. *News and Courier*, December 14, 1887. The judiciary committees of both House and Senate supported Izlar's constitutional arguments. *Ibid.*, February 8, 1888.

128. *Ibid.*, December 14, 1887.

The regime's triumph in 1887 ended reapportionment attempts during the Conservative hegemony, but it did not end the reapportionment struggle. The regime had successfully stopped the reapportioners, but in the long run theirs was a pyrrhic victory. Up country-men smoldered over the wrong they felt their fellow Democrats had done them. Their dissatisfaction erupted again in 1890 when Benjamin Tillman used the reapportionment struggle, especially the state Senate battle in 1887, to great advantage against the Conservative Democrats.[129]

The Conservative leadership had defended their system from three attacks originating within the Democratic party. As quickly as one suggested change had met defeat or obstruction, another had taken its place. That only one of the three proposals would have directly affected sectional political strength in the Democratic party seems to have had little effect or influence on the dissidents. The agitations disturbed Dawson because, although he could find " very little tangible cause for complaint against the State . . . officers in general," he did discover " a nervousness and restlessness in the Democratic party which [might] become dangerous." That same kind of opposition to the regime worried Governor Thompson. To a friend he wrote that the dissatisfaction consisted " chiefly in vague hints and insinuations against the present State Government." He believed that " the fact that no definite charges [were] made [was] the best evidence that none [could] be made." Still, " whatever the cause," Thompson admitted " that much dissatisfaction exists among our people." [130] Against restlessness so general and vague, effective

---

129. *Infra*, chap. v. Tillman accused state senators who voted against reapportionment in 1887 of having committed perjury because they had failed to uphold their oath to support the state constitution, which according to Tillman, required a yea vote on the 1887 measure. This accusation was certainly exaggerated if not untrue, for the constitutionality of the 1887 reapportionment plan was highly dubious.

130. *News and Courier*, September 9, 1885; Thompson to E. Croft, June 7, 1886, Thompson Letterbook D, Executive File, SCA.

It is my feeling that Dawson and Thompson were largely correct in their analysis of the dissent in the up country. That section, to be sure, was underrepresented in the legislature. But a mathematically perfect reapportionment would have left it underrepresented because the lower counties had more Negroes, and no one suggested eliminating the Negro from apportionment calculations.

To find a specific reason for their unrest is impossible. The chief state officers chosen since 1876 had not been up countrymen, but neither had they been low countrymen. All three elected Governors and both United States Senators came from the midlands. But the other two men who had served as Governor, William D. Simpson, who became

defense was difficult; absence of vigorous leadership made the conduct of that defense even more difficult.

Responsible for the lack of direction in the Conservative leadership was Wade Hampton. Since leading the party to victory in 1876, he had commanded the Democrats of South Carolina. The generals who had followed him in the war years obeyed him in peace. When one of their number, Martin Gary, struck out against Hampton and the regime, the others remained loyal to Hampton, who used his prestige to destroy Gary's political aspirations. Hampton's removal to the United States Senate in 1879 did not decrease his prestige or power in the party. In 1880, he intervened on behalf of his loyal lieutenant Johnson Hagood to ensure the political death of Gary, and after 1880 Hampton retained his predominant position in the party. No Democratic opposition contested his re-election to the U.S. Senate in 1884; as the Columbia *Daily Register* asserted, it would be " utterly useless for anybody to oppose him for the Senatorial seat." [131] After 1880, the General did not exert or attempt to keep his authority in the state. When the bitter contest between two of his friends and subordinates threatened in 1882 to disrupt the Democratic party, he replied with general pronouncements about the excellent capabilities of both men.

No one took Hampton's authority from him; he gave it up willingly. Public life did not suit him. Prior to the Civil War he had not been active in South Carolina politics, and he spent most of the Reconstruction years in Mississippi looking after his farming interests. Upon returning to South Carolina, he assumed command of a military campaign, termed political, to restore the government of South Carolina to its native white citizens. He remained active from 1877 to 1880 to ensure the permanency of the victory of 1876

Governor when Hampton went to the U.S. Senate, and Thomas B. Jeter, president *pro tempore* of the state Senate, who became Governor when Simpson was elected Chief Justice of the state Supreme Court, were both from up-country counties.

Moreover, up-country forces had led the effort that made Hugh Thompson Governor in 1882. That the convention chose Thompson over Bratton or Kennedy delighted the up-country editors. Yet, before Thompson's tenure had ended, many of the same people who had worked for him in 1882 spoke out against him. I have been unable to discover any particular issue that caused that change of attitude except reapportionment. And on that question Thompson tried to have a census taken, but was thwarted by the Senate. Always the up country demanded more power within the Democratic party; it never said what it would do with that power.

131. *News and Courier*, December 10, 1884; *Daily Register*, August 25, 1883.

both in the party and in the state. By 1880 he had eliminated the only important internal opponent to the Conservative Democrats; by 1882 the national Republican party and the Republican administration in Washington had ended attempts to renew the struggle of 1876. With both party and state safe, Hampton no longer felt called upon to take an active role in state affairs.

Other than external events influenced Hampton's abdication. No longer a young man, he had been weakened by the loss of his leg in 1878.[132] Frustrations with the normal political activities of a senator and lack of interest in the decade's issues, such as trusts, labor, and financial questions, disheartened him. Physical infirmity and discouragement in his office drained his zeal for activity and brought a general melancholy. In 1880 Hampton wrote to his sister: " Life seems closed to me, and I have nothing but duty to live for. It is very hard, but I try to say, God's will be done." [133] When, in the old general's mind, no battles remained that required his services, he retired from the field.

When Hampton abdicated his position of leadership, the Conservative Democrats could offer no successor. His lieutenants— Conner, Hagood, Bratton, and others—had served together as subordinates in war and in 1876. No one had tried to assert any authority over his comrades—and it is doubtful that any one of them would have succeeded. Senator Butler had never commanded a respect and loyalty equal to Hampton's, for he too had always been a Hampton lieutenant. To have assumed the leadership position, Butler would have needed Hampton's public blessing. Of course by such intercession Hampton might have conferred on any individual the claim to the loyalty of leading Conservatives, yet he named no one. He left on the field in South Carolina several commanders but no commander in chief.

From a purely political view, Francis W. Dawson, editor of the Charleston *News and Courier*, represented the most logical choice for the top post in the Conservative Democratic party. The voice of the most powerful newspaper in South Carolina, and one of the

132. Hampton to Thomas Bayard, March 12, 1880, Thomas F. Bayard Papers, LC.
133. Hampton to Thomas F. Bayard, November 7, 1880, *ibid.*, and Hampton to A. H. Garland, June 12, 1885, Cleveland Papers, *ibid.*; also see Johnson Hagood to James Conner, April 29, 1883, Conner Papers, SCHS and N. G. Gonzales to Miss Emily Elliot, May 18, 1882, Eliott–Gonzales Papers, SHC; Hampton to Anna Preston, March 20, 1880, Wade Hampton Papers, SCL.

most influential in the South, the politically astute Dawson was South
Carolina's representative on the Democratic National Committee, a
position that automatically gave him a seat on the state party's
Executive Committee.[134] Dawson had been consistent: he always stood
with Hampton against Gary, and he strongly supported Johnson
Hagood for Governor in 1880.

Although he had been an effective supporter of Hampton in the
Gary fight, personal difficulties with the General tarnished his reputation among certain of Hampton's closest associates. An altercation
arose apparently over Dawson's belief that Hampton had opposed his
election to the National Committee in 1880. A more lasting difference came from Hampton's continued support of Thomas F.
Bayard of Delaware for the Democratic presidential nomination.
Both in 1880, when Dawson backed General Winfield Scott Hancock,
and in 1884, when he worked for Grover Cleveland, his interests
and goals conflicted with Hampton's.[135] Even though their animosity
never caused a break between them,[136] it did lessen Dawson's chance
of being accepted as the leader of the Conservative Democrats.

Besides his differences with Hampton, the editor's personal history
worked against him. That as a young Englishman he ran the
blockade to fight for the Confederacy endeared him to Conservative
chieftains. But his foreign birth and Roman Catholic religion added
to his failure to attain high rank in his adopted army hindered his
political acceptance within a group of old South Carolina families
that almost worshiped high military rank gained in Confederate
service. Dawson realized the difficulties of his position; writing to
his protégé and friend, N. G. Gonzales, Dawson acknowledged that
many " Carolinians resented the success of a ' carpet-bagger ' like

134. For comments on Dawson's political power in South Carolina, see the *New
York Times*, March 30, 1880, and the *Daily Register*, September 15 and 17, 1885.
Also numerous letters in the Francis W. Dawson Papers, Duke, testify to his influence
in the Conservative Democratic party: e. g., Joseph Earle to Dawson, August 12, 1886,
Charles Simonton to Dawson, August 26, 1886, and John Bratton to Dawson, June 15,
1881, in Scrapbook I; also Dawson to his wife, June 27, 1884.

135. Hampton to Dawson, May 25, 1881, and December 17, 1884, Scrapbook I,
Dawson Papers, Duke; Dawson to Hampton, May 14, 1881, Letterbook 1879–84;
memorandum by Dawson on his election as national committeeman in 1880 in a note-
book. *Ibid.* See also Hampton to James Conner, March 1, 1881, Conner Papers, SCHS.

136. Even so, Dawson felt that Hampton had "always disliked" him. Dawson to
his wife, October 15, 1886, Dawson Papers, Duke. That feeling did not prevent
Dawson from atempting to remain in Hampton's good graces. Dawson to his wife,
June 27, 1884, *ibid.*; *Daily Register*, June 26, 1884.

myself." [137] Dawson's lack of respect for the idols of South Carolina's Conservative leaders provided even more of an impediment. He had little use for lamentations of " the fallen structure " of the past.[138] Thus, with no hesitation, he had given complete public support to Daniel Chamberlain and the Republicans in early 1876. Of course, once the Democrats decided to make a fight in that year, his columns aided them. Still, he could never erase his public endorsement of Chamberlain and the Republican party.[139]

Hampton's virtual abdication and the absence of any successor prevented the Conservative Democrats from presenting a unified front to attackers. So long as dissidents made their protests within the Conservative regime, as did the up countrymen who proposed a variety of changes, they did not threaten its very existence. But the leaderless party faced mortal danger if a strong political force which operated outside of the rules and mores of the Conservative Democrats were to declare war on the regime.

137. Dawson to N. G. Gonzales, May 28, 1882, Letterbook 1879–84, Dawson Papers, Duke; see also Dawson to Grover Cleveland, May 27, 1885, Cleveland Papers, LC.

138. S. Frank Logan, "Francis Warrington Dawson, 1840–1889; South Carolina Editor," *The Proceedings of the South Carolina Historical Association* (1952), p. 20.

139. Other Democrats, to be sure, had connived with Republicans during Reconstruction, but Dawson's support had been public and remained public at a time—1876 —when opinion was moving the other way with intensity.

CHAPTER III

THE PROBLEM OF RACE

I

When in 1876 Wade Hampton accepted the Democratic nomination for Governor he declared, " I shall be the Governor of the whole people, knowing no party, making no vindictive discriminations, holding the scales of justice with firm and impartial hand, seeing, as far as in me lies, that the laws are enforced in justice tempered with mercy, protecting all classes alike." As far back as 1867, Hampton expressed his assent to limited Negro suffrage. He took particular pride in this stand and in campaign appearances emphasized his desire to bring the Negro into the Democratic party. At Darlington he promised, "*Not one single right enjoyed by the colored people to-day shall be taken from them. They shall be equals, under the law, of any man in South Carolina.*" [1] Hampton wanted honest, efficient government, in which the Negro should participate. Concern for the Negro so pervaded Hampton's speeches that one student of the campaign concluded Hampton directed his orations largely to the Negroes. [2]

The state Democratic party followed the Hampton campaign program. The platform adopted at the August convention, which nominated Hampton, accused the Republicans of " arraying race against race." " In perfect good faith " it accepted the Thirteenth, Fourteenth, and Fifteenth Amendments, and called upon all citizens

---

1. John S. Reynolds, *Reconstruction in South Carolina, 1865–1877* (Columbia: The State Co., Publishers, 1905), pp. 352–53; Wade Hampton to Armistead Burt [n. d., but probably late 1867], Wade Hampton Papers, Duke University Library, cited hereafter as Duke; *Free Men! Free Ballots!! Free Schools!!!: The Pledge of Gen. Wade Hampton, Democratic Candidate for Governor, to the Colored People of South Carolina,* p. 6.
2. Francis Butler Simkins and Robert Hillard Woody, *South Carolina during Reconstruction* (Chapel Hill: University of North Carolina Press, 1932), p. 497.

" irrespective of race or past party affiliation, to join with us in restoring the good name of our State, and in elevating it to a place of dignity and character among the commonwealths of this great country." Prompted by continuing concern for the Negro voter, the state Executive Committee in October issued a pamphlet of excerpts from eleven Hampton letters and speeches dating back to 1867, which disclosed his interest in the welfare of the Negro.[3]

After the Democratic victory in 1876, Hampton persisted in his campaign promise.[4] While in Washington attempting to arrange the withdrawal of Federal troops from South Carolina, he wrote to President Rutherford B. Hayes that he desired to establish " a government which will secure to every citizen, the lowest as well as the highest, black as well as white, full and equal protection in the enjoyment of all his rights under the Constitution of the United States." Returning to Columbia in early April, he reiterated his pledges that " every citizen of South Carolina, white or black, would be equal before the law; " he closed with an appeal for all South Carolinians to unite in working for the benefit of the state. To a New York reporter in the summer of 1877, Hampton defined his platform as one of friendship and co-operation between the races.[5]

United States Senator Matthew Butler supported Hampton on the race question. Speaking in his home county of Edgefield, Butler pronounced the issue facing the state no longer " a question of race." He advocated using Negro Democrats to speak against Republicans. Looking ahead to the national election of 1880 as the true crisis for the South, he avowed a Democrat had to win, and Negro Democrats could and would help carry the day in South Carolina.[6]

The 1878 elections generated Democratic determination to gain Negro support. The state Executive Committee in August implored Negroes to join the Democratic efforts to govern South Carolina

3. Reynolds, *Reconstruction*, pp. 354–55; *Free Men! Free Ballots!! Free Schools!!!*, *passim*.

4. Hampton M. Jarrell, *Wade Hampton and the Negro: The Road Not Taken* (Columbia: University of South Carolina Press, 1949), pp. 99–103, argues that the Negro vote gave the Democrats the victory; for a contrary opinion, see Joel Williamson, *After Slavery: The Negro in South Carolina during Reconstruction, 1861–1877* (Chapel Hill: University of North Carolina Press, 1965), pp. 408–11.

5. Hampton to Hayes, March 31, 1877, quoted in Harry Barnard, *Rutherford B. Hayes and His America* (Indianapolis: The Bobbs-Merrill Company, Inc., 1954), p. 427; Charleston *News and Courier*, April 7, 1877; *New York Herald*, June 21, 1877, quoted in the Columbia *Daily Register*, June 25, 1877.

6. *News and Courier*, July 28, 1878.

honestly and effectively. In a speech to the Barnwell county Democratic convention, Comptroller General Johnson Hagood entreated, " Invite the negro to the ranks of the Democracy as you invite the white man; and within the ranks of the party accord him every right that you accord the white man—neither more nor less." The state Democratic convention, as Hampton had requested, reaffirmed its interest in the Negro by unanimously adopting the entire 1876 platform.[7]

Governor Hampton courted the Negro vote during his campaign tour through the state. In the blackest South Carolina county, Beaufort, the Governor defied whites or Negroes " to put their finger upon one pledge I have violated." He urged Negroes " to reciprocate the good feeling offered by the best men in our party " and aid the Democrats. He reminded them that the Democrats had lowered their taxes; he promised better educational facilities. Returning to a familiar theme, Hampton proclaimed that " the Democratic party was elevated to power in '76 by the vote of the colored man, so will it be sustained in power by that same vote." When he repeated this claim in Greenville, he impressed a large number of Negroes, who maintained a great interest throughout the address.[8]

Hampton's exertions paid well. In 1878, he received 25,000 more votes than in 1876; at the same time, the Republican vote dropped by 90,000.[9] A resolution endorsing the Democratic ticket narrowly failed in the Republican state convention of 1878, but the Republicans did not put up a state ticket to oppose the Democrats.[10] A Republican Negro state Supreme Court Justice who had resigned under pressure told a Philadelphia reporter in the summer of 1877 that Hampton would be re-elected Governor " almost unanimously. He will get nine-tenths of the colored vote . . . There is not a decent Negro in the state who will vote against him." A prominent white Republican assured D. T. Corbin, a former Republican United States Senator from South Carolina, that Hampton took

7. *Ibid.*, August 23, 1878; Spartanburg *Herald*, May 22, 1878; *Daily Register*, August 2, 1878, and Sumter *Watchman*, August 8, 1878.

8. *News and Courier*, September 20 and October 31, 1878.

9. Appendix B.

10. *News and Courier*, August 8 and 9, 1878; James Welch Patton, " The Republican Party in South Carolina, 1876–1895," in *Essays in Southern History*, ed. Fletcher Melvin Green, in *The James Sprunt Studies in History and Political Science*, XXI (Chapel Hill: University of North Carolina Press, 1949), 93.

seriously his overtures to the Negroes.[11] President Cooke of Claflin University wrote to a Northern friend that the white Democrats did not oppose " negro suffrage or negro office-holding or the rights of manhood which the constitutional amendments secure." Many years afterward, Thomas E. Miller, a Negro Republican who sat in the United States House of Representatives asserted that Hampton " was sincere when he said that he intended to make a part of the government of our State mixed as to race." [12]

The overwhelming Democratic triumph of 1878 did not change the party's racial stand. The Executive Committee's address of thanks, not ignoring the future, found it " especially gratifying that so many thousands of colored people of the State have united with us in perpetuating home rule and good government." [13] Before the 1880 campaign, Hampton, by then a United States Senator, urged the party Executive Committee to begin work in doubtful counties, for with an early start " they [could] secure thousands of colored voters " for the Democratic party. Francis Dawson, in the *News and Courier*, affirmed that " proper efforts " would bring " great numbers of blacks to the support of the Democratic ticket." In his inaugural address in 1880, Governor Johnson Hagood continued the pattern of assuring Negroes that South Carolina Democrats would maintain their rights. Democratic Congressman Michael P. O'Connor advocated to a party worker in Greenville the enrollment of Negroes in the Democratic party: " I have always been in favor of that policy best suited to secure his [the Negro's] alliance and co-operation with the Democratic party." [14]

As late as 1882, the Democratic party actively solicited Negro support. In that year, 2,000 Negroes were " regularly enrolled and members of Democratic Clubs " in Barnwell county.[15] In July, 1882,

11. *Philadelphia Times*, quoted in the *Daily Register*, August 21, 1878; William Earle to D. T. Corbin, March 9, 1878, Source Chronological File of the Justice Department, Record Group 60, National Archives; cited hereafter as NA. Also, all other NA citations in this chapter come from Source Chronological File of the Justice Department, Record Group 60.

12. *The Springfield Republican*, December 18, 1878, quoted in the *News and Courier*, December 30, 1878; George Brown Tindall, *South Carolina Negroes, 1877–1900* (Columbia: University of South Carolina Press, 1952), p. 43.

13. *News and Courier*, November 15, 1878.

14. Hampton to James Conner, May 30, 1880, James Conner Papers, South Carolina Historical Society, cited hereafter as SCHS; *News and Courier*, September 18 and December 1, 1880; Mary Doline O'Connor, *The Life and Letters of M. P. O'Connor* (New York: Dempsey and Carroll, 1893), pp. 203–4.

15. Georgetown *Enquirer*, July 12, 1882.

the Orangeburg county convention of the Democratic party unanimously resolved that the county's Negroes "be accorded representation upon our ticket, in proportion to their assistance and co-operation with us, in the cause of good government;" then it voted to issue a public address informing the citizens of its action. Georgetown Democrats arranged with Republicans, largely Negroes, to share county offices. The "momentous question of preserving a pure and efficient administration of public affairs" promoted their alliance.[16]

To secure Negro members, the Democrats did more than make friendly gestures from the public platform. Hampton took pride in appointing former Republican Lieutenant Governor Richard Gleaves as a trial justice. The Democratic party of Clarendon county included one Negro in its group of three men recommended for election managers. The Governor appointed a Negro captain of a state militia company in Abbeville county; he also appointed the Negro postmaster of Columbia to the board of the state orphan asylum.[17] A recent survey indicates that Hampton appointed at least eighty-six Negroes to office.[18]

The Democrats also placed Negroes on legislative delegations. When the Charleston county Democratic convention in June, 1877, nominated candidates for the legislature, those chosen included three Negroes. No Negro Democrats served in the South Carolina Senate, but between 1878 and 1882 as many as six at one time sat in the state House of Representatives. The News and Courier, the state's most powerful Democratic newspaper, spoke truthfully in 1881: "Far from the Democratic leaders in South Carolina being determined to maintain the 'color line' they have worked assiduously and patiently to obliterate it." [19]

16. Orangeburg Times and Democrat, July 20, 1882; Georgetown Enquirer, August 2, 1882.

17. New York Herald, June 21, 1877, quoted in the Daily Register, June 25, 1877; Brown Manning to Wade Manning [Hampton's private secretary], November 28, 1877, Wade Hampton Papers, Incoming Correspondence, Box 7, Executive File, South Carolina Archives, cited hereafter as SCA; William Arthur Sheppard, Red Shirts Remembered: Southern Brigadiers of the Reconstruction Period (Atlanta: Ruralist Press, 1940), pp. 216–17; Tindall, Negroes, p. 23.

18. Tindall, Negroes, p. 22, n. 8. It must be said that for the most part, these appointments were not to important positions but they served to make Negro Democrats feel that the party at least knew of their existence. Also, after 1880 the number of Negroes appointed to any office decreased.

19. Charleston Journal of Commerce, June 20, 1877; Tindall, Negroes, pp. 309-10; News and Courier, July 12, 1881. Dawson's statement sums up the official position of

II

Wade Hampton's attitude toward the Negroes in the state did not go unchallenged. Martin Gary, as early as 1874, had declared that South Carolina political contests posed " a question of race, and not of politics." In January, 1876, he blamed the failure to break up radical rule on not appealing to the white man as a white man. Gary envisaged victory only in the " unescapable issue of race against race." [20]

Gary's plan for the campaign embodied his verbal attacks. He admonished Democratic speakers to remember " that *argument* has no effect" upon Negroes; " they can only be influenced by their *fears*, superstition, and cupidity." He exhorted them to show Negroes " that their natural position is that of subordination to the white man," and to encourage among white men any method necessary " to control the vote of at least one negro." [21] When Daniel Chamberlain, Republican candidate for Governor, reached Edgefield for a campaign speech in August, 1876, armed riflemen on horseback greeted him. As some 800 horsemen rode through the small town, the rebel yell reverberated in the streets. Democratic enthusiasts tore down the platform intended for the Republican speakers and re-erected it " with Democratic guidons." At Newberry, white riflemen surrounded Chamberlain while he sat on the speakers' platform.[22] In Aiken county a major race riot was narrowly averted.

Bitter about being passed over for the United States senatorship in 1876, Gary decided to use the Negro question against Hampton. To an alliance with Negroes Gary attributed the victory of the Hampton program in the regular legislative session of 1877.[23] He said white Democrats voting with Negroes upheld the bond settle-

---

the party. Those statements, however, cannot be accepted without an investigation of election practices discussed below.

20. Jarrell, *Hampton*, p. 57, n. 51; David Duncan Wallace, *History of South Carolina* (New York: American Historical Society, Inc., 1934), III, 306. Gary's most ardent defender, William A. Sheppard, wrote in his *Red Shirts Remembered*, p. 192, that Gary " would as soon sing Psalms to a dead mule as to deliver a speech to them [Negroes]."

21. Simkins and Woody, *Reconstruction*, pp. 564–69.

22. Sheppard, *Red Shirts Remembered*, pp. 94–109, 123–24.

23. Gary to Hugh Farley, May 9, 1878, Martin Witherspoon Gary Papers, South Caroliniana Library, University of South Carolina, cited hereafter as SCL.

ment and reopened South Carolina College against the express wishes of the up country.[24]

Gary bristled when Hampton supported a constitutional amendment providing a two-mill tax to support public education for both races. He fought it unsuccessfully in the legislature and arraigned the plan in a public addresss in Abbeville. Although he opposed the amendment because the constitution of 1868 forbade segregation in public schools, he argued his case on other grounds: "Nine-tenths of this tax would be paid by white people, and three-fourths of it would be spent in educating piccaninnies." [25]

In his attempt to have the legislature of 1878 elect him United States Senator, Gary returned to his 1876 generalizations on race. Speaking before the Edgefield county Democratic convention in June, Gary named the real political issue in the South and South Carolina " an antagonism of race." At a huge meeting in Edgefield during the county canvass prior to the elections in November, Gary asserted that in his " judgment the mistake that our leaders were making was in considering the differences between the negro and white man a difference of politics, instead of a difference in point of fact of *race*." According to Gary, human nature, philosophy, and especially, the history of Santo Domingo and Haiti verified his racial stand.[26]

Later in August, Gary took his campaign to Greenville where he declared the Edgefield Plan responsible for victory in 1876, and judged the deciding issue in the future, as in the past, to be race. In the review of Greenville militia companies, the occasion of Gary's address, an incident swept him to an open personal attack on Hampton as the architect of a disastrous racial policy. A captain of one of the militia brigades had invited the Negro Mountain City Guards to participate in the review. Upon seeing Negro troops marching in line with white, Gary told the crowd the combining of races in the review exemplified Hampton's race policy. Such mingling would not stop with racially mixed military reviews, for " we will next hear of dining or dancing with the colored brothers and sisters, as events [which are] the natural result of *Hampton* Democracy." [27]

24. Cf. *supra*, chaps. i and ii.
25. Sheppard, *Red Shirts Remembered*, pp. 215–16. Of course, no Conservative leader contemplated integration of public schools.
26. *News and Courier*, June 4 and August 15, 1878.
27. *Ibid.*, August 29, 1878.

Gary hoped to discredit Hampton by publicizing critical articles on the Claflin University dining episode. In Orangeburg in 1878, Superintendent of Education Hugh S. Thompson and Governor Hampton had accepted a dinner invitation from President Cooke of Claflin. Upon their arrival in Cooke's home they found two Negro guests but, after a moment's hesitation, Hampton and Thompson both sat down. Using "White Supremacy" as a nom de plume, Gary wrote an article attacking Hampton as being pro-Negro.[28] His eating with Negroes did not surprise "those who have watched Governor Hampton's political course." The Governor "has again and again boasted" he supported Negro suffrage before any other man in the South. He was the first white Democrat to sit on the rostrum with Negro radicals; he supported the bill that joined South Carolina College and Claflin University. Gary never published the "White Supremacy" article because one of his chief political advisers feared it would backfire. Henry Farley argued that publicizing the dining affair would afford Hampton an opportunity to explain and "the blame will be thrown on Cooke who is ready to shoulder it." At first, Gary refused to be swayed from publication but finally yielded to Farley's advice.[29]

Gary discovered that others disapproved of his harsh attitude on the race question. Circuit Judge Joshua H. Hudson of Marlboro county, a strong Gary supporter, cautioned Gary not to "come down too heavy on the *race issue.*" Advising on the kind of speech he should give in Bennettsville, Hudson warned Gary that he was too extreme on the race question for most of his supporters; he should "temper the language" in his speeches. He told Gary that his Greenville speech excited "unfavorable comment as being too harsh on the negro." The *News and Courier* condemned his Greenville speech because "the issue in South Carolina, as made by the Democratic party, is not an issue of race." Unless Gary modified his position, Dawson vowed, "He must be treated like any other Democrat who is in open rebellion against the Democratic party." [30]

When Edgefield county Democrats formally adopted Gary's Negro policy, opposition arose in every section of the state. As chairman

28. The manuscript is in the Gary Papers, SCL.
29. Henry Farley to Gary, September 23 and October 11, 1878, *ibid.*
30. J. H. Hudson to Gary, September 9, 1878, and William Wallace to Gary, September 21, 1878, *ibid.*; *News and Courier*, August 29, 1878.

of the county party and as the most important political figure in the county, Gary had prompted a resolution adopted by the June convention of the Democratic party of Edgefield county: " that we regard the issues between the white and colored people of this State, and of the entire South, as *an antagonism of race*, not a difference of political parties." By barring Negro voters from Democratic primaries, the convention formalized its May decision to refuse to recognize the existence of any Negro Democratic clubs in the county.[31] The up-country *Laurensville Herald*, which " could hardly stomach " Edgefield's anti-Negro policy, declared Democrats could not afford to ignore Negro voters; the Democratic party needed them in every election. Because Negroes had supported the Democratic ticket in 1876, " it would be unwise, impolitic, and ungrateful in us not to countenance those who assisted in redeeming the State." When Negroes come to join Democratic clubs, " we are honor bound to receive them, and should by all means, do so, and vote them with us." In Newberry county, a neighbor of Edgefield and Laurens, the *Herald* concluded that the logical outcome of the Edgefield Resolutions would be a race war none could want. Furthermore, in adopting proscription and violence, " we sink ourselves to the level of any half-civilized people." In up-country Anderson county the *Intelligencer* invited Negroes to vote Democratic: " They should now cast off their bad leaders [the Radicals] and make friends with those with whom they are identified in interest." In predominantly white York county, the Democratic convention adopted a resolution praising Hampton for remembering his promises to " our colored citizens." [32]

Midlands and low-country papers joined the assault on the Edgefield Resolutions. The *Kingstree Star* said that even with its Negro majority, Williamsburg county must remain in Democratic hands. " They [Edgefield Resolutions] are impolitic and they are not Democratic. The negro is as much a party in the politics of South Carolina as the white man, and for those having a Democratic majority to ignore his existence, is to throw the whole burden of negro rule upon us in the low country." The best interests of white and

31. *News and Courier*, June 4 and September 25, 1878.

32. *Laurensville Herald*, May 31, 1878; Newberry *Herald*, quoted in the *Daily Register*, May 26, 1878; Anderson *Intelligencer*, October 31, 1878; Yorkville *Enquirer*, June 27, 1878.

Negro required the Negro to join " his former master " in the Democratic party. Though admitting the Negro possessed rights, the *Star* concluded " it is the part of political wisdom to use the negro as we can for their [Republican] injury and not our own." The *Daily Register* of Columbia warned its readers that " we must not become lax in our efforts to further increase the army of colored Democrats." Because Negroes in the midlands rallied " to the support of honesty and home rule," white Democrats in Sumter would never forget that " the colored Democrats stood by us in our time of need." [33]

Although Wade Hampton's moderate policy has been documented, most students have agreed with the contemporary observations of Laura Towne, the abolitionist schoolteacher, that he was not able to keep his pledges to the Negro in the face of the widespread opposition to Negro rights in the party. The *New York Times* echoed Miss Towne: Hampton could never defeat " the unquenched fire-eaters of his party." [34] Yet Gary, the leader of the anti-Negro element in the party, completely failed to alter Hampton's policy. Often, he alone fought the administration's program in the legislature. Both of his tries for high state office and his attempts to profit from a harsh racial policy ended disastrously. His advisers counseled against anti-Negro speeches, and reaction to the Edgefield Resolutions showed that they recognized the popular temper better than Gary. Even after Gary's death in 1881, the Democratic party continued to cultivate the Negro.[35]

33. *Kingstree Star*, quoted in the Sumter *True Southron*, June 18, 1878; *Daily Register*, September 20, 1878; Sumter *Watchman*, April 11 and 18, 1878.

34. Rupert Sargent Holland (ed.), *The Letters and Diary of Laura M. Towne: Written from the Sea Islands of South Carolina, 1862–1884* (Cambridge, Mass.: The Riverside Press, 1912), p. 264; *New York Times*, August 24, 1878.

35. The most notable account of Hampton's race policy is Jarrell, *Hampton*. George Tindall, the historian of the South Carolina Negro after 1877, generally agrees (*Negroes*, pp. 19–22) with Jarrell on Hampton. But Tindall voices the opinion of Laura Towne when he says that Hampton's policy " was opposed by the majority of whites and upheld only by the immense prestige of Hampton." (*Ibid.*, p. 39.) To prove either this theory or its converse is all but impossible. The state party's official announcements and the editorials of most newspapers supported the Governor, not Gary. Gary's advisers warned him to curtail his anti-Negro activity. At the same time, whites took any measures they thought necessary to prevent a resurrection of the Republican party.

The question of hypocrisy is equally difficult. Undoubtedly some Conservative spokesmen had no intentions of carrying out the programs enunciated by their party. Yet most

III

Even though the Conservative Democrats repudiated Martin Gary's ideas on race and officially and publicly adopted the moderate policy espoused by Wade Hampton, the years from 1877 to 1882 proved no blissful era for Negroes in South Carolina. The Democratic party's appeal to the Negro met with some success; however, the great majority of Negro voters remained stanch Republicans. Legislative action eliminated most Republicans from the General Assembly and made more difficult the election of Republican candidates. Outside of legislative halls, in towns and in countryside, fraud and violence held down the Republican vote.

In the regular legislative session beginning in November, 1877, the Democrats wrote and passed a new election law that provided for two different ballot boxes and tickets at each polling place. One box served for congressional candidates and presidential electors, the other for " State, Circuit, and County Officers." The two boxes were kept " separate and apart and not in the same apartment." In addition to divorcing federal and state boxes, the legislature drew up a new list of county voting precincts that drastically reduced the number of polling places in predominantly Negro counties. This provision handicapped the average Negro, the average Republican, in reaching the polls during the voting hours between 8 A.M. and 5 P.M., because the trip to the polling place often entailed a day's journey.[36]

In their reports to Washington, officials of the United States Department of Justice recounted numerous devices used to thwart Republican voters and ensure Democratic success. The federal District Attorney for South Carolina, Lucius Northrop, a white Republican, called the election of 1878 " a farce." In Charleston on election day, managers of the election arbitrarily refused Negroes the right to vote; by 1 P.M. " over one thousand Colored men, whose right to vote cannot be disputed, [had] been denied the privilege." The United States Marshal reported to the Attorney General that

---

observers—contemporary and subsequent—have found Hampton sincere in his concern for the Negro. The truth probably lies between Hampton and Gary. Most white South Carolinians were not so sincere as Hampton in their determination to accord the Negro equal treatment with the white; but, on the other hand, most did not accept the harsh, bitter attitude of Martin Gary. Almost two decades passed before they did.

36. South Carolina, *Statutes at Large*, XVI, 565–69; cf. *ibid.*, XV, 981–85.

Democrats "carried all the strong Republican counties by Stupendous frauds." [37] According to E. W. M. Mackey, Northrop's assistant, the Democratic election managers at Palmetto Engine House Poll #1 in Charleston's First Ward stuffed in 2,500 false ballots after the box was closed. They did not throw out any ballots, and returned a vote of 3,108 for the Democrat to only 461 for the Republican. Mackey doubted that 3,500 votes could have been cast when the manager had to swear in each prospective voter. On Edisto Island, where 1,000 Republicans but only 50 Democrats resided, the polls never opened.[38]

From 1878 on, Democrats often employed stronger voting restrictions. To show their disregard for federal authority, Democrats in Marion and Chesterfield counties ripped badges from United States marshals. In Aiken county, cannon covered the streets opposite polling places. On election eve, all of Greenville county " resounded with reports of cannon and firearms." Armed Democrats prevented Republican voting in Camden. In Fairfield county, where some 600 to 900 Negro Republicans came to the polls, Negro and white Democrats " dressed in red shirts and armed with knives and pistols formed a line around the door of the polling place and forcibly and violently threw back every Republican voter who . . . endeavored to reach the door." [39]

Harassment of Republicans was not peculiarly an election day event. Democrats intimidated Republicans trying to hold campaign meetings and used force to disperse them. Sumter Democrats became so violent that Governor Hampton called out the militia. When Republican congressional candidate Robert Smalls attempted to hold a meeting in Gillisonville in the closing days of the 1878 canvass, 800 red shirts galloped on the scene with rebel yells, scattered the crowd, and peppered with gunfire a store where Smalls and some of his supporters had retreated.[40]

37. Lucius B. Northrop to Charles Devens, November 5, 1878; E. W. M. Mackey to Charles Devens, November 5, 1878; R. M. Wallace to Charles Devens, November 5, 1878, all NA.

38. *New York Times*, November 11, 1878.

39. *Ibid.*, November 9, 1880; Lucius Northrop to Charles Devens, November 5, 1878; C. C. Levy [Republican in Camden] to Charles Devens, November 5, 1878; Samuel Melton to Benjamin Brewster, December 21, 1883, all NA.

40. R. M. Wallace to Charles Devens, October 21, 1878, NA; Rupert Holland (ed.), *Diary and Letters of Laura Towne*, pp. 289–90.

Although it found a general plan where none existed, Northrop's allegation that acts of intimidation and fraud formed "the result of a deliberate and desperate conspiracy of the whole democratic organization to defraud the acknowledged republican majority of the use of the suffrage" described events with more than a little accuracy.[41] A Marlboro county Democrat recounted to the party's congressional candidate the action at the polls in his county: "The negroes were sullen and stubborn and came to the polls today in mighty force. But hard work early and late, and bold, determined, and aggressive action broke their ranks and gave them a Waterloo."[42] The state furnished attorneys for Democrats prosecuted for violations of federal election laws.[43] State Executive Committee Chairman General J. D. Kennedy handled the Democratic case during the Charleston hearings by a congressional committee formed to investigate reports of fraud and violence during the 1878 elections in South Carolina.[44] In 1883 the legislature honored Governor Hugh Thompson's request and appropriated $10,000 to defray the legal expenses of Democrats being prosecuted in the federal courts.[45]

Simultaneously, the Democratic party solicited the Negro voter and hounded him if he tried to use the ballot outside the party. A contemporary observer understood this phenomenon. In the *International Review* in 1880, Edward Hogan noted that if the Negro became a Democrat, he would remain "perfectly safe"; but if he persisted in his Republicanism, "no amount of peaceful profession or kindly consideration toward him . . . [would] save him from being pushed aside by men who indignantly deny him to be their political equal."[46] Wade Hampton, architect of the Conservatives' racial program, displayed these sentiments in numerous speeches. He warned Negroes against making race an issue—that is, voting

41. Lucius Northrop to Charles Devens, December 9, 1880, NA.
42. J. H. Hudson to John S. Richardson, November 5, 1878, John S. Richardson Papers, SCL.
43. United States Marshal Wallace complained to Attorney General Devens that "the best lawyers in the state [would] volunteer" to defend accused Democrats. Wallace to Devens, October 17, 1878, NA.
44. *News and Courier,* January 31, 1879. The committee was named for its chairman, Senator Henry Teller of Colorado.
45. *Ibid.,* November 28, 1883, and Kennedy to James Conner, April 2, 1879, Conner Papers, SCHS.
46. Edward Hogan, "South Carolina Today," *The International Review,* VIII (February, 1880), 110.

Republican—for if they drew that line, "they would be drawing it for their own destruction." Because South Carolina whites would never again let the Republican party dominate the state, he admonished Negroes to join the Democrats. The *News and Courier* chorused approval. Editor Dawson, commenting on the Teller committee hearings, wrote that " white civilization, and all that it implies, must rule in South Carolina "; at the same time he invited Negroes to become members of the Democratic party, the vehicle of white domination.[47]

Though Hampton and the Conservatives intended to retain their hegemony at all costs, they condemned many methods used against the Republican party. The *News and Courier* called for laws to end the carnival of fraud that existed during elections. U.S. District Attorney Northrop felt sure that " a sober second thought [was] at work seriously among the democrats [sic]. They know that the State cannot live on public dishonesty in defiance of the federal laws." William L. Mauldin, a prominent up-country legislator and later Lieutenant Governor, feared that " our people [the Conservative Democrats] are placed in a bad light " because of their violent and fraudulent behavior at election time.[48] As early as 1878, Hampton voiced concern about election violence in South Carolina. In a published interview, he admitted knowledge of irregularities then added, "No one can regret this more than I do." Such practices he regarded as impolitic. To his friend L. Q. C. Lamar, Hampton acknowledged 1878 "irregularities" but denied that he approved of them or even knew of them until after the election. In the United States Senate, Hampton again confessed that frauds and violence had marred South Carolina elections in 1878 and 1880. In the same speech, he " announced his unalterable determination to try . . . to rectify the wrong that had been done." [49]

47. *News and Courier*, March 21, 28, July 28, and October 3, 1878; January 31, 1879; January 12, 1881.

48. *Ibid.*, November 19, 1880; Northrop to Devens, November 27, 1880, NA; William L. Mauldin Diary, entry of November 2, 1880, Southern Historical Collection, University of North Carolina.

49. Yorkville *Enquirer*, January 23, 1879; Hampton to Lamar, September 12, 1879, L. Q. C. Lamar Papers, Mississippi Department of Archives and History; *New York Times*, April 23, 1881, and *News and Courier*, April 23, 1881.

IV

This acknowledgment by party leaders of illegal and wrongful activity moved the state government to act. Concerned about violence, Governor Thomas Jeter in 1880 wrote the chief state constable that he was " very anxious to have the public peace preserved during the next General Election and for this purpose I think it important that you appoint in each County where there is any apprehension of a disturbance a sufficient number of special deputy Constables to maintain the peace." [50] The General Assembly in its regular session of 1880 intended to do more than just maintain peace; it set up a joint committee to investigate the entire electoral problem and make recommendations for new legislative action at the 1881 session.[51]

The committee's recommendations largely embodied the ideas of attorney Edward McCrady, Jr., former Confederate officer and member of an old Charleston family. A keen student of history who wrote important volumes on colonial South Carolina, McCrady turned to classical and English constitutional history in his search for an answer to the South Carolina suffrage dilemma. McCrady pondered the Conservative problem—how could a minority govern without violence and fraud when universal manhood suffrage prevailed? Fraud and violence decay civilization, but education, he reasoned, could provide the base of lawful political dominance by an intelligent minority. " History will not excuse us, if having a remedy in our hands, we prefer fraud to the legitimate exercise of our legislative power." [52]

This legislative power derived from American constitutions, federal and state, " based upon the fundamental assumption that our people can read and write." The state provided a system of

50. Jeter to Colonel Alfred Rhett, October 23, 1880, Simpson–Jeter Letterbook, Executive File, SCA.

51. *News and Courier*, December 3, 1881, and *New York Times*, February 16, 1880.

52. The sources for this exposition of McCrady's view are two of his pamphlets: *The Necessity of Education as the Basis of Our Political System: an Address Delivered before the Euphemian Society of Erskine College* [June 28, 1880] (Charleston: Walker, Evans and Cogswell Publishers, 1880) and *The Necessity of Raising the Standard of Citizenship and the Right of the General Assembly of the State of South Carolina to Impose Qualifications upon Electors* (Charleston: Walker, Evans and Cogswell Printers, 1881). The latter was his report to the joint committee, and formed the basis of the committee's report to the legislature.

public education financed by a two-mill levy on all taxable property in a county and by a one-dollar poll tax. Therefore, in providing for secret ballots the state assumed literate voters. "Is it not then right and proper that having gone so far, and done so much to secure the freedom of the voter," McCrady asked, "that the State should go one step further and require each and every elector to read and write, as the condition and qualification of the exercise of his right to vote? Is not this the logical result of the theory and system of the [written] constitution?" To McCrady there appeared only one possible answer to these questions.

For another part of his program, he turned to the South Carolina constitution, drafted in 1868 by the despised Radicals. Article VIII required the state to register voters "from time to time." For McCrady this stipulation served two purposes. To register meant to write a prospective voter's name in the registration books. Requiring the prospective voter to write his own name, rather than having the registrar do it for him, would add another literacy qualification. A strict registration policy would handicap the voting of the ignorant, the transient, the criminal, as well as the Negro.

McCrady's program specifically intended to disfranchise great numbers of Negroes, but opposition arose to protest no loopholes for illiterate whites. McCrady replied unequivocally: "The public good" required the enactment of such a measure even if the disfranchised included whites. They could learn; the state had provided a free school system. "We deprive no man of his franchise where we impose a condition of its existence with which he can comply."

McCrady accepted John C. Calhoun's idea of the existence and necessity of levels in society. The whites should rule, but those Negroes who met the strict requirements for citizenship, as McCrady termed them, could cross the line. Likewise those whites who did not meet the requirements must stay on the other side. Even though convinced of its impossibility, McCrady feared the day when Negroes would attain sufficient education to dominate under such a system as he devised; thus he challenged white South Carolinians:

We complain of the great and cruel injury done to the white race in the South by forcing upon us the ignorant negro vote . . . The remedy is in our hands. Raise the standard of citizenship; raise the qualification of voters. But raise them equally. If we are the superior race we claim to be, we surely, need not fear the test.

When the legislature assembled in November, 1881, the joint committee submitted a comprehensive report on the suffrage question. Following McCrady's thinking, the report envisioned a vigorous registration system coupled with voting procedures that made literacy essential. Initial registration and maintenance of registered status required payment of various fees, ranging from twenty-five cents to five dollars, plus prompt notification to the supervisor of any change of address, even if that change occurred in the same precinct or voting district. This provision disfranchised the very poor along with those who for lack of education or lack of industry failed to understand thoroughly the complex features of the law. The voting procedure itself consisted of a system of eight boxes, one for each classification of office. The voter had to place the proper ballot in each box; a wrong placement voided his entire vote. No one could render assistance by reading the names on the boxes or otherwise aid the illiterate voter.[53]

In the state Senate, the bill based on the report encountered little trouble. An effort to strike out the entire registration section failed. Thomas E. Miller, a Negro Republican from Beaufort county, led the tiny contingent opposed to all aspects of the proposed legislation, which would disfranchise " poor whites and struggling blacks." On his motion to strike out the enacting clause, Miller had only two supporters; twenty-seven opposed him. On December 13, the bill passed intact except for the money features of registration.[54]

The House attacked the committee's proposals from several sides. Difficulty in the House had not been expected because a Democratic caucus had pased on the bill by a substantial majority.[55] The bill's

---

53. *News and Courier*, November 24, 1881. The different classifications of offices (*Statutes at Large*, XVII, 1117) were:

    (1) Governor and Lieutenant Governor
    (2) Other state officers
    (3) Circuit solicitor
    (4) State senator
    (5) Members of the state House of Representatives
    (6) County officers
    (7) Representatives in Congress
    (8) Presidential electors.

54. *News and Courier*, December 3, 1881.

55. *Ibid.* The course of the debate in the House can be followed through the columns of the *News and Courier* for December, 1881, and January, 1882; that source should be supplemented by the *Journal of the House of Representatives of the General Assembly of the State of South Carolina* (1881–82).

supporters managed to rebuff a proposed increase in the number of supervisors and a decrease in the number of boxes. The leader of the opposition in the House, W. H. Parker of Abbeville, found strong sympathy for throwing out the registration section. Defending his work from its chief antagonist, fear of white disfranchisement, McCrady argued that any voter disfranchised by the bill " did not deserve to have a vote."

McCrady's plea did not suffice. The Christmas recess evidently allowed the representatives to hear adverse opinions; Parker commanded enough strength to defeat the bill by five votes on January 17. Many who voted against the bill personally favored it yet wanted to stand in a good political position should the bill prove unpopular.[56] After two party caucuses had given strong support to the bill, its defeat came as an especial shock. The bill's managers, who regrouped their forces and gained a reconsideration, could at best only arrange a committee composed of supporters and opponents to restudy the bill.

This committee did its work quickly and on January 20 reported to the House. Signed by nine of the ten committee members, the report cleared the House by fifty-seven to thirty-nine votes. When the House bill reached the Senate, some senators had objections, but " they [did] not think it would be safe to risk further argument upon the matter." Passing the Senate without a recorded vote, the bill was signed into law by Governor Johnson Hagood on February 9.[57]

The law differed both from the ideas McCrady had publicized and from the report the joint committee had made in November, 1881. In its journey through the legislature, McCrady had to yield ground to the bill's opponents, although the end product remained satisfactory enough for him to vote aye on the final roll call. The major change came in voting procedure. The special House committee inserted an amendment that required the election manager, on demand of the voter, " to read to him the names on the boxes." This revised provision created wide opportunity for fraud on the part of the manager. Knowing that " no vote for any office other than that for for which such box shall be designated and labeled

---

56. *News and Courier*, January 18, 1882.

57. *Ibid.*, January 27, 1882; no vote was recorded in the *Journal of the Senate of the General Assembly of the State of South Carolina* (1881–82).

shall be counted," the manager could choose to misinform an illiterate voter.[58] That the prohibition against aid to voters was deleted while the often attacked registration requirement was retained suggests that the bill's proponents agreed to accept the read-on-demand amendment in order to retain the registration section. Thus, they granted possible assistance for the illiterate white at the polling place while making his arrival there improbable.[59]

Even without the fee system, the registration provisions bred real difficulties. All citizens eligible to vote in 1882 had to register in either May or June of that year or remain perpetually disfranchised. For those who became eligible after 1882, the books opened one day in each month up to July before a November election. The county Supervisor of Registration alone could ascertain the legal qualification of each applicant for registration; more important, he could refuse to register any applicant. Upon such refusal, the prospective voter could appeal to the circuit court, provided he informed the Supervisor in writing within five days after his rejection. The Supervisor gave a newly registered voter a certificate stating his name, age, place of residence, and occupation. Any change, no matter how slight, in any of those particulars required a report to the Supervisor, who issued a corrected certificate. Provided he informed the Supervisor of his new status, the holder easily obtained a new certificate.[60]

The new law drew generally favorable reactions from the South Carolina press. Both the Yorkville *Enquirer* and the Edgefield *Chronicle* supported the law; the *Enquirer* thought a better one unlikely, considering all the pressure to omit and include specific sections. The powerful *News and Courier* favored the bill; recognizing the Supervisor as the key figure, it called on Governor Hagood to appoint upstanding men to the position. The extremely con-

---

58. *Statutes at Large*, XVII, 1118.

59. In roll call analyses of key House votes, I could find—with one exception, the Negro representatives—no meaningful groupings among the opponents of the election law. Their ranks did not hold firm through the long debate. Certainly there was no up-country fight to ensure the ballot for the illiterate white. Legislators did oppose the measure because they felt it would disfranchise whites, but they came from all sections of the state. For example, on Murray's motion to table Parker's motion to strike out the registration section, 43 representatives voted nay. Of those, 15 came from up-country counties, 11 from midlands counties, and 18 from low-country counties. *House Journal* (1881–82), pp. 138–39. Of the 18 from the low country, eight were Negroes. Every Negro in the House, both Republican and Democrat—except for J. A. Owen, a Negro Democrat from Barnwell county—voted against the bill at every opportunity.

60. *Statutes at Large*, XVII, 1111–17.

servative Georgetown *Enquirer* sounded a note of disharmony when editor Walter Hazzard favored the report of the joint committee but opposed the final form of the legislation. He called it "an intellectual anomaly and a political monstrosity, and opens wide the door to fraud of the most unblushing kind." [61]

The Election Law of 1882 did not stand alone in the Conservative arsenal against fraud and violence. The census of 1880 gave South Carolina two new congressmen, increasing the total to seven. As early as April, 1882, the *News and Courier* called for a special session of the legislature to redistrict the state. [62] Many other papers concurred, but a few preferred to have the two new congressmen run at large in the November elections. Governor Hagood considered redistricting essential, and called a special session in June.

The special session met on June 27; by July 5 it had redistricted the state. Senator J. F. Izlar of Orangeburg introduced a bill to divide the state into seven congressional districts. When the Democrats caucused to consider Izlar's proposal before it reached the floor of either body, no real opposition developed; except from the Republicans, no resistance appeared on the floor. Speaking for the Republicans, Senator Miller said his party did not object to the bill as a gerrymander, but to the obvious Democratic determination to exterminate Republicanism. He had hoped for a more conciliatory plan. Gladly would he have given four districts to the Democrats in turn for three Republican ones, but a six-one split he declared unfair. [63]

The bill introduced by Izlar, passed by the legislature, and protested by the Republicans, did propose an obvious gerrymander. Named after its chief author, Samuel Dibble of Orangeburg, formerly a member of the legislature and from 1882 to 1890 a member of Congress, the Dibble plan divided the state to give Democrats control of as many seats in the national House of Representatives as possible without fraud or violence. Worked out in detail prior to the convening of the legislature, Dibble's proposal fulfilled the assignment in ingenious fashion.

Dibble founded his plan on the relative number of Negroes in

61. Yorkville *Enquirer*, February 16, 1882, and Edgefield *Chronicle*, June 21, 1882; *News and Courier*, January 28, 1882; Georgetown *Enquirer*, February 15, 1882.
62. *News and Courier*, April 22, 1882, and *Daily Register*, April 8, 1882.
63. *News and Courier*, June 28 and July 1, 1882.

SOUTH CAROLINA CONGRESSIONAL DISTRICTS
(AS DRAWN IN 1882)

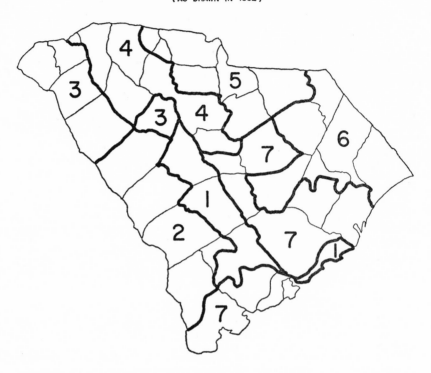

South Carolina counties. He intended to group the blackest counties
into a single Republican district, which the Democrats would not even
contest. The three counties having the heaviest Negro population
—Beaufort, Berkeley, and Georgetown—stretched along the coast
intersected by Colleton and Charleston counties. By adding the lower
part of Colleton—also heavily Negro—and connecting Colleton
with Berkeley, the three were aligned into one. To that heart of
the district, he appended the Santee sections of Williamsburg,
Clarendon, Orangeburg, Sumter, and Richland counties. Each of the
added counties had a heavy Negro population, most of whom lived
in the Santee sections. This proposal, besides creating " a congressional District for the colored people," made possible legitimate
Democratic control of the remaining sections of the counties not
wholly in the Negro district, because it left whites in the majority

in the parts of the counties outside that district. Dibble thought
" any other sub-division of the State, [would] involve the sacrifice
of strong white sections in colored Districts, and [would] not appre-
ciabily benefit the remaining Counties." [64]

The Democrats expected to carry six of the seven districts. " If
the full white and colored Democratic vote be cast for Congressman," Francis Dawson asserted, only the Seventh District, which
quickly received the name Black District, would go Republican.[65]
The Democrats, in 1882, fully intended to give the Republicans
this District containing 25 per cent of the state's Negroes. The
newspaper accounts of the special redistricting session announced
that the Democrats would not contest the Black District seat, and
none did oppose Republican E. W. M. Mackey in the 1882 election.[66]

After the heated activity of the winter and summer of 1882, the
concern of white South Carolinians with the race issue declined. By
the summer of 1882, those Democrats dissatisfied with the registration sections of the election law had adjusted themselves to it.[67]
The opposition to the McCrady law showed some local unwillingness
to disfranchise certain whites as part of a general Negro disfranchisement, but the fight stirred up no anti-Negro feeling. Between 1882
and 1886, the Democratic press rarely mentioned the Negro; race
questions occupied few legislative days. In general, quiet prevailed.
Election violence and fraud decreased after the election law of 1882
and the creation of the Black District.

The federal government and the Republican party of South
Carolina helped induce this relaxation. The continuing federal
prosecutions for election law violations had troubled the state

---

64. Dibble to John S. Richardson, June 21, 1882, Richardson Papers, SCL, and a
memorandum in the Williams-Chestnut-Manning Papers, *ibid.*

65. *News and Courier*, July 4, 1882. In that same issue, the *News and Courier* gave
the approximate number of voters in each district:

District	White	Negro
First	11,953	13,223
Second	11,392	17,096
Third	13,952	13,756
Fourth	17,696	17,519
Fifth	12,031	13,433
Sixth	12,879	14,685
Seventh	7,008	31,152

66. *Ibid.*, and Port Royal *Palmetto Post*, July 27, 1882.
67. *News and Courier*, June 27, 1882.

government and roused public opinion.[68] By the end of 1882, however, President Chester A. Arthur and his Attorney General Benjamin H. Brewster decided to give up the prosecutions. Receiving little assistance from the Justice Department in Washington, the Republican party in South Carolina degenerated into squabbling factions. Their conventions, described by Democratic correspondents as ludicrous, seemed "models of tediousness and longevity." They ran no candidate for statewide office, and their attempts to unite with independent movements proved futile. The party stopped offering congressional candidates except in its special preserve. Even in the Black District, feuds and factions wracked the party.[69]

Originally the fear of renewed Republican or Negro domination precipitated most Democratic anti-Negro activity. After 1882 the Democrats saw little reason to harp on the race issue. They had achieved their goal—the elimination of a politically potent Republican party.

Even though general fraud and violence did not recur in South Carolina elections in the 1880s,[70] the Democratic party by the middle of the decade began to doubt the wisdom of staying out of the Black District. No Democrat contested that district in 1882; two years later Colonel William Elliott of Beaufort carried the party's banners. Elliott's candidacy had been much questioned even before Robert Smalls defeated him. One paper had advised the Democratic party not to offer a candidate, for in a fair fight only the Republicans could win, and the *Daily Register* thought such a contest had "doubtful utility." [71] Still, the *Register* pledged to back the District's Democrats should they decide to run a candidate. They did convene and

68. The federal government attempted to try cases growing out of both the 1878 and 1880 elections. Because of difficulties with juries and with the law (see the discussion on this question in chap. i), the federal cases had met with little success.

69. Patton, "Republicans," p. 95 and *passim*; George Gage [a white Republican in Beaufort county] to ——— Wilson, August 10, 1889, Letterbook 1884–94, George Gage Papers, Duke University Library, cited hereafter as Duke; Port Royal *Palmetto Post*, 1882–90 *passim*.

70. Letters from Chief Justice Morrison R. Waite to his wife contain valuable comments on South Carolina conditions. Talk of violence and intimidation disappeared; quiet rather than turmoil pervaded the political and social atmosphere. This change in attitude can be traced through the letters of May 20 and 24, 187., May 23, 1880, May 14, 1886, in the Morrison R. Waite Papers, Library of Congress, cited hereafter as LC.

71. Orangeburg *Times and Democrat* quoted in the *Daily Register*, August 19, 1884, and the *Daily Register*, August 2 and 19, 1884.

nominate Elliott for Congressman,[72] not hoping to capture the District for the party but to provide a full Democratic ticket so as to gain the strongest possible vote for Grover Cleveland.[73] Two years later in 1886, when the party decided to take the District, Elliott again ran against Smalls. This second time he won. The *Greenville News* cried fraud: " The State will be put before the country as being party to a plain, deliberate fraud." The *News and Courier* countered that there had been little counting out; quite to the contrary, Elliott owed his election to the intelligent Negroes, who, tired of Republican corruption, turned to the candidate of good government.[74] Probably some Negroes did vote for Elliott, but without a doubt fraud helped.

At the same time, some Democrats throughout the state began again to question the wisdom of soliciting the Negro vote. The proliferation of primaries adversely affected the Negro's position in the Democratic party. The Barnwell county Democrats in 1884 made Negro voting in their primaries practically impossible. Speciously arguing that Negro clubs had violated party rules, they reasoned the party could ill afford " to countenance irregularities." Yet they assured the Negro that they had no intention of casting him aside " as a practically useless factor in county politics." The Democratic convention of the Fifth Congressional District, meeting in Lancaster in September, 1886, professed no such feelings; it simply barred the Negro from the District primary.[75] Two years later, the Laurens county Democratic convention passed what became a model resolution: " No negro shall vote in the next primary election who cannot prove by five responsible white Democrats that he voted with the Democracy for Hampton and the State ticket in 1876, and has been a Democrat ever since." [76]

72. *Daily Register*, October 11, 1884, and *News and Courier*, October 10, 1884.

73. *News and Courier*, June 28, 1884. Francis Dawson to S. H. Rogers [editor of the Port Royal *Palmetto Post*] August 19, 1884, Letterbook 1879–84, and Dawson to Samuel Dibble, January 26, 1885, Letterbook 1884–87, Francis W. Dawson Papers, Duke.

74. *News and Courier*, December 2, 1886.

75. *Ibid.*, August 11, 1884; *Daily Register*, September 25, 1886.

76. *Laurensville Herald*, May 18, 1888. This is not to say that after 1885 no Negroes became Democrats or received appointments from the party. For example, Democrats organized new Negro clubs in Hampton county as late as 1888. (Anderson *Intelligencer*, June 6, 1888.) In that same year, white Democrats welcomed disaffected Negroes from the Republican party who helped them win the Beaufort county elections.

Even though local Democratic organizations had begun to exclude Negroes, the Conservative leadership continued to voice allegiance to Hampton's program. Hampton himself, campaigning for Cleveland at Anderson in 1884, implored Negroes to vote for the national Democratic ticket, because the national party would protect them as the state party had done. He told his Negro listeners: "As I stand here in the sight of people and of God, I say we have carried out every pledge made to you as a part of the people of South Carolina." Governor Thompson, in his inaugural of that year, reiterated the Conservative promise to give the Negro impartial consideration. Speaking before a Negro Teachers Institute in the summer of 1887, Governor Richardson declared the white Democrat to be the Negro's best friend in South Carolina and the Democratic party to be no hinderer of Negro progress.[77]

V

Although the agitation begun in the autumn of 1885 by Benjamin Tillman culminated in the overthrow of the Conservative regime, the issue of race played no part in Tillman's success. Neither Tillman nor his followers openly attacked the Conservative racial position. Demands and platforms growing out of the Tillman-dominated Farmers' Association conventions made no mention of race. The Negro question occupied a singularly unimportant place in the gubernatorial canvass of 1890.[78]

Indirectly, Tillman caused anti-Negro action by demanding primaries for every office from Governor to coroner; normally the elimination of the Negro from the Democratic party became an adjunct of the primary system. A top Tillman leader, J. L. M. Irby, dominated the Laurens county Democratic convention that in 1888

Port Royal *Palmetto Post*, November 8, 1888. But the decreasing number of Negro Democrats in the legislature illustrates the direction of the general trend. By 1886, only two remained in the House; they would stay there until 1890. Tindall, *Negroes*, p. 310. For a discussion of Negro voting, see Appendix C.

77. *News and Courier*, September 27 and December 5, 1884; *Daily Register*, July 9, 1887.

78. Neither Tillman nor the Conservatives made any sort of plea to—or against—the Negro. The Negro himself played no significant part in the campaign. The Colored Farmers' Alliance did endorse Tillman, but it made no public campaign for him. That endorsement brought no Conservative reaction. Joseph Church, "The Farmers' Alliance and the Populist Movement in South Carolina, 1887–96" (unpublished Master's thesis, Dept. of History, University of South Carolina, 1953), p. 47.

required any Negro wishing to vote in a primary to produce five whites who would swear that he had voted for Wade Hampton in 1876. Led by another prominent Tillmanite, Dr. Samson Pope, the Newberry county Democratic convention in 1890 overwhelmingly adopted a resolution that called for a statewide Democratic primary for whites only. The action by Laurens and Newberry heralded the change that came in the 1890 party constitution, written by a Tillman-controlled state convention, which made a statewide primary mandatory in 1892, and required any Negro who wished to vote in that primary to have voted for Hampton in 1876 and to have remained a Democrat ever since.[79]

Other indications of the vehement anti-Negro course Tillmanism would take by 1895 became evident. Tillman's attitude toward the Negro obviously differed from that of Hampton and the Conservative leadership.[80] A friend visiting Tillman in 1889 remembered his host's saying, "We cannot work free negroes without cussing." In an 1888 campaign speech at Hodge's Depot in Abbeville county, Tillman alleged that "the negroes had been pitched overboard," and the only pertinent question asked which group of whites should rule. His inaugural address in December, 1890, made no pretense about his estimation of the Negro's place in South Carolina. "We deny," Tillman told his audience, "without regard to color, that all men are created equal." "The whites have absolute control of the State government, and we intend at any and all hazards to retain it." A Tillman newspaper, the Charleston *World*, asserted that Tillmanism had no desire to proscribe any class but insisted that "all white men in the record of the ballot box shall stand upon the same footing." [81] In yet another way, Tillmanism struck at Conservative racial policy. When, in 1888, a prominent young Tillmanite lawyer from Aiken county, John Gary Evans, introduced in the legislature a bill to repeal the state's civil rights law, this attempt failed. Evans reintroduced his bill in 1889 and obtained its passage, though not without a fight.[82]

79. Newberry *Herald and News*, July 3, 1890; *Constitution of the Democratic Party of South Carolina* (1890), Art. 6.

80. *Infra*, sec. VI.

81. Thomas J. Kirkland, "Tillman and I," Columbia *State*, June 30, 1929, p. 40; *News and Courier*, July 21, 1888; Francis B. Simkins, *Pitchfork Ben Tillman: South Carolinian* (Baton Rouge: Louisiana State University Press, 1944), p. 171; Charleston *Weekly World*, June 24, 1890.

82. *News and Courier*, December 17, 1888, and December 22, 1889.

Although the bitter racist aspects of Tillmanism attracted little attention before 1890, a close student of South Carolina affairs could foresee the Negro and his complete proscription becoming a political issue. Anticipating the racists, certain important Conservative leaders turned to an idea they had never before considered. With their political and social structure collapsing from Tillmanite pressure, a pressure the Conservative Democrats seemed unable to combat successfully, Senators Hampton and Butler spoke out for Negro emigration from the country. Harking back to old American Colonization Society proposals, they campaigned for federal legislation and funds for such a program. By 1888, Butler believed colonization offered the only hope for Southern salvation;[83] a year later, Hampton expressed his belief that for the South "to escape disasters greater than those inflicted by the war" there appeared "but one preventive and that is the removal of the negro from America." In the summer of 1890 Hampton contended in a national magazine that deportation of the Negro with his consent provided the only possible way to solve the Southern racial problem.[84]

Both men carried their fight to the floor of the United States Senate. Butler, keenly aware of Tillman's progress, found the key to the race issue in "an unrelenting, unforgiving, incurable race prejudice." He professed his concern over the future welfare of the Negro race; in that future the Negro could expect little or no change in the prejudice against him. His best hope lay in moving to a new land, Central America or Africa, where he could develop on his own without white suppression.[85] Hampton thought the Negro race needed to work out its destiny outside the United States because in this country too many obstacles checked "aspirations for equality and independence." He appealed to Union sentiment and declared that the presence of the Negro prevented the "perfect union" dreamed of by the founding fathers. The specter of racial bloodshed haunted him; the national interest demanded a liberal emigation policy.[86]

83. For several Butler letters on this topic, see the Matthew C. Butler folder in the Yates Snowden Papers, SCL.

84. Hampton to Jonathan Doolittle, November 12, 1889, Wade Hampton Papers, Personal Miscellaneous File, LC; Wade Hampton, "The Race Problem," *Arena*, II (July, 1890), 132–38.

85. *The Negro Problem* (n. p., n. d.), a collection of pamphlets in SCL.

86. *Negro Emigration. Speech of Wade Hampton, a Senator from the State of South Carolina, in the Senate of the United States, Thursday January 30, 1890* (Washington,

By 1890 emigation was impractical. But, confronted with Till-manism and an attitude toward the Negro of which they dis-approved, the Conservatives had little room in which to maneuver. Unchecked Tillmanism also meant the end of Southern politics as Hampton and Butler knew them. The demagogue who thrived on denunciation of the Negro lurked just ahead. Hampton and Butler advocated the only way of preventing his rise and dominance, the removal of the ultimate source of his strength, the Negro. Their proposals generated little response; Benjamin Tillman soon over-whelmed the Conservative regime.

VI

Outside the political realm the Conservative Democrats displayed little official interest in the Negro. A pattern of racial politics with white politicians vying to champion the white man did not develop. Neither did a systematic body of statute law create a society with rigid legal definitions of social separation. Racial segregation undoubtedly marked the general pattern of race relations in South Carolina but the urge to place custom in a legal code did not develop. No responsible white Democrats advocated anything like racial inte-gration, however; to a man, Conservative politicians believed in the superiority and the necessary supremacy of the white race. Although the white demanded that the Negro remain subservient, he did believe the state had obligations to its Negro citizens.[87]

1890). The most important Conservative paper in the state, the *News and Courier*, supported the scheme propounded by Butler and Hampton.

In the U.S. Senate, Hampton and Butler failed to obtain any significant backing for their bill, even from other Southerners. Rayford W. Logan, *The Negro in American Life and Thought: the Nadir, 1877–1901* (New York: The Dial Press, Inc., 1954), pp. 135–36.

87. George Tindall in his *Negroes*, chaps. xvi and xvii, reached this conclusion which C. Vann Woodward in his *Strange Career of Jim Crow*, Galaxy edition (2d ed. rev.; New York: Oxford University Press, 1966), chaps. ii and iii, agreed with and used on a broader canvas. Recently, however, Joel Williamson in his *After Slavery* (esp. chaps. ix and x), has registered a strong dissent. Writing about Negroes in South Carolina during Reconstruction, Williamson argues that the harsh line in race relations was established during those years and never changed. Williamson goes on to say that even Wade Hampton was a firm believer in white supremacy. I, too, have pointed to Hampton and his party as champions of white supremacy. But I disagree with William-son's conclusions. In fact, it seems to me that the Tindall-Williamson argument is semantic. No one denies that practically all whites believed the Negro to be inferior

The Conservatives maintained public education for Negroes. State Superintendent of Education Hugh Thompson, who held the post from 1877 to 1882, worked to establish on firm foundations a public school system for both races. By 1880, Thompson had succeeded in fulfilling Hampton's promise to place education within the reach of all classes. In 1879–80, white schools received $168,516 ($2.75 per capita), and Negro schools received $182,899 ($2.51 per capita). Between 1877 and 1880 the per capita expenditures were relatively equal, and the appropriations for public education increased every year up to 1890.[88]

The Conservative leadership fought opponents of public education for Negroes. In a letter to the *News and Courier*, a white South Carolinian questioned free schools for Negroes. He approved the Eight Box Law with its literacy qualifications as the perfect system for maintaining white supremacy. To educate Negroes seemed to him paradoxical; education would allow them the ballot. Editorially Dawson replied that Negroes composed a part of the body politic, that education would help them to exercise their rights as citizens capably and wisely. He told his correspondent that the ignorant Negro would be more dangerous than the educated one. Superintendent of Education Thompson asserted that "true philanthropy and sound statesmanship alike teach the best way to elevate the negro . . . is to educate him." [89]

Realizing their lack of financial resources, the Democrats of South Carolina requested assistance from Washington even before Senator Henry W. Blair introduced his ill-fated bill on federal aid to education.[90] An address from the state Democratic Executive Committee in August, 1882, asked the federal government for " liberal appropriations " to assist in converting " the present and rising generation

---

to the white. At the same time, the absence of a systematic body of statute law requiring racial segregation in every area of social contact cannot be pushed aside and minimized. To say that the lack of segregation laws meant a racial paradise existed is surely wrong. But white supremacy did not have to mean the complete proscription of the Negro. The opposition met by Martin Gary in his attempts to use that issue supports the claims of Tindall and myself.

88. Tindall, *Negroes*, p. 214. Professor Tindall asserts that "the state dealt generously with Claflin," the Negro college. *Ibid.*, p. 288.

89. *News and Courier*, May 10, 1884; *Reports and Resolutions of the General Assembly of the State of South Carolina* (1879), p. 365.

90. Allen J. Going, "The South and the Blair Bill," *Mississippi Valley Historical Review*, XLIV (September, 1957), 267–90.

of freedmen into intelligent and responsible citizens." A plank in the state party platform of 1882 included similar expressions, as did Governor Thompson's inaugural.[91] In the U.S. Senate, Hampton endorsed the Blair Bill and told the Senators that South Carolina did not have sufficient funds to educate her young. Hampton's remarks pleased Governor Thompson, who repeated his support for federal aid in his second inaugural.[92] Support of the Blair Bill did not end with Senator and Governor, for newspapers in all sections of the state voiced approval.[93]

When in 1883 the United States Supreme Court declared the Civil Rights Act of 1875 unconstitutional, no rush occurred to repeal the state civil rights law. Certain newspapers advocated repeal, but the most powerful papers ridiculed such thinking.[94] A repeal bill introduced in the legislature induced some support from legislators who feared the Supreme Court's decision would involve the state in litigation unless they repealed the state law; however it died with little fanfare. Senators Hampton and Butler heartily approved the Court's action yet reasoned the decision would have little real effect in South Carolina, because, according to them, the state already protected the Negro's constitutional rights.[95]

Maintaining the state civil rights law on the statute book did not enforce civil rights. In fact no record exists of any convictions

91. *News and Courier*, August 22, 1882; *Daily Register*, August 3, 1882, and *News and Courier*, December 6, 1882.

92. *Speech of the Hon. Wade Hampton of South Carolina, in the Senate of the United States, on Senate Bill No. 398 to Aid in the Establishment Ane* [sic] *Temporary Support of Common Schools, March 27, 1884* (Washington, 1884); Thompson to Hampton, March 28, 1884, Thompson Letterbook D, Executive File, SCA; *News and Courier*, December 5, 1884.

93. *News and Courier*, March 28, 1884; *Daily Register*, March 30, 1884; Anderson *Intelligencer*, April 3, 1884.
This attitude, however, did not survive the decade. By 1889, both the *News and Courier* and the *Daily Register* had changed their editorial policies. Now they opposed the bill as unconstitutional; it represented another step in the march towards centralization. *News and Courier*, November 1, 1889. No longer did the platform of the Democratic party ask for federal funds.
One possible reason for this shift which might be a signpost to the hardening of racial attitudes was the editorial position of the Charleston *World*. The *World*—an anti-regime paper that supported Tillman—called Blair's proposal " a bill of abominations " that would lead to federal control of education. Charleston *World*, February 17, 1888.

94. *Aiken Recorder*, quoted by the *Daily Register*, November 9, 1883; *News and Courier*, November 5, 1883.

95. *News and Courier*, October 24, November 29, and December 3, 1883.

under it.[96] At the same time, Negroes did have equal access with whites to certain public accommodations during the Conservative period. The Charleston Academy of Music and bars and ice cream parlors in Columbia accepted Negroes and whites as patrons. Railroads provided accommodations for both races without discrimination; the *News and Courier* ridiculed the idea of segregated railroad cars.[97] Establishments that accepted Negroes on an equal basis with whites undoubtedly were fewer in number than those not doing so. Still, such Negro contact with whites occurred more extensively during the 1880s than it did later.

The Conservative government of South Carolina treated its prisoners, mostly Negro, more humanely than did its counterparts in other Deep South states. The notorious convict lease system never became so entrenched in South Carolina as it did elsewhere.[98] In 1879 the *News and Courier* exposure of the condition of prisoners leased to the Greenwood and Augusta Railroad led to public outrage and to investigations by prison officials and the legislature. In 1880 the legislature enacted a law empowering the Governor to revoke any contracts for prisoners "whenever it appeared that prisoners were being cruelly treated." [99] The law required that each prisoner be examined by a prison physician at least once every month. Four years later, the legislature stipulated that guards for prisoners must be responsible to the state rather than to private contractors. During the eighties, the state penitentiary began to farm for itself with convict labor; this system of state-owned farms expanded until in 1897 convict leasing was abolished.[100]

Lynching of Negroes did occur in the Conservative years, but not so frequently as in future years. Leading spokesmen of the state govern-

96. Tindall, *Negroes*, p. 292.

97. *Ibid.*, pp. 294–95, and Woodward, *The Strange Career of Jim Crow*, pp. 36–40; *News and Courier*, November 5, 1883, and August 1, 1887.

98. Tindall, *Negroes*, chap. xiii; Fletcher Melvin Green, "Some Aspects of the Convict Lease System in the Southern States," *Essays in Southern History*, ed. Fletcher Melvin Green, in *The James Sprunt Studies in History and Political Science*, XXXI (1949), 119. In 1890 there were 732 Negroes in the state penitentiary but only 59 whites. *Appleton's Annual Cyclopedia* (1890), p. 778. The preceding decade had the same disparity in numbers.

99. *News and Courier*, November 23-24, 1879; Tindall, *Negroes*, p. 272.

100. Tindall, *Negroes*, pp. 273–76. See also Governor Johnson Hagood to the president of the Edgefield and Trenton Railroad, February 3, 1881, Hagood Letterbook A, Executive File, SCA, and Governor Hugh Thompson to C. R. Miles, June 26, 1885, Thompson Letterbook D, *ibid.*

ment and powerful newspapers strongly denounced all lynching—with one exception. Almost all white opinion condoned lynching for the Negro man who had allegedly raped a white woman. Public pronouncements of the state officials were more than platitudes. Governor John P. Richardson in 1889 ordered that the state militia reinforce the York county sheriff's department to prevent the lynching of Negro prisoners.[101]

The argument advanced by C. Vann Woodward that Southern Conservatives or Bourbons were tolerant white supremacists has substantial validity in South Carolina outside of politics.[102] One can argue that nobody insisted on statutory racial proscription during the 1880s because the Negro had already been suppressed. But, if Negro suppression were a fact, South Carolina political leaders of the mid-1890s thought otherwise, because only then did they begin to erect a system of legal discrimination.

---

101. *News and Courier*, March 29, 1889. See also William E. Gonzales [Governor Richardson's private secretary] to J. E. McDonald [solicitor of the Sixth Circuit], March 23, 1889, and Gonzales to E. A. Crawford [sheriff of York county], March 26, 1889, both in Richardson Letterbook E, Executive File, SCA.

102. Woodward, *The Strange Career of Jim Crow*, chaps. ii and iii.

CHAPTER IV

THE ECONOMICS OF CONSERVATISM

I

" The industrial progress of South Carolina in the last ten years almost surpasses belief," declared the *New York Times* in 1884.[1] Industry substantially aided South Carolina's effort to recover from the calamity of military defeat and physical devastation. By 1880 capital invested in manufactures was almost double the 1860 amount.[2] New and larger manufacturing establishments hired more workers, paid more wages, and significantly increased the value of their finished products.

The decade following 1880 witnessed even greater growth than had the twenty previous years. In 1890, capital invested in manufactures approached $30,000,000, almost three times that of 1880, while the value of manufactured products almost doubled the 1880 total. The number of employees in industrial enterprises increased by more than 30 per cent; their wages rose almost two-fold. Railroads, cotton mills, and phosphate mining—these three enterprises dominated South Carolina industry.

Railroads had long advanced the state's development. In 1833 the South Carolina Railroad, covering a distance of 136 miles be-

1. *New York Times*, February 4, 1884.
2. The following table contains the statistics cited here and in the following paragraph:

	1860	1870	1880	1890	1900
Invested capital	$6,931,756	$4,320,235	$11,205,894	$29,276,261	$62,750,027
Value of products	$8,615,195	$7,886,185	$16,738,008	$31,926,681	$53,335,881
Wages paid	$1,380,027	$1,234,972	$ 2,836,289	$ 5,474,739	$ 9,130,269
Number of employees	6,994	8,141	15,828	22,748	47,025

These figures come from South Carolina, Department of Agriculture, Commerce and Immigration, *Handbook of South Carolina* (Columbia: The State Company, 1907), p. 396, cited hereafter as *Handbook* (1907).

tween Charleston and Hamburg, was the longest railroad in the world. Between the completion of the South Carolina Railroad and the beginning of the Civil War, leading Carolinians worked assiduously to increase the railroad mileage in the state and to connect Charleston with the West. Although their efforts to link the South and West by rail failed, the state had 987 miles of railroad by 1860.[3]

Four years of war wrecked railroads in South Carolina, but peace brought a new era of railroad building. Construction was renewed in 1868, when a friendly state government granted charters and encouraged railroaders. Railroad men responded; by 1877 mileage stood at 1,356, an increase of 25 per cent over the 1865 total of 1,007.[4] The most important addition to the state's railroads, the Atlanta and Richmond Air Line built by Pennsylvania Railroad interests, crossed the northwestern part of the state and passed through Spartanburg and Greenville on its way from Charlotte to Atlanta.

The end of Republican political control in the state did not halt railroad construction. In fact, roads spread at a more rapid rate in the decade after 1877; by 1890, mileage in South Carolina totaled 2,297, an increase of 41 per cent over 1877.[5] By then a new road connecting Atlanta with the northeastern United States competed with the older Atlanta and Richmond Air Line in the piedmont— with numerous smaller roads and branches acting as feeders from the chief cotton-producing areas. The state had become a railroad gridiron.

Cotton mills, like railroads, in South Carolina antedated the Civil War. In fact the South's pre-eminent ante-bellum industrialist, William Gregg, lived and operated his famous mills in Graniteville, South Carolina. Prior to the establishment of the Graniteville mill in 1845, cotton manufacturing had been a small scale, relatively unimportant enterprise. Gregg's efforts brought personal business success but did not incite a cotton mill boom. In 1860 South Carolina

3. John F. Stover, *The Railroads of the South, 1865–1900: A Study in Finance and Control* (Chapel Hill: University of North Carolina Press, 1955), p. 5.

4. Francis Butler Simkins and Robert Hilliard Woody, *South Carolina during Reconstruction* (Chapel Hill: University of North Carolina Press, 1932), p. 188, and Ernest McPherson Lander, Jr., *A History of South Carolina, 1865–1960* (Chapel Hill: University of North Carolina Press, 1960), p. 97.

5. Lander, *South Carolina*, p. 193.

MAJOR RAILROAD LINES IN SOUTH CAROLINA
(1890)

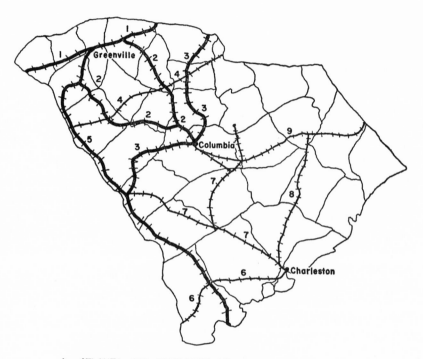

1 ATLANTA AND CHARLOTTE AIR LINE
2 GREENVILLE AND COLUMBIA (WITH BRANCHES)
3 CHARLOTTE, COLUMBIA AND AUGUSTA
4 SEABOARD AIR LINE
5 PORT ROYAL AND WESTERN CAROLINA
6 SAVANNAH AND CHARLESTON
7 SOUTH CAROLINA
8 NORTHEASTERN
9 WILMINGTON AND MANCHESTER

NOTE: ALL ROADS SHOWN IN HEAVY LINE WERE CONTROLLED BY
THE RICHMOND AND DANVILLE SYSTEM

had seventeen cotton mills, only one more than in the year of Graniteville's founding; and Graniteville remained the only significant mill.[6]

Between 1865 and 1880 cotton mills made substantial progress but not until the decade of the 1880s did they rival railroads as the most important industry in the state. Although the depression of 1873 dealt cotton manufacturing a severe blow, toward the end of the decade a real boom was beginning and by 1883 the number of mills had risen to twenty-six. After a recession in 1884 and 1885, cotton manufacturing began a decade and a half of astounding growth. By 1900, with an invested capital of almost $40,000,000, textiles had become South Carolina's dominant industry.[7]

Phosphate mining, unlike railroads and cotton mills, had few ante-bellum antecedents. That phosphate rock existed in the Charleston and Beaufort areas had been known for years. Edmund Ruffin, in his 1843 geological survey of South Carolina, reported marl deposits extremely rich in carbonate of lime. By 1860 mining operations had begun, but the onset of war forced their suspension. Actual mining began soon after 1865. The first phosphate mining company, the Charleston Mining and Manufacturing Company, was organized in 1867 and by 1870 thirteen companies were engaged in mining phosphate and manufacturing the material into fertilizers. Throughout the years of Conservative rule, the industry had fairly consistent growth. After 1885 production never fell below 170,000 tons; the high point came in 1890 with 247,150 tons.[8]

Phosphates never became so important an industry as railroads or cotton mills. With the deposits located chiefly along coastal river beds from Charleston to Beaufort, few people or communities became interested in mining phosphate. Also, after 1890 and richer discoveries in Florida, the industry in South Carolina began a fatal decline. Even so, for the years between 1877 and 1890, phosphate mining assisted in the economic recovery of the Charleston-Beaufort area and greatly benefited the finances of the state.[9]

6. Gustauvus Galloway Williamson, Jr., "Cotton Manufacturing in South Carolina, 1865–1892" (unpublished Ph.D. dissertation, Dept. of History, The Johns Hopkins University, 1954), p. 4.
7. *Ibid.*, pp. 63, 68, 92, 94, 105, and Lander, *South Carolina*, p. 83.
8. Philip E. Chazal, *The Century in Phosphates and Fertilizers, a Sketch of the South Carolina Phosphate Industry* (Charleston, 1904), pp. 55–56.
9. *Infra*, sec. III.

II

The Conservatives welcomed industry to South Carolina and worked to create a favorable atmosphere for its growth. Governors' messages consistently pointed with pride, at times with exaggeration, to the state's industrial achievements and they emphasized the soundness of the state's credit. To future investors they repeatedly pledged an economical state government that would insure them a friendly and profitable home in South Carolina.[10]

Francis W. Dawson through his *News and Courier* led the cry for a new age in South Carolina. Summarizing his philosophy Dawson declared, " Charleston cannot live by cotton and rice alone." Describing the location of a new cotton mill in Columbia, Dawson prophesied that the state capital would become " the Southern Manchester." He continually talked about the state's need for " a new impetus in the direction of further progress." Almost any mention of a new industrial project for Charleston or any other community in South Carolina gained his editorial support and drew his praise for the capitalists, local or foreign, making the investment.[11]

Although not so ecstatic over industry as Dawson, other leading Conservatives did more than write paeans on state credit and economy. Acting through the General Assembly, the Conservative Democrats took specific steps to encourage manufactures in their state. When the Democrats regained control of the state in 1877, they did not investigate, throw out, or repeal all of the Republican party's handiwork. They took as their own the law exempting manufactures from taxation. Enacted in 1873, this statute absolved " any individual or association of individuals " from payment of any taxes levied by state, county, or municipality " upon the property or capital employed or invested in such manufactures or enterprises." The tax exemption extended for ten years " after the commencement or extension of such manufacture or improvement." [12]

This legislation retained practically unanimous public support until the mid-1880s. When opposition charged that the law freed corporations from paying taxes whereas no law allowed poor citizens to

---

10. For example, see Governor Thomas B. Jeter's message of 1880 in the Charleston *News and Courier*, November 25, 1880.
11. *Ibid.*, December 20, 1877; March 13 and May 2, 1879; July 17, 1888.
12. South Carolina, *Statutes at Large*, XV, 513–14.

escape the tax collector, proponents of tax exemption called these critics opponents of progress. Pointing out that the act did not exempt the lands on which factories were built, the supporters of exemptions asserted that tax money that would otherwise be nonexistent came from higher assessments on industrial lands.[13]

The battle raged through two legislative sessions. Governor Hugh Thompson took no part in the fight.[14] In fact the press, led by Dawson's *News and Courier*, seemed to be the main force behind retaining the law. A repeal measure passed the state House of Representatives in 1884 by more than a two-to-one margin, only to fail in the Senate by a single vote. A year later, when the Senate reversed itself and joined the House to repeal the tax-exemption law, no one became very excited. Even the *News and Courier*, noting the divided opinion in the state and asserting the law had done its intended work, readily acquiesced in repeal.[15]

Almost simultaneously with the repeal of tax exemption the legislature passed a measure eagerly desired by the pro-industry men. Prior to 1886, incorporation of any manufacturing enterprise in South Carolina required a special act of legislature. In 1886 the legislature, with little fanfare or opposition, enacted a general incorporation law that allowed the South Carolina Secretary of State to grant a charter to any applicant who fulfilled the requirements of the law.[16]

The General Assembly also acted to aid specific enterprises. One of the first resolutions passed by the special session of the 1877 legislature directed the state Attorney General to investigate the charters of the several companies mining phosphate in the rivers of the state and to report his findings to the legislature at its regular session. Attorney General James Conner complied and submitted to the legislators in January of 1878 a lengthy document recommending that the state grant, for a specified time period, exclusive rights to a company to mine in a specific area. Conner thought the exclusive rights guarantee was needed because of the capital necessary to equip and run an efficient mining operation.[17] The legislature

13. *News and Courier*, February 5, 1878; December 4 and 11, 1884; Columbia *Daily Register*, December 4, 1884.
14. *News and Courier*, November 27, 1884, and November 25, 1885.
15. *Ibid.*, December 23–24, 1885.
16. *Ibid.*, December 24, 1886; *Statutes at Large*, XIX, 540–50. The statute excluded railroads.
17. *Statutes at Large*, XVI, 320–21; *News and Courier*, January 18, 1878.

accepted the Attorney General's opinion and enacted a comprehensive law based on the exclusive rights idea, which permitted the companies granted these rights to carry on their affairs free of concern over the possibility of competition.[18]

State assistance to railroads declined substantially after the Civil War. Lack of available money after 1865 retarded the ante-bellum policy of generous state aid to railroads, but railroad frauds perpetrated by certain leading Republican officials after 1868 convinced the state not to renew its aid program. Popular reaction to the frauds brought about the constitutional amendment, ratified in 1873, that forbade the state's guaranteeing by loans, endorsement, or any other procedure, the bonds of any railroad without the approval of two-thirds of the qualified voters.[19]

Although no aid came from the state, the Democratic legislature did enthusiastically support measures enabling local governments to assist railroads. Any municipal or county help that included bond issues, public stock subscriptions, or the like required authority that only the legislature could give, and each request meant a special act because no general law covered that contingency. Between 1865 and 1900 the legislature passed 117 acts authorizing local governments to aid railroads.[20]

The Conservative regime refused to rely solely on legislation to encourage manufactures; the state government conducted a program dedicated to publicizing the natural and material resources of the state. Direction of its public relations fell to the state Agriculture Bureau, headed by Andrew P. Butler, who relied on two means: publications and exhibits. The prime element in the publicity campaign, a massive handbook, detailed all aspects of the state's economic features from physical geography to vital statistics. Conceived in 1882 and published a year later, *South Carolina, Resources and Population, Institutions and Industries*, edited by Harry Hammond, was basically a compendium of South Carolina material in

18. *Statutes at Large*, XVI, 615–24.
19. Frank Willie Putnam, "An Analysis of Public Aid to Railroads in South Carolina, 1865–1900" (unpublished Master's thesis, Dept. of Economics, University of South Carolina, 1957), pp. 23–25, 34, 75. Also see Carter Goodrich, *Government Promotion of American Canals and Railroads, 1800–1890* (New York: Columbia University Press, 1960), pp. 216, 219–21.
20. Putnam, "Public Aid to Railroads," p. 41. Sixty-one per cent of those acts were passed between 1880 and 1890.

the United States Census of 1880.[21] To this information Hammond added extensive reports of climatic, agricultural, and geological conditions in all sections of the state.

Though Hammond's work constituted its major effort, the Agriculture Bureau, carried on other publicity work. In 1887 Commissioner Butler contributed to a promotional volume on the South a twenty-page review that glowingly recounted the state's material progress since 1877.[22] The wide distribution given that book placed Butler's article within reach of almost everyone who might want to invest in South Carolina. Aside from his literary efforts, Butler planned the South Carolina exhibits in numerous expositions and fairs held in the South during the 1880s.

The official acts of the state government and the General Assembly received broad and enthusiastic support from the citizens of South Carolina. If any difference existed between the state and local government on the question of attracting industrial enterprises, the local areas were even more eager than the state administration. Citizens embraced with their gratitude and money any new industry established in their communities.[23] Even though they welcomed all types of enterprises, most communities concentrated on railroads and cotton mills.

Local governmental units feared that failure to get a railroad or, even better, railroads, would lose their competitive position to neighboring towns. The nature or financial soundness of a road normally made little difference to a county or town. Practically no local opposition challenged community aid for railroads. The railroad promoters, readily understanding this feeling, emphasized local projects and encouraged and assisted prominent men in different communities to form committees for attracting railroads. These committees, through public meetings and local press support, became the best promotional agents any railroad could hope for.[24]

21. South Carolina, State Board of Agriculture, *South Carolina. Resources and Population, Institutions and Industries*, ed. Harry Hammond (Charleston: Walker, Evans and Cogswell Printers, 1883). Cited hereafter as *Handbook* (1883).

22. *The New South: Its Resources and Attractions*, ed. M. B. Hillyard (Baltimore: The Manufacturers' Record Co., 1887), esp. pp. 143–62.

23. The local newspapers I went through consistently supported all industry, whether manufacturing, transportation, or any other kind.

24. Putnam, "Public Aid to Railroads," pp. 49, 50, 58–59, 62, 68–70. See also the William L. Mauldin Diary, *passim*, Southern Historical Collection, University of North Carolina Library, cited hereafter as SHC; William Herman Patterson, "'Through the

Local support for cotton mills paralleled that for railroads. In the 1879–82 boom that saw growth of small textile plants, citizens " rallied to support these enterprises in a paen [sic] of local patriotism and ' boosterism.' ".[25] The depression that hit the mills in 1884 and 1885 brought a temporary halt to the formation and construction of new mills, but increased local efforts in behalf of cotton mills accompanied the return of prosperity in 1887. Between 1888 and 1890 " numerous attempts [took place] in small towns to organize and finance cotton mills . . . for the benefits that were expected to accrue to the towns involved."[26]

The advent of Tillmanism caused little change in the attitude toward industry. Benjamin Tillman, himself a farmer, had little to say about industry. Certainly he never challenged the Conservatives on an anti-industry issue; moreover, he maintained a close friendship with Daniel A. Tompkins, one of the South's premier pro-industry spokesmen. Important Tillman leaders like Daniel K. Norris and Ira Jones invested heavily in cotton mills; one of the most prominent Tillmanites, John Gary Evans, was a vigorous promoter active in numerous railroad schemes.[27]

The feeling that industrial enterprises offered an economic boon to South Carolina continued unabated in the late eighties. In 1889 N. G. Gonzales, the *News and Courier*'s chief reporter, wrote to his editor: " There is more manufacturing activity than ever before, and it should be encouraged to the fullest." An anti-regime newspaper that supported Tillman in 1890 declared the interest capitalists had shown in South Carolina and the South one of " the pleasing signs of the times."[28] When Tillman gained control of the state in 1890,

Heart of the South ': A History of the Seaboard Air Line Railroad Company, 1832–1950 " (unpublished Ph. D. dissertation, Dept. of History, University of South Carolina, 1951), pp. 222–25.

25. Williamson, " Cotton Manufacturing," p. 78. In the eighties, South Carolina mills—unlike the railroads—were financed largely with native capital. For example, the Newberry Cotton Mill was organized in 1883 with a capital stock of $150,000; 87.2 per cent of the money came from South Carolina sources, with Newberry county alone providing 80.7 per cent of the total. *Ibid.*, pp. 106–8.

26. *Ibid.*, pp. 119–20, 122.

27. *Infra*, chap. v, and Gustavus G. Williamson, Jr., " South Carolina Cotton Mills and the Tillman Movement," *The Proceedings of the South Carolina Historical Association* (1949), pp. 45–46; the John Gary Evans Papers in the South Caroliniana Library at the University of South Carolina, cited hereafter as SCL, contain much material on Evans's promotional schemes, e. g., see Evans to George Potts [New York City], November 14, 1887.

28. Gonzales to J. C. Hemphill, March 23, 1889, N. G. Gonzales Papers, SCL; Charleston, *World*, July 18, 1888.

he did nothing to inhibit industrial growth, which exploded in the decade between 1890 and 1900.[29]

III

Though the government—state and local—avidly courted industry, neither believed that industry should operate free of public scrutiny and some type of public control. Even Francis Dawson, South Carolina's leading disciple of Henry Grady's New South gospel, refused to deny any need for governmental regulation of industrial enterprises. On numerous occasions Dawson emphasized that corporations had a distinct responsibility to the people. Therefore, the public ought to maintain watch over corporations to prevent them from abusing the public trust.[30]

The state supervision fell mainly on two major industries. Promptly upon gaining control of the state, the Conservative Democrats took steps to examine the phosphate companies mining river rock. Because those companies operated with state charters on state-owned property, the creation in 1877 of a phosphate commissioner aroused no protest. The duties of this single commissioner included inspection of company operations to ensure that firms worked within their charters. But more important, he had the responsibility of collecting the royalties for the state.[31]

The state required each company mining in a river or navigable stream to pay for that privilege. In 1870, the state government had set the fee at one dollar per ton of phosphate rock mined. When the Democrats enacted their comprehensive law on phosphates in 1878, they retained the one dollar per ton royalty, and these royalty payments constituted a significant portion of the state's revenues. By 1879 phosphate companies had contributed over $500,000 into the state treasury.[32] In that year the royalty totaled more than $98,000; by 1885, the payment exceeded $175,000; in 1890, the state received $237,149.06.[33]

29. *Supra*, n. 2.
30. *News and Courier*, July 8, 1881. Cf. *infra*, n. 64.
31. *Statutes at Large*, XVI, 491, and XVII, 75.
32. Simkins and Woody, *Reconstruction*, p. 309; *Statutes at Large*, XVI, 781; Charles A. Shepard, Jr., M.D. [chemist in the Agriculture Bureau], *South Carolina Phosphates and Their Principal Competitors in the Markets of the World* (Charleston: Laboratory for Analytical Chemistry, 1880), p. 66.
33. *Reports and Resolutions of the General Assembly of the State of South Carolina* (1879), p. 116; (1885), II, 37; (1890), II, 657.

No leading Conservative advocated abolition of the royalty charges, but when Benjamin Tillman accused the Conservatives of allowing the phosphate companies to profit at state expense, the royalty question came up for public discussion. The General Assembly of 1886 appointed a commission to investigate the phosphate industry. Its report in 1887 advocated that the mining companies pay a set fee to the state of $175,000, with a one dollar royalty on every ton over 175,000.[34] The state Senate vote on the bill derived from the commission's recommendation does not show a Tillman-Conservative split. Leading Conservative senators like James F. Izlar and Lawrence W. Youmans voted with the majority that killed the measure, while other Conservatives like Augustine Smythe and Edwards Murray found themselves in the minority along with the two most prominent Tillmanites in the Senate, W. Jasper Talbert and Jefferson A. Sligh.[35]

As railroads affected more people than any other enterprise, they received more attention from the state government than any other industry. Two changes caused the initial Conservative concern over railroads. First, more and more of the state's railroad mileage had come under the control of capital and interests outside the state. In a state with strong local feelings, a state that had largely controlled its ante-bellum roads, this alien direction caused alarm.[36] Second, high freight rates accompanied outside domination. The Panic of 1873 compounded the perilous financial condition of many roads. Attempting to save their property, railroad men raised rates, especially on freight,[37] but increases went unnoticed in the political

---

34. *News and Courier*, November 30 and December 3, 1887. The available evidence does not show the companies getting rich at state expense. Normally, the phosphate rock brought $6.00 per ton; in 1880 Dr. Shepard thought the royalty contributed significantly to the industry's low profits. Shepard, *South Carolina Phosphates*, p. 65. The 1887 commission felt that a $1.00 per ton royalty with a $6.00 per ton price equitable, but the commission wanted the companies to pay to the state one-third of the value of all rock that sold over $6.00 per ton. *News and Courier*, November 30, 1887.

35. *News and Courier*, December 8, 1887.

36. Stover, *Railroads of the South*, chaps. vi and xi; for local opinion, see the Anderson *Intelligencer*, January 29, 1880, and the *News and Courier*, August 4, 1877; also see Samuel Melanchton Derrick, *Centennial History of South Carolina Railroad* (Columbia: The State Company, 1930), chap. xv, esp. pp. 255–57.

37. Albert Neely Sanders, "State Regulation of Public Utilities by South Carolina, 1879–1935" (unpublished Ph.D. dissertation, Dept. of History, University of North Carolina, 1956), p. 11.

storms of 1876 and 1877 when all attention was riveted on the fight between Democrats and Republicans.

In 1878, with the state securely in their hands, the Conservative leadership considered the railroad question. Long interested in the problem of high rates, the state Grange petitioned the legislature in 1878 to create a railroad commission to supervise and regulate the roads.[38] D. Wyatt Aiken, an important Grange leader and a Democratic congressman, publicized the freight rate situation by showing that the cost of shipping cotton from his native Abbeville county to Charleston was so expensive that farmers instead took their cotton to Greenville on wagons. Aiken pointed to the power exercised by the " great railroad magnates," and called for a regulatory commission.[39] The *News and Courier*, asserting that a commission offered " to the public a mode of correcting abuses which are known to exist," supported Congressman Aiken and the Grange.[40]

The legislature of 1878 responded to the cries for action. Hesitant about making a frontal attack on the railroads, it created a one-man commission with only advisory and supervisory powers.[41] The commissioner could examine a railroad's books and make recommendations to the legislature in his annual report. If he discovered serious wrongs, such as violation of a charter or conditions detrimental to the public, he had authority to request that the railroads make the necessary changes. Should a road fail to comply, he could apply to a state circuit court for a restraining order.

The man chosen as railroad commissioner proved to be a diligent, dedicated official. Although Milledge Luke Bonham, a Confederate brigadier and wartime governor, had no previous railroad experience, he made an effort to educate himself in railroad affairs. Working

38. J. H. Easterby, " The Granger Movement in South Carolina," *The Proceedings of the South Carolina Historical Association* (1931), p. 29.

Of course the problem of high freight rates and the pressures for some type of regulation were not peculiar to South Carolina; they were common across the South and also in the West. Maxwell Ferguson, " State Regulation of Railrods in the South," in *Columbia University Studies in History, Economics and Public Law*, LXVII, No. 2 (New York, 1916).

39. *News and Courier*, September 13, 1878.

40. *Ibid.*, November 25, 1878; see also the *Daily Register*, November 10, 1877, and the *Laurensville Herald*, August 16, 1878.

41. *Statutes at Large*, XVI, 789–92. Of the twenty-five Democrats who voted in the Senate on the bill, only five cast their ballots against it. *Journal of the Senate of the General Assembly of the State of South Carolina* (1878), p. 167.

with energy, he made the law of 1878 as effective as possible. Quickly, however, Bonham realized that the commission needed more power to control rates. In his 1880 report, a lengthy review of railroad conditions in South Carolina, Bonham asked the legislature to amend the 1878 law and give the commission more authority, including the power to set rates.[42]

By 1880, Bonham's crusade for a stronger commission had found powerful allies. Convinced that their economic difficulties could be remedied only by tighter control of railroads, Charleston interests took command of the fight for state regulation. Dawson spoke for Charleston when he declared " the public must not be at the mercy of corporations," chiefly " the railroad octupus [sic]." Following up Dawson's newspaper campaign and the resolutions of public meetings, Senator Augustine Smythe in 1880 introduced a resolution calling for a legislative commission to investigate the railroad problem and make a report, including possible legislation, at the next session.[43] When the legislature appointed a commission, it made Senator Smythe chairman.

Charleston had cause for alarm. By the early eighties, the main lines in the state had been absorbed " into railway systems which were fundamentally north-south lines." [44] The chief culprit, for Charleston, was the Richmond and Danville, which controlled almost 40 per cent of the mileage in the state.[45] Working to control a trunk line from Atlanta to the northeast, the Richmond and Danville had no interest in Charleston. Competition became so fierce among the north-south lines that they formed a pool, the Associated Railroads of the Carolinas. The only major road outside the pool, the South Carolina, designed to bring freight, especially cotton, from the up country and midlands to Charleston, found itself hauling less freight and consistently losing money.[46] It had to rely on other roads as

42. Albert Neely Sanders, " The South Carolina Railroad Commission, 1878–1895 " (unpublished Master's thesis, Dept. of History, University of North Carolina, 1948), pp. 19, 54–55. Bonham's report is in *Reports and Resolutions* (1880).

43. Derrick, *South Carolina Railroad*, pp. 249, 263; *News and Courier*, June 19, 1879, and October 16, 1882; Sanders, " Railroad Commission," p. 20.

44. Sanders, "Regulation of Public Utilities," p. 30.

45. *Ibid.*, p. 28; Stover, *Railroads of the South*, chap. xi. Francis Dawson to Major Peyton Randolph, May 25, 1887, Letterbook 1884–1887, Francis W. Dawson Papers, Duke University Library, cited hereafter as Duke.

46. Sanders, " Regulation of Public Utilities," p. 30; Derrick, *South Carolina Railroad*, chaps. xv and xvi, esp. p. 249, where he declares that " competition was without doubt the major cause of reducing the business and receipts of the company."

feeders from the cotton areas, and rates set by the Association discriminated against Charleston. It cost $0.46 per mile to ship a 500-pound bale of cotton from Abbeville to New York; to Charleston the cost was $1.50.[47]

With Senator Smythe as their spokesman, Charleston interests looked to the legislature for assistance. In 1881 the Smythe Commission submitted a recommendation asking for a strengthened railroad law to give the state Railroad Commission power to regulate both passenger and freight rates as well as control schedules and general operations.[48] The Smythe bill received strong support from Governor Johnson Hagood. Calling attention to the extent of outside control of South Carolina roads, the Governor thought it " highly important that the Legislature . . . provide through a Board or otherwise for a regulation of freight and passenger tariffs which [would] protect the local patrons of the roads in this State." [49]

Only after two legislative sessions did the Smythe recommendations become law. A comprehensive railroad law written by the legislature of 1881 but passed in February, 1882, neither gave the Railroad Commission power to make rates nor increased the number of commissioners.[50] It empowered the commissioner to investigate rates and, if he found serious discriminations, to issue an order with the force of law to cover the specific situation. Of course, the railroad could seek relief from the courts. In addition, the law prohibited charging less for a long haul than a short one. Even though this law was much stronger than the 1878 one, Bonham and the Charleston interests still pressed for rate control. Agitation for a stiffer law spread across the state during 1882,[51] and when the legislature met again in November, the adherents of an even more stringent law prevailed. The December law increased the membership of the state Railroad Commission to three men—with power to set rates.[52]

47. Extensive comparisons of rates per mile can be found in the News and Courier, October 16, 1882. Of course the total cost to New York exceeded that to Charleston, but when sea rates from Charleston were added the two charges were not so disparate.
48. Ibid., November 29, 1881.
49. Senate Journal (1881–82), p. 25.
50. Statutes at Large, XVII, 791–843.
51. Sanders, "Railroad Commission," p. 30, and Anderson Intelligencer, October 19, 1882.
52. There was surprisingly little opposition. The measure passed the House by 72 to 35. Journal of the House of Representatives of the General Assembly of the State

The laws passed in February and December, 1882, gave Commissioner Bonham full powers to regulate railroad activity. Vested with real authority, Bonham managed to get tangible results. When the Commission published its rate schedule in mid-1883, the new rates were lower than any in force in the state.[53]

Even this legislation failed to satisfy everyone. The refusal of the Commission to push rates down farther, below a point which the economic condition of the roads warranted, aroused public opinion against the law.[54] On the other hand, state business groups feared that the new regulations, especially the rate schedule, would cripple the roads and prevent future railroad development in the state. Demanding repeal of the 1882 laws, smaller communities blamed the Commission for stifling proposed railroads.[55]

Pleased with this popular outburst, the railroad forces encouraged the agitation and prevailed upon the 1883 legislature to repeal rate-making powers.[56] Three men led the railroad attack on the 1882 laws. William P. Clyde, who dominated the Richmond and Danville, came to Columbia to direct railroad strategy. Clyde's chief lieutenants were the Haskell brothers—Alexander, former chairman of the state Democratic Executive Committee, and former member of the state Supreme Court, now president of the Columbia and Greenville, a Richmond and Danville subsidiary, and John, an attorney for the Columbia and Greenville and chairman of the Committee on Railroads of the state House of Representatives.[57] Beginning their campaign before the legislature convened, the railroad men told the people of South Carolina that retention of rate-making powers by the state Railroad Commission would doom future railroad construction in the state. Clyde, in calling such powers "disastrous"

of South Carolina (1882), pp. 252–53; the Senate passed the bill without a division. News and Courier, December 9, 1882; Statutes at Large, XVIII, 10–19.

53. Sanders, "Regulation of Public Utilities," p. 27, and Milledge Louis Bonham [grandson of Milledge Luke], "The Life and Times of Milledge Luke Bonham" (unpublished manuscript biography, Milledge Luke Bonham Papers, SCL), chap. vi; New York Times, June 30, 1883.

54. Sanders, "Regulation of Public Utilities," p. 41; see also M. L. Bonham, Jr. to Bonham, December 18, 1883, and John D. Kennedy to Bonham, October 16, 1883, both in Bonham Papers, SCL.

55. New York Times, July 5, 1883; Edgefield Chronicle, October 24, November 7 and 14, 1883.

56. John D. Kennedy to Bonham, October 16, 1883, Bonham Papers, SCL.

57. Bonham to Dawson, December 8, 1883, and to William Porcher Miles, May 9, 1884, ibid.

for both roads and the state, predicted an indefinite halt to all future investments in South Carolina. Alexander Haskell and other South Carolina railroad officials informed the House Committee on Railroads that existing legislation threatened the financial safety of the roads.[58]

When the railroad fight reached the floor of the General Assembly, Charleston legislators again directed the anti-railroad forces.[59] Senator Smythe took up his post as the roads' chief antagonist; Smythe's counterpart in the House was Charles H. Simonton, also of Charleston. Smythe and Simonton enlisted the assistance of Governor Thompson, who asked the legislature to retain the 1882 legislation; but after a vicious legislative battle, the railroad interests succeeded in depriving the Commission of its rate-making powers.[60]

They prevailed by the narrowest of margins. The state House passed the bill by seven votes; the Senate, by a margin of only two. The losers accused railroad interests of resorting to bribery and corruption; they charged one prominent Democrat representative, E. B. Murray, of switching his vote only after he had been made a director of the Columbia and Greenville.[61] The *News and Courier's* capital correspondent, N. G. Gonzales, wrote his editor that the vote of Democratic Senator Madison Howell had been "bought or unduly influenced by the syndicate"; Clyde and his assistants, according to Gonzales, had bought the votes of the Negro legislators with free passes.[62] These charges can neither be proved nor disproved, but William Clyde was present in the legislature when it enacted a railroad bill that pleased him.

The law of 1883 retained most features of the comprehensive law of February, 1882, but repealed the part of the December, 1882, statute that allowed the Railroad Commission to fix rates. The new law permitted the roads to set their own freight rates subject, however, to Commission approval. Moreover, the roads had the right

---

58. *News and Courier*, November 27 and December 7, 1883.

59. *Ibid.*, December 15, 17, 20, and 21, 1883.

60. *Senate Journal* (1883), p. 52; *Statutes at Large*, XVIII, 480–88.

61. *News and Courier*, December 17 and 21, 1883.

62. N. G. Gonzales to Dawson, December 22, 1883, Elliott-Gonzales Papers, SHC; *News and Courier*, December 17, 1883. Eleven of the twelve Negroes (nine Republicans and three Democrats) in the House voted with the railroads as did all three Negro senators (all Repubicans). Thus, of fifteen Negroes in the legislature, fourteen (the other one did not vote) voted for the bill. Of course, it is impossible to prove or to deny Gonzales's allegation that free passes bought their support.

to appeal any Commission decision to the state courts, where the burden of proof rested with the Commission.

After the great battle of 1883, public and governmental interest in railroad regulation declined. In 1884 John Haskell wrote Clyde that he " heard very little of the [railroad] law " while on a trip through the piedmont.[63] A year later Francis Dawson, who supported regulatory legislation but at the same time privately advised Richmond and Danville officials on policy, told Clyde that if the railroad interests kept their peace, public opinion would remain quiet.[64] And until the depression of the 1890s public opinion did remain relatively tranquil.[65]

Thus, the story of industry in South Carolina from 1877 to 1890 is that of a poor state trying to improve its economic position. Generally, the Conservative regime welcomed industry and capitalists; no one feared that the promotion of industry would endanger the well-being of agriculture.[66] Local governments and citizens joined the state government in an effort they hoped meant progress and promised the alleviation of poverty. In this industrial campaign a few individuals undoubtedly became rich, but the evidence does not support the conclusion that industrialists and politicians colluded to enrich each other at the expense of the general welfare.[67] Neither

63. Haskell to Clyde, January 9, 1884, Letterbook 1883–87, John C. Haskell Papers, SCL.

64. Dawson to Clyde, December 7 and 17, 1884, Letterbook 1884–87, Dawson Papers, Duke. Dawson told Clyde that his sympathy lay with Clyde's plans but he could not discount altogether opinion in Charleston, and Charleston thought of the Richmond and Danville as an enemy. At the same time, Dawson had supported strong railroad laws, and Bonham thought him to be a friend and ally. Bonham to Dawson, December 8, 1883, Bonham Papers, SCL.

Dawson seems to have maintained successfully his double role. As late as 1887, his paper still supported Charleston and the South Carolina Railroad against the Richmond and Danville. Writing to J. C. Hemphill [Dawson's assistant] on June 6, 1887, John C. Haskell protested the *News and Courier*'s opposition to the Richmond and Danville. Letterbook 1883–87, Haskell Papers, SCL. Only two weeks earlier, Dawson had given advice to a Richmond and Danville official on the road's policy in South Carolina. Dawson to Major Peyton Randolph, May 25, 1887, Letterbook 1884–87, Dawson Papers, Duke.

65. Sanders, " Railroad Commission," p. 73.

66. For general comments, see Edward Delor Beechert, Jr., " Industrialism in the Southeast, 1870–1914 " (unpublished Ph. D. dissertation, Dept. of History, University of California, Berkeley, 1957), pp. 13–14, 31, and 94, n. 3.

67. C. Vann Woodward does not include South Carolina in the same category as Georgia and Alabama in his discussion of collusion between industrialists and Bourbon politicians. C. Vann Woodward, *Origins of the New South, 1877–1913*, Vol. IX of

does the evidence show that the regime although it both courted industry and supported state regulation, formulated any definite theory about the role of government in the economy.[68]

IV

Even with the industrial growth of the 1880s, South Carolina remained overwhelmingly agricultural. Seventy-five per cent of the state's labor force worked on farms.[69] that in 1880 produced two-and-one-half times more wealth than did industry.[70] Although manufactures improved their position during the following decade, the value of industrial products in 1890 still fell short of the value of agricultural products by some $20,000,000.[71] Francis Dawson, the

---

A History of the South, ed. Wendell Holmes Stephenson and E. Merton Coulter (Baton Rouge: Louisiana State University Press, 1951), chap. i. But Professor Woodward does assert (*ibid.*, p. 19) that the South Carolina Conservatives stood with the capitalists against the people " with striking consistency." It seems to me that the story told in this chapter suggests that Professor Woodward's conclusion is extreme. Moreover—according to my findings—most South Carolinians of the Conservative period generally looked upon the capitalists as men who could materially increase the welfare of their state, not as men who might harm them or their state.

68. The South Carolina Conservative Democratic party did not represent the revival of Whiggism. That idea has often been used, e. g., C. Vann Woodward, *Reunion and Reaction: The Compromise of 1877 and the End of Reconstruction*, Anchor edition (New York: Doubleday and Co., Inc., 1951), pp. 39–42, to characterize Southern Bourbons. The main reason for no return to Whiggism in South Carolina was that no Whig party of any consequence existed in John C. Calhoun's commonwealth. The ante-bellum state government did assist industrial projects, especially railroads, but by the end of the 1840s both the clamor for industrial projects and state aid subsided. Harold S. Schultz, *Nationalism and Sectionalism in South Carolina, 1852–1860* (Durham: Duke University Press, 1950), p. 85, and Alfred Glaze Smith, Jr., *Economic Readjustment of an Old Cotton State: South Carolina, 1820–1860* (Columbia: University of South Carolina Press, 1958), chaps. iv and vi.

69. *Handbook* (1883), p. 562. Between 1880 and 1890, the number of landowners remained relatively stable.

Farms	1880 (per cent)	1890 (per cent)
Owned	49.7	44.7
Rented	23.5	27.8
Sharecropped	26.8	27.5

U.S. Bureau of Census, *Tenth Census: 1880. Statistics of Agriculture*, pp. 84–85; *Eleventh Census: 1890. Statistics of Agriculture*, pp. 178–79. Hereafter, U.S. Bureau of Census is omitted in all citations referring to the Census.

70. The value of agricultural products in 1880 was $41,969,749. *Compendium of the Tenth Census: 1880. Part I*, p. 725. For the value of manufactures, see *supra*, n. 2.

71. The value of agricultural products in 1890 totaled $51,337,985. *Eleventh Census: 1890. Statistics of Agriculture*, p. 226.

state's most vocal advocate of industrialism, recognized that "agriculture . . . [was] the bed-rock and foundation of State prosperity." [72]

Staple crops grown mainly for export had always predominated in South Carolina agriculture. Rice, along with indigo, had brought wealth to the state during the eighteenth century. Although the loss of the British Empire's bounty on indigo after the American Revolution doomed that crop, by 1800 another crop had appeared in the state to buttress the rice culture. After 1820 rice fell behind the new mainstay of South Carolina agriculture—cotton.

Two decades after the Civil War found cotton more dominant among state crops than it had been prior to 1860. Cereals and grains, not important money crops during the ante-bellum period, remained unimportant during the 1880s. Rice, the one exception, failed to regain its ante-bellum prominence; rice production in 1880 was less than half of that in 1860.[73] Cotton followed a reverse pattern. In 1880, the state produced 516,000 bales of cotton on 1,526,000 acres—163,078 more bales than in 1860.[74] In 1890, over 2,000,000 acres of cotton yielded almost 750,000 bales.[75] In that year cotton accounted for over 60 per cent of the total value of agricultural products grown in the state.[76]

The economic health of agriculture determined the economic well-being of the entire state; therefore in the 1880s South Carolina

72. News and Courier, August 1, 1881.

73. Rice production in 1860 totaled 119,100,528 pounds. Smith, Economic Readjustment, p. 64. By 1880, it had fallen to 52,077,414 pounds. Handbook (1907), p. 263. Rice showed some improvement during the eighties, but the 1890 crop brought only $1,702,298. Reports and Resolutions (1890), II, 648.

A memoir by Duncan Clinch Heyward, scion of an old rice-planting family, Seed from Madagascar (Chapel Hill: University of North Carolina Press, 1937) offers a good picture of postwar rice planting. Heyward says that even though rice planting never prospered after 1865, the major decline came after 1885.

74. Handbook (1883), p. 11. For the acreage planted, see U.S. Department of Agriculture, Agricultural Marketing Service, Cotton and Cottonseed, Statistical Bulletin No. 164 (1955), p. 9, cited hereafter as Cotton.

75. Cotton, p. 9; Eleventh Census: 1890. Statistics of Agriculture, p. 396.

76. The value of the 1890 cotton crop was $30,422,912. I arrived at this figure by multiplying the average yield per acre times the number of acres harvested. Then I multiplied that product by the average farm price per pound in 1890. Cotton, p. 9, gives the number of acres harvested and the average yield in pounds of lint per acre. Fred A. Shannon, The Farmers' Last Frontier: Agriculture, 1860–1897, Vol. V of The Economic History of the United States, ed. Henry David et al. (New York: Farrar and Rinehart, Inc., 1945), p. 415, lists the average prices.

The figure given above does not include the value of cotton seed.

depended chiefly on cotton for income. Farmers, aware of their dependence on that staple, increased their cotton acreage by 25 per cent between 1880 and 1890. That increase did not result from high prices or profits, for cotton prices declined from 9.8 cents per pound in 1880 to 8.6 cents in 1890.[77] With prices declining, hard-pressed farmers tried to maintain their income by planting more cotton. The attempt was doomed. To increase acreage meant, in part, use of marginal land, and that led, even with an increasing use of fertilizers, to a decrease in the amount of cotton produced per acre.[78] That decrease, along with low cotton prices, left most farmers operating at a substantial loss.[79]

Even though no single condition placed the South Carolina farmer in so disastrous a position, most students agree that the crop lien system must absorb much of the blame.[80] The crop lien system, basically a credit arrangement, allowed the farmer to place a mortgage on his future crop with the person or persons who advanced him supplies for his operations. Normally those who made advances only accepted liens on an easily salable crop which was inedible and difficult to steal. Only with that type of crop, the lien merchants argued, could they entertain reasonable hopes of making a profit in the hazardous lien business. No other crop planted in the lower South so completely satisfied these requirements as did cotton. Thus, Southern agriculture became more and more dependent on it. Although scholars have absolved most lien merchants from nefarious practices that kept the farmer at their mercy,[81] they have

77. *Cotton*, p. 9; Shannon, *Farmers' Last Frontier*, p. 415.

78. Shannon, *Farmers' Last Frontier*, p. 115, and R. H. Taylor, "Commercial Fertilizers in South Carolina," *South Atlantic Quarterly*, XXIX (April, 1930), 185–87. In 1890, South Carolina farmers used 168,679.4 tons of fertilizer (*Reports and Resolutions* [1890], II, 630); in 1880, they used only 100,000 tons. *Ibid.* (1880), p. 480.

The pounds of lint produced per acre declined from 186 in 1880 to 174 in 1890. *Cotton*, p. 9.

79. Appendix D.

80. M[atthew] B[rown] Hammond, *The Cotton Industry: An Essay in American Economic History, Publications of the American Economic Association, New Series, No. 1* (New York: The Macmillan Company, 1897), pp. 145–50; Woodward, *Origins of the New South*, pp. 180–82; Shannon, *The Farmers' Last Frontier*, pp. 89–95.

81. Thomas D. Clark, "The Furnishing and Supply System in Southern Agriculture Since 1865," *Journal of Southern History* (1946), XII, 24–31, and *idem, Pills, Petticoats, and Plows: The Southern Country Store* (reprint, Norman: University of Oklahoma Press, 1964), chap. xviii; also Woodward, *Origins of the New South*, pp. 184–85.

concurred in Matthew Hammond's description of the lien system:
" When one of these [lien] mortgages [had] been recorded against
the southern farmer, he [had] usually passed into a state of helpless
peonage to the merchant who [had] become his creditor." [82]

The crop lien system had come to South Carolina in the wake of
military defeat and the emancipation of slaves. Even with slavery
abolished and money practically non-existent, the demand for agricultural credit remained. The first lien law, passed in 1866, represented an attempt to provide for that credit by allowing the farmer
to use his future crop as his security. The lien law, when enacted, was
termed a temporary expedient, but the Republicans retained the
law, which remained the basis of agricultural credit in the state after
the Democrats triumphed in 1876.

The Democratic party discovered that the lien law had become
indispensable to the state's farmers. In the special legislative session
of 1877 the Democrats, with little opposition, repealed the eleven-
year-old law,[83] but by the time repeal took effect, January 1, 1878,
difficulties in obtaining agricultural credit forced the legislature to
undo its work of the previous summer and to repeal its repeal.
The new lien law was to have expired after one year, but in
December, 1878, the legislature made the law permanent.[84]

The legislation of 1878 continued throughout the 1880s as the
basis of the lien system in South Carolina. The law provided that
any person who advanced " money or supplies " should have a lien
upon the projected crop, " *provided*, an agreement in writing shall
be entered into before such advance is made . . . in which shall
be specified the amount to be advanced." The person holding the
lien, should he suspect his debtor of devious ways, was permitted
to present an affidavit stating his suspicions to the county clerk of
court, who could issue a warrant empowering the county sheriff
to seize the crop and sell it for cash to pay the lien merchant.

Although Democratic legislators protected lien merchants, they
took more care than had the Republicans to guard and to strengthen
the legal position of the landlord. The 1878 law stated that the

---

82. Hammond, *Cotton Industry*, p. 149.
83. The repeal measure passed the House by a vote of 51 to 28 (*House Journal*
[Special Session, 1877], p. 98) and the Senate without a division. *Senate Journal*
(Special Session, 1877), pp. 245, 269. For the repeal law itself, see *Statutes at Large*,
XVI, 265.
84. *Senate Journal* (1878), p. 22; *Statutes at Large*, XVI, 410–11, 713–14.

landlord "leasing lands for agricultural purposes" had "a prior and preferred lien for rent" on at least one-third of the value of all crops raised on his land. This lien had validity without any written agreement; however, for the landlord's lien to exceed one-third of the crop value, a written agreement had to be filed in the county court house. The only important lien legislation after 1878 emphasized the rights of the landlord. The Priority Lien Law of 1885 specifically provided that "the landlord shall have a lien upon the crop of his tenant in preference to all other liens." [85]

Opinion in the state never agreed on the need or usefulness of the lien law. Commenting on the question of reviving the law in December, 1877, the *Keowee Courier* asserted that the lien law had been "more destructive of the material wealth of the State than all other causes combined." In agreement, the Yorkville *Enquirer* termed the law "the great tumor on the laboring class of our country." The Barnwell *People*, dissenting vigorously, argued that repeal had been "ill-advised"; the Newberry *Herald* declared that repeal had caused much hardship and called for the re-enactment of the lien law. [86]

Proponents of the law emphasized the small farmer's need for it. The *News and Courier* thought that without the lien system the small independent farmer and the renter would be unable to continue farming because of their inability to find credit elsewhere. [87] Fighting a repeal bill in 1881, one representative declared that the abolition of the lien system would end credit for four-fifths of the state's farmers. [88] A report from Barnwell county stated that repeal of the lien law would mean "the crushing out of more than one-half of the one-horse farmers [in that county], both white and black." The Edgefield *Advertiser* pictured a countryside filled with "boundless hardship, want, sorrow, and humiliation" should the lien law be repealed. [89]

85. *Statutes at Large*, XVI, 411, and XIX, 146.
86. *Keowee Courier*, quoted in the *Daily Register*, December 5, 1877; Yorkville *Enquirer*, January 10, 1878; Barnwell *People*, January 10, 1878; Newberry *Herald*, January 2, 1878.
87. *News and Courier*, December 18, 1882, and December 20, 1884.
88. *Ibid.*, December 9, 1881.
89. *Ibid.*, August 24, 1881; Edgefield *Advertiser*, September 1, 1881.
The available evidence seems to substantiate the claim that the lien system was the small operator's system. In 1885, the value of liens in South Carolina was $6,595,000 but the average lien was only $99.00; in 1886, the value of liens dropped to $5,037,968

Often important agricultural spokesmen opposed the lien law, which " instituted a system of slavery." Commissioner of Agriculture Andrew P. Butler saw the lien system damaging hopes for long term agricultural improvement. Agreeing with Commissioner Butler, the state Agricultural Society in 1881 petitioned the legislature to repeal the obnoxious and harmful legislation. Johnson Hagood, the state's most agriculturally-minded governor, told the legislature in that same year that the lien system " result[ed] in disadvantage to the individual and serious damage to the best interests of the State." [90]

Farmers themselves failed to agree on whether the lien law represented a threat to the state's agricultural prosperity. Voting on lien law proposals in the legislature found farmers in favor of the lien system, though not unanimously. Only two farmers joined the minority of seven senators who opposed the lien law enacted in 1878. Over one-half of the farmers voting in the state House of Representatives on the lien law repeal measure sponsored by the Grange and state Agricultural Society in 1881 cast their ballots for retention of the system. Four years later, when the Priority Lien Law passed the state Senate, 56.2 per cent of the farmers in that body voted aye.[91]

Even Benjamin Tillman, the self-appointed champion of the farmer, refused to mount a major assault against the lien system. None of his Farmers' Association platforms recommended repeal of the lien law.[92] In his 1890 campaign for the governorship, Tillman did label the lien law " damnable," but once in power he did nothing to remove lien legislation from the statute book.[93]

Both individuals and organizations at times changed their positions. The News and Courier advocated repeal in 1881, then argued for retention a year later. The Grange petitioned the legislature for

while the average increased by only $4.00. Reports and Resolutions (1885), II, 107 and (1886), I, 158–59.

90. News and Courier, November 24 and December 10, 1881; Edgefield Chronicle, August 10, 1881; Senate Journal (1881), pp. 27–28.

91. Senate Journal (1878), p. 22, and (1885), p. 323; House Journal (1881), p. 202.

92. News and Courier, May 1 and November 11, 1886, and December 1, 1887; also, the Daily Register, March 28, 1890.

93. News and Courier, July 19 and August 6, 1890. The law on agricultural liens remained in 1900—ten years after Tillman's triumph—exactly what it had been fifteen years earlier. Code of Laws of South Carolina (1902), I, 1151–56.

repeal in 1877 and in 1881, but in 1878 its Master, James Lipscomb, voted in the state Senate to re-enact the recently repealed lien law.[94] Although agricultural leaders normally spoke out against the system, farmers in the legislature speaking for their counties voted to retain it. With no other credit system available, some kind of lien law appeared almost essential.[95]

V

The Conservative Democrats, especially since three of their elected Governors were farmers, had no intention of ignoring the claims of the land.[96] The major Conservative effort on behalf of agriculture produced a state Agriculture Bureau. In 1877 the state Grange had appointed a committee to talk with Governor Hampton about organizing a state Bureau of Agriculture that would serve the interest of the farmer, and thus the whole people. Through his column in the *News and Courier*, D. Wyatt Aiken constantly pointed out the benefits such an organization would bring to the state.[97] Francis Dawson placed his paper behind Aiken and the Grange when he declared that a state Agriculture Bureau " could accomplish incalculable good for the state." [98]

In 1879, a bill providing for a state Agriculture Bureau operated by a commissioner who had to be an active farmer, under the direction of a state Board of Agriculture, met little opposition in the legislature.[99] To support the department, a tax of twenty-five cents per ton was placed on all persons or companies in the state engaged in the manufacture or sale of commercial fertilizers and manures. The legislature chose as state Commissioner of Agriculture Aiken county Senator Andrew P. Butler, a former Confederate lieutenant colonel and member of an influential family.

Commissioner Butler in various ways assisted the state's farmers. The collection and publication of accurate agricultural statistics from

94. *News and Courier*, August 1, 1881, and December 18, 1882; Easterby, " The Granger Movement in South Carolina," p. 29, and *Senate Journal* (1878), p. 22.

95. Woodward in his *Origins of the New South*, pp. 181–83, treats the difficulties of replacing the lien system with anything that would be an improvement.

96. Among Wade Hampton, Johnson Hagood, Hugh S. Thompson, and John P. Richardson only Thompson, an educator, was not a farmer.

97. *News and Courier*, April 7, 1877, and April 19, 1878.

98. *Ibid.*, January 29, 1878, and September 18, 1879.

99. *Statutes at Large*, XVII, 72–76.

every county enabled farmers to compare their performances with their fellows across the state. In an attempt to increase agricultural profits, the Bureau disseminated new information on seeds and fertilizers. The inspecting and stamping with chemical analyses of all commercial fertilizers permitted farmers to know the quality of fertilizer they purchased. Investigations and reports on new crops and different types of agriculture were intended to reduce the reliance on cotton.

Through the years, the Bureau undertook other services. In addition to inspecting fertilizers, the Bureau made chemical analyses of any samples sent by farmers to its laboratories.[100] Veterinary services and a broader range of botanical work offered information and assistance on livestock and seeds. In conjunction with the United States Signal Service, the state Agriculture Bureau through local stations endeavored to make weather predictions and maintain complete meteorological records.

The Bureau's activities satisfied state agricultural leaders, who urged its public support. Speaking in Charleston in 1880, state Grange Master Lipscomb predicted the department would be "a great and magnificent success." Lipscomb called on his listeners to give Commissioner Butler and his organization their "confidence and support, in return for which [the Bureau would] prove a blessing to this State and people." [101] In his annual message of 1882, Governor Hagood endorsed "the unquestionable service" of the state Agriculture Bureau which would increase in efficiency and value to the farmers. In that same year, a general report on the state recorded that "under earnest and judicious management, its [the Bureau's] great usefulness is already manifest." [102]

The state government also subsidized the South Carolina Agricultural and Mechanical Society, a descendant of the ante-bellum state Agricultural Society. Through joint summer meetings with the Grange in different towns, this society provided a social outlet for farmers and a forum for the discussion of agricultural topics.[103]

100. *News and Courier*, January 19, 1887.

101. Patrons of Husbandry: First State Grange of South Carolina: Minutes, 1873–1905, SCL.

102. *Daily Register*, December 5, 1882; *Appleton's Annual Cyclopedia* (1882), p. 745.

103. By the end of the 1870s the Grange, suffering from decreases in membership, decided to meet jointly with the state Agricultural Society. This union lasted through

Prior to 1860, impressive papers on agriculture predominated in the Society's proceedings, but after the war " records of experiments and addresses upon agricultural topics " gradually declined.[104] In their place, the Society devoted its energies to promoting a state fair for display of the products and methods of South Carolina farms. Held annually in Columbia, this fair evolved from its 1869 beginning into a social and political holiday rather than an occasion for serious agricultural discussion. Describing the Society's meetings, D. Wyatt Aiken spoke harshly though with some truth: " Seldom have we ever experienced, or seen, any substantial benefit resulting from a convention of farmers." [105]

This governmental support for an Agriculture Bureau and a state Agricultural Society did not change the most important fact on most South Carolina farms—depression. The *News and Courier* filled many columns with discussions of " the low country problem." The decline of rice culture had practically destroyed the prosperity of what was formerly one of the richest regions in the state. Headlining suggestions on new crops as " the road to fortune," the *News and Courier* supported efforts to turn to wheat, oats, olives, or any other item anyone might suggest.[106] The Columbia *Daily Register* found agrarians across the state suffering from low prices and a glut of cotton. To the legislature of 1881, Governor Hagood accused the lien law of inflicting permanent damage on the state's agriculture. The alarming increase in the number of acres forfeited for non-payment of taxes troubled Governor John P. Richardson, who told the legislature of 1887 that the farmers must be aided.[107]

The question of assistance brought forward the problem of relief. The *Daily Register* had no doubt that the Republican tariff policy lay behind the ills of the state's farmers. Governor Richardson proposed a postponement of the tax deadline as the method of preventing forfeiture of land.[108] No other solution, except that of more

the 1880s. When the Grange took this step, it lost its impetus for political action because the state Agricultural Society had no interest in politics. Easterby, " The Granger Movement in South Carolina," pp. 29–30, and Francis Butler Simkins, *The Tillman Movement in South Carolina* (Durham: Duke University Press, 1926), p. 17.

104. *History of the State Agricultural Society of South Carolina, 1839–1916* (Columbia: R. L. Bryan Company, 1916), pp. 32–33.

105. *Ibid.*, pp. 27–28; News and Courier, August 10, 1877.

106. *News and Courier*, July 13, 1877, and April 16, 1879.

107. *Daily Register*, September 21, 1887; *Senate Journal* (1881), pp. 27–28, and (1887), pp. 6–8.

108. *Daily Register*, September 21, 1887; *Senate Journal* (1887), pp. 6–8.

diversified farming, came from either the agricultural or the state leadership. Even Governor Hagood made no suggestions.

Johnson Hagood, who illustrated the shortcomings of the Conservative leadership, refused to admit that a serious depression confronted the farmer. A year after describing the lien law as damaging and potentially destructive, he declared that the state was in the midst of an agricultural prosperity even without lien law repeal. Forfeiture of lands distressed Governor Richardson only momentarily. At the close of his annual message in 1887, he denounced those who claimed the state's prosperity had ebbed away. According to the Governor, the statistics warranted no such impression, but instead revealed " a steady advance in all material . . . interests." [109] Neither glowing words depicting agriculture nor the knowledge that his tax deadline had been postponed comforted the average South Carolina farmer. Doubtlessly, on a state level the Conservatives were helpless to remedy a problem—low cotton prices—concerned with international economics and politics. But their lack of comprehension of the situation ensured inaction and led to their denials that anything serious was wrong.

That same feeling influenced their reaction to Benjamin Tillman's agitation. Tillman, like the Conservatives, had few economic solutions for agricultural problems, but being on the outside of political power, he emphasized the real hardships endured by South Carolina farmers.[110] Tillman conveniently blamed all agricultural problems on the Conservative regime. To defend itself, the Conservative regime on the one hand blamed any problems on Republican tariff policy, and on the other hand, valiantly tried to convince the South Carolina farmer—as it had convinced itself—that no serious problems existed.[111]

---

109. *Daily Register*, December 5, 1882; *News and Courier*, November 23, 1887.

110. *Infra*, chap. v.

111. In the campaign of 1890 Joseph Earle and John Bratton, the Conservative candidates, assured their listeners that agriculture had " always been regarded as the prime interest in this state." While Earle told the farmers that state laws assisted them, Bratton declared that even though the Republican tariff policy was oppressive he could " find no adequate cause for the unrest of the people so far as their material interests are concerned." *News and Courier*, July 12, 19, and August 2, 1890.

CHAPTER V

THE CHALLENGE OF TILLMANISM: ISSUES

I

At a rural county seat one hot August day in 1885 the smoldering unrest in the Conservative Democratic party broke into the open. A warmer political atmosphere enveloped South Carolina when Benjamin Ryan Tillman forcibly injected himself into state affairs.

Captain Benjamin Tillman, in 1885, was a thirty-eight-year-old farmer who had rarely been outside of his native Edgefield county. Youth and illness had prevented his participation in the Civil War. Lacking the title, General or even Colonel, that South Carolina political figures of the 1880's proudly displayed as indisputable badges of personal honor and leadership abilities, he won his captaincy commanding an Edgefield militia company during the violent campaign of 1876. He initially attracted attention in 1885, not in his own right, but as the younger brother of George D. Tillman, a prominent Conservative Congressman.

For most of his life he had farmed, as had his parents, in Edgefield county. His family had prospered in the ante-bellum years and in 1860 owned more than one hundred slaves. They had believed in education and had sent George to South Carolina College and Harvard College, but the war and his illness had denied Benjamin a college education. Even so, he was an avid reader, particularly of English novels. His farming operations after 1865 made him a reasonable living, and in 1882, according to his own account, he bought more land and began extending himself. Although optimism had earlier prevailed on Tillman's acres, bad years from 1883 to 1885 soured him. Failures in cotton left him with little return, not even enough to meet interest payments. More important, he decided that neither he nor the majority of farmers in South Carolina really knew how to farm. He called himself and his agricultural comrades land-butchers, whose poor methods had caused rapidly deteriorating land values.

143

To promote self-help, Tillman attempted to organize Edgefield county farmers. His first effort, the Edgefield Agricultural Club, failed in 1884 before it got underway, but in January, 1885, he successfully organized the Edgefield County Agricultural Society. As president of this society, he had a platform from which to preach about the farmers' ills. When President D. P. Duncan of the state Agricultural and Mechanical Society invited Tillman to speak at the joint session of his society and the state Grange in Bennettsville in August, the aroused farmer readily accepted.[1]

Tillman's speech of August 6, 1885, made him " a flaming power in South Carolina affairs." [2] The assembled delegates had heard papers on tile drains and other elements of proper farming along with glowing words about South Carolina's agricultural prosperity when the Edgefield farmer rose to speak. He was no traditional South Carolina orator. With an empty left-eye socket—the result of an 1864 abscess and surgery—staring from a large head bare of the usual flowing beard, the rudely dressed Tillman could effectively paint a morbid picture of the state's agricultural condition. Farmers in his county found themselves poorer in 1885 than they had been fifteen years earlier, and Edgefield did not suffer alone. Decay had set in and had begun to destroy the independence of the farmers. The state government had facilitated this " descent into hell." " The people [had] been hoodwinked by demagogues and lawyers in the pay of finance." He condemned the agricultural department of South Carolina College as " a sop to Cerberus, a bribe to maintain the support of farmers in the legislature." Although he refrained from advocating abolition of the College, he did pronounce many of its alumni " drones and vagabonds."

He admitted that many of those who had gone to the legislature and passed laws were farmers, but with stinging irony he accused the regime of subverting the good intentions of the agriculturalist:

He enters the State House a farmer; he emerges from it in one session a politician. He went there to do something for the people. After breathing the polluted atmosphere for thirty days he returned home intent on doing something for himself. The contact with General This and Judge That and

1. Francis Butler Simkins, *Pitchfork Ben Tillman: South Carolinian* (Baton Rouge: Louisiana State University Press, 1944), pp. 90–91.
2. William Watts Ball, *The State that Forgot: South Carolina's Surrender to Democracy* (Indianapolis: The Bobbs-Merrill Company, 1932), p. 210; Charleston *News and Courier*, August 5–8, 1885; Simkins, *Tillman*, pp. 92–95.

Colonel Something Else, who have shaken him by the hand and made much of him, has debauched him. He likes this being a somebody; and his first resolution, offered and passed in his own mind, is that he will remain something if he can.

At the end of his speech Tillman offered four resolutions. He proposed an experimental farm; he wanted to make South Carolina College " a real agricultural institution " with more farmers on its board of trustees. His last two suggestions concerned changes in the Board of Agriculture and the establishment of farmers' institutes. The convention adopted his first resolution without debate, and with little more, tabled the others.[3]

Upon returning to Edgefield, Tillman continued his attacks on the status quo. In long letters published in the *News and Courier,* he pressed his scathing assault on those who ruled the state. Focusing on such agencies as the Agriculture Bureau, whose work directly affected the farmer, he found extravagance and incompetence in all of them. The true purpose of assisting farmers had been forgotten by men desperately clinging to office.[4]

In these letters Tillman maintained the general style of his Bennettsville speech. His attacks on the regime consisted of general insinuations made more pointed by his forceful language denouncing greedy politicians. He found them in every office and always they worked against the farmer, not for him. Roundly condemning the Agriculture Bureau and the state Agricultural Society as havens for political appointees who cared little, if at all, for the farmers, he paraphrased Alfred Lord Tennyson:

> Politicians to the right of us,
> Politicians to the left of us,
> Politicians in front of us,
> Volley and Thunder!

In the autumn of 1885, Tillman alone cried reform. He railed against a system he felt " rotten with politics," but he stood without firm support.[5] He expected to arouse the state's farmers to his cause but had no organization to assist him. Dependent on friends to get

3. *News and Courier,* August 7, 1885.
4. *Ibid.,* November 19 and 30, and December 3, 1885.
5. *Ibid.,* November 30, 1885.

his speeches circulated in newspapers,[6] he realized his debt to Francis W. Dawson for publishing his letters in the *News and Courier;* without Dawson, Tillman would have been an agitator without audience.[7] But as early as November, the idea of a state-wide farmers' organization "uniting our forces, to exert that influence and control over legislation affecting our interest as farmers" had formed in his mind.[8]

Tillman worked throughout the winter, and in March, 1886, issued a call for a statewide farmers' convention to be held in Columbia on April 29.[9] Proclaiming that the farmers, 76 per cent of the population, no longer governed the state, the call urged that "thoughtful and intelligent" farmers must act to ensure beneficial laws from future legislatures. Tillman called for the "wisest and best of our farmers" to assemble in Columbia to "find remedies for those evils" that beset the agriculturist. Tillman argued that politicians in South Carolina divided along up-country–low-country lines, but among farmers the common occupation of agriculture and the shared problem of economic hardship eliminated such divisions. "Our interests are one. Let us come together from the mountains to the sea . . . and obliterate this [sectional] line forever."

At this stage Tillman thought of his movement not as political action but as the only way for farmers to help themselves.[10] General agricultural depression forced all farmers to think as one and, Tillman reasoned, with the Grange practically defunct and the state Agricultural Society failing to generate much interest, most farmers had no organizational ties. The March call, signed by 92 farmers— including such men as Harry Hammond, son of one of ante-bellum South Carolina's most distinguished planters and leaders, James H. Hammond—was directed toward the landowners whom it referred to as wise, best, and thoughtful farmers. On the other hand, the

6. Tillman to Luther [Ransom], September 2 and October 9, 1885, Clemson History File, Clemson University Library, cited hereafter as CUL.

7. Tillman to Luther [Ransom], November 17, 1885, *ibid.;* B. R. Tillman to Francis W. Dawson, May 11, 1886, Francis W. Dawson Papers, Duke University Library, cited hereafter as Duke.

8. From a Tillman letter read at the November 7, 1885 meeting of the Beech Island [Aiken county] Farmers' club, recorded in the Beech Island Farmers' Club Minutes, 1846–93 held by the South Caroliniana Library, University of South Carolina; cited hereafter as SCL.

9. Edgefield *Chronicle,* March 17, 1886.

10. Tillman to Ransom, September 2, 1885, Clemson History File, CUL; Tillman to Dawson, May 17, 1886, Dawson Papers, Duke.

vituperative language and harsh attacks on lawyers and politicians aroused the less educated landowners and perhaps some sharecroppers, even though Tillman never at this point or later directly appealed to the latter.[11] He feared the impoverishment of all white landowners and envisioned their combining to protect mutual interests.

On the prescribed April day, over 300 delegates from thirty of South Carolina's thirty-four counties heeded Tillman's call to Columbia.[12] According to the *News and Courier* reporter, " intelligent South Carolina farmers " made up the bulk of the convention, and a goodly number of delegates combined merchandising with agriculture. Older men " predominated in numbers " but " a fair sprinkling of the younger generation participated."

The chief address came from the man who had called them to Columbia. Tillman lashed out at the " little and contemptible " politicians who criticized any attack on the status quo and at office holders infested with the " political leprosy which now permeate[s] our entire governmental fabric." He disparaged those advising that the convention stick to agricultural matters and leave politics to the officials. He challenged his listeners to assert their rights: " Say, you men who own the soil of South Carolina, who pay three-fourths of the taxes, whose devotion and courage have made South Carolina Democratic and have kept her so, how do you like this wet-nursing, this patronizing, this assumption of superiority, this insufferable insolence? "

At the same time, he chided farmers for lack of initiative. The one-crop system imprisoned them and subservience to the past kept agrarians in mental bondage. Since 1865 the whole South had been shackled by the Confederacy; farmers had to throw off this bondage and realize that appeals to the past would not help them in the present. Tillman asserted that he " must reform the farmers . . . Above all there must be more brain work, more mind-phosphate." He discerned an " almost spontaneous uprising of the people " behind

11. Tillman felt that he spoke for the state's farmers, and many supported him; but, on the other hand, others stood by the Conservative banner even in 1890. In contemporary usage, however, both in newspapers and private correspondance any reference to farmer legislators or farmer delegates meant those supporting Tillman. I have just continued this practice. In the second place, to pinpoint the date when Tillman's agitation received the name Tillmanism is impossible; therefore, for clarity, I have used it from the beginning.

12. *News and Courier*, April 29 and 30, 1886.

his movement that indicated they had begun to wake up and throw off their chains.

Even after this declaration, Tillman refused to sentence to oblivion men who were not farmers. He implored the delegates to return to their homes and convince other citizens of the truth in their movement. "I care not what profession they belong to—lawyers, preachers, doctors or merchants—so they are true men and stand on our platform." He urged his listeners to "let moderation and harmony guide our counsels."

Tillman invited all classes to join his movement, but he left no doubt about his disenchantment with the Conservative regime. Conservative delegates, led by J. J. Dargan, moved to have the convention invite Governor Hugh S. Thompson for an address which they believed would add dignity to their gathering. In defeating Dargan's motion, Tillmanites countered that a convention of South Carolina farmers had dignity enough; besides, according to N. G. Gonzales who covered the convention for the *News and Courier,* the farmers wanted nothing to overshadow their deliberations.

After their show of strength and purpose, the Tillmanites relented and allowed an invitation to the Governor, who accepted. Thompson said he had never feared a farmers' movement because he could not believe that farmers "who shouldered their muskets in 1861" and elected Hampton in 1876 could do "anything that would militate against the prosperity of the state they love so well." [13]

The convention treated the Governor courteously, but in its platform formalized demands Tillman had been making since Bennettsville. Overwhelmingly endorsed by an enthusiastic gathering of South Carolina farmers, this platform defined the issues that would dominate the political arena for the next four years.[14] Bennettsville had broadcast the name of Benjamin Tillman across the state. His platform and his convention gave him a strong base from which to assume the political offensive. Except for brief moments, after April, 1886, the Conservative regime remained on the defensive. Even when they checked Tillman's immediate goals, he retained the initiative. Public discussion and controversy focused on the four major elements in his platform.

13. *Ibid.,* April 30, 1886.
14. The vote was 140 to 26. *Ibid.,* May 1, 1886.

II

A major section of the convention platform called for an end to extravagance in the state administration and a return to honest, frugal government. Tillman followed two courses for implementing his demand that the state cut expenditures. First, he worked to lower the salaries of various officials in order to make state officers public servants rather than feeders on the " public pap." [15] Second, in an attempt to arouse the farmers against a regime that he thought had little interest in their welfare, Tillman accused the government of extravagance. This charge appealed to hard-pressed, taxpaying farmers.

Even before the April convention, the economy element in Tillmanism had made itself known. Prior to the convening of the legislature in 1885, a number of reformers, both admitted Tillmanites and other discontented legislators, organized the Economic Caucus, a group that grew out of a caucus of reformers held on November 29. Of course, at this early date no tight organization existed; those legislators dissatisfied with the regime had banded together to gain strength. A member of the caucus told the *News and Courier* capital correspondent of their decision to " lop off " the salaries of officials at the penitentiary, on the Railroad Commission, and connected with the judiciary. The reformer made no mention of cutting the salary of members of the legislature.[16]

The Economic Caucus decided to concentrate its efforts against the Lieutenant Governor. The economists thought that his salary of $1,000 was too much for his services. He worked for the state during the legislative session, and that service alone, they argued, should determine his remuneration. To implement their ideas, they introduced a bill that would pay the Lieutenant Governor $10 per day during the session, plus travel expenses. Opposition led by William Munro of Union county quickly argued that such a law would demean the second office. The state had a duty to support its elected officials; moreover, $1,000 was certainly a small sum. The economists' salary-reduction bill lost by only one vote.[17]

After 1885, the legislature continued to witness fights for salary

15. Simkins, *Tillman,* p. 109.
16. *News and Courier,* November 30, 1885.
17. *Ibid.,* December 3, 1885; *Journal of the Senate of the General Assembly of the State of South Carolina* (1885), p. 89.

reduction as the reformers pressed their attack on a broader front. In 1888, in the state House of Representatives they moved to reduce the salaries of circuit judges from $3,500 to $2,500. The reduction forces saw little sense in paying a judge so much. But the lawyers in the House struck back; led by William Brawley of Charleston and Ernest Gary of Edgefield—the attack on the judiciary united all lawyers, for Brawley was a stanch Conservative and Gary an ardent Tillmanite—they decried "cheap judges." The court system was too sacred to be subjected to petty and partisan politics; lowering salaries would reduce the caliber of judges, cause a deterioration of justice, and lose respect for the courts. The lawyers attempted to maintain the $3,500 salary but the economy-minded reformers simply overwhelmed them in a victory that proved fruitless because the House bill received an unfavorable committee report in the Senate and died.[18]

Although the reformers failed to have their economy measures enacted, their leader had success with his charges of extravagance. In a fight that drew its battle lines not in the legislature but on public platforms and in newspaper columns, Tillman's tactics differed from those of his followers engaged in salary reduction. His Bennettsville charges of excess he repeated at the Farmers' Association conventions in 1886 and 1887.[19] In his letters to the *News and Courier* he claimed that taxes had almost doubled between 1880 and 1885. Expenditures as well as taxes made him angry; speaking at the state Democratic convention in May, 1886, he declared that state expenses in 1887 had increased by one-quarter-of-a-million dollars over those in 1879. Tillman substantiated his charges by using the reports of the comptroller general as authority.[20]

Tillman carefully differentiated between his charge of extravagance and that of corruption. In the Farmers' Association conventions of April, 1886, he emphasized that he had not accused state officials of peculation. Speaking in Abbeville county prior to the 1888 nominating convention, he "denied that he had accused the State

18. *News and Courier*, December 5, 6, and 12, 1888; cf. *ibid.*, December 1, 1889.
19. *Ibid.*, April 30 and November 10, 1886, and December 2, 1887. After the April, 1886 meeting, the Farmers' Association convened two more times prior to 1890. The first annual meeting occurred in November, 1886, and the second annual session in December, 1887. From that date until the famous March, 1890 convention, no other state-wide conventions were held, but the association's executive committee was active in 1888 and 1889.
20. *Ibid.*, October 21, 1886, and Columbia *Daily Register*, May 18, 1888.

Government of Corruption, but of extravagance." [21] Tillman had no evidence on which to base any charge of corruption even though state expenses had increased. By impugning the character of public officials and then revealing rising governmental costs, he let his audiences draw their own conclusions.

Tillman's strategy forced the Conservatives into a predicament. They could not deny that expenses had gone up in the years between 1878 and 1887; they had to explain the reasons. Dawson, through his editorials in the News and Courier, tried to counter Tillman in a general way. He told his readers that " lack of complete success in farming, or insufficient profit, is no proof of the existence of either corruption or extravagance on the part of the State Government." Other Conservative sheets adopted his view. The Yorkville Enquirer did not believe the situation to be as Tillman pictured it; the Darlington News flatly rejected any talk of extravagance or abuses in the government.[22] This line of defense tried to dissociate the farmers' condition from rising expenses but did not explain why costs had gone up.

To that task Dawson and Governor Richardson addressed themselves. Dawson tried to explain in his paper that " an increase in expenditure is not censurable in itself." He pointed out that the great majority of the increase in costs between 1878 and 1887 lay in heavier appropriations for South Carolina College and the Citadel along with those for improvements on the State House.[23] Richardson took his campaign against Tillman's " vague and irresponsible charges " to the people. In every speech Richardson made during the 1888 canvass, the major portion concerning state affairs dealt with the extravagance issue.[24] He argued that tax receipts had in-

21. News and Courier, April 30, 1886, and July 21, 1888.
22. Ibid., September 22, 1887; Yorkville Enquirer, February 4, 1886; Darlington News, September 30, 1886.
23. News and Courier, October 21, 1886; May 28 and June 4, 1888.
24. Ibid., July 21 and August 2 and 4, 1888.
In an attempt to discover the validity of Tillman's charges, I analyzed the reports of the comptroller general in Reports and Resolutions of the General Assembly of the State of South Carolina for 1878–80, and for 1886–87. Tillman's claim that expenses rose was correct; but the Conservatives did not distort the facts when they claimed that increasing appropriations for the South Carolina College and the Citadel were the major element in the rise. For example, in fiscal year 1880 South Carolina College received only $2,100, but by fiscal year 1886 the College and the Citadel (reopened in 1882) received $40,000, and educational appropriations continued to rise after 1886. Salary scales showed no significant increases, e. g., the appropriation

creased because the state had made economic progress; land values had risen and the phosphate royalty had kept pace with that industry's progress. Both he and Dawson emphasized that in the late 1870s the debt had been funded, but that now it was being paid off in cash.

The Conservatives made a valiant effort to challenge Tillman's motives on the extravagance issue. Even while pointing out the " misleading character " of his statements, they remained on the defensive. In the legislature they might stop attempts to reduce salaries but they could not match Tillman on the stump. He spent his time condemning the government and identifying with his audience by calling himself " a plain, simple farmer." Such images made a much greater impression on rural South Carolina political meetings than did two-hour speeches filled with figures.

III

A second major plank in the farmers' convention platform demanded changes in state agricultural agencies. On November 30, 1885, Tillman had begun his attack in a letter to the *News and Courier* condemning both the state Agricultural Society and the Agriculture Bureau as the " veriest humbugs " controlled by " professional men or politicians." He asserted that those agencies existed only to provide offices for politicians and did little to benefit farmers.[25]

President D. P. Duncan of the state Agricultural Society rushed to the defense of his organization.[26] Refuting Tillman's charges that politicians and professional men dominated the Society, Duncan termed such accusations "wilful and malicious slander." After testifying that most of the leading officers of the Society were active farmers, Duncan demanded that Tillman retract his " vile slander or furnish the public with his proof that the society is saturated, permeated, rotten with politics."

Besides attempting to prove Tillman's assertions false, Duncan pointed out that both he and the Society had welcomed Tillman and

---

for the Governor's office remained practically the same from 1878 to 1887. Because in the final analysis both Tillman and the Conservatives spoke the truth, the chief issue became which side of the question had greater public appeal.

25. *News and Courier,* November 30, 1885.
26. *Ibid.,* December 14, 1885.

his criticism. After he had personally invited Tillman to speak at Bennettsville, the Society had asked Tillman to join its ranks. By refusing to join the Society and make his reforms from within, Tillman, according to Duncan, admitted his own selfishness and lack of true interest in assisting the farmers. Furthermore, said Duncan, Tillman was an ingrate. When Duncan offered to guide him around the state fair Tillman replied, " D—n the fair, I'm hunting figures on you fellows." Perhaps Duncan's moral deductions had little justification, yet Tillman confessed to his friend Luther Ransom that he had " some big bombs and [would] make somebody sick ere long." [27]

Tillman took intermittent shots at the state Agricultural Society and Duncan, but he fired his heavy barrages at the Agriculture Bureau and its commissioner, Colonel Andrew P. Butler. In a November, 1885, letter, he called the Bureau absurd and extravagant. The platform of the November, 1886, Farmers' Association convention indicted the Bureau as one wedded to " politics and politicians " that neither knew nor attempted to supply the needs of the farmers. His old accusation of no interest in the farmers' welfare applied to Butler as it did to his department. Moreover, Butler exemplified those incompetents eating from the " public crib." According to Tillman, Butler knew so little about his department's work that he merely signed his name to letters and reports drafted by his subordinates; he never read the contents. In reply, Butler attempted first to snub Tillman and later to challenge him to back his words with action. Though their threatened gunfight in the railroad station at Barnwell failed to materialize, Butler's reactions show that Tillman was making good his boast that he would make " somebody sick." [28]

After defending his personal honor, Butler vigorously defended his department. As early as December, 1885, he argued that the work of his department had " accomplished great good for all classes of our people, and particularly for the farming interests." Borrowing Duncan's tactics, he pointed out that, with only one exception, farmers sat on the executive board of his department, and he himself had farmed all of his life. In an 1887 interview granted to the *News and Courier,* Butler detailed the various activities of the Agriculture

27. Tillman to Luther [Ransom], September 2, 1885, Clemson History File, CUL.
28. *News and Courier,* November 11, 29, and January 28, 1886, and Simkins, *Tillman,* pp. 109–10.

Bureau and, among its valuable aids to farmers, he listed fertilizer inspection, weather reporting, and veterinary services. At the conclusion of the interview Butler emphasized his chief goal: " Our desire is to make the department of the greatest benefit to the farmers, and we are endeavoring to keep them informed and interested in its work, in order to secure their cordial co-operation." [29]

Tillman's charges against the Society and the Agriculture Bureau resembled his attack on extravagance. He centered his assault on alleged lack of interest in the farmers' welfare; just as in other branches of the state government, desire for office and politics motivated action. These agencies squandered the farmers' tax money on meaningless projects that returned him little benefit. Again, Tillman neither advocated specific reforms nor listed particular charges. Instead, he insisted that farmers should control the department, or in other words, that true farmers, those in the Farmers' Association, should determine the membership of the board that conducted the department's affairs.

Tillman gave the title " farmer " only to those men who stood behind his banner; others engaged in agriculture who opposed him, such as Duncan and his associates, Tillman defined as politicians. As Duncan and A. P. Butler repeatedly reminded him, the leading men in their organizations were certainly farmers. Tillman never contrasted farmers and planters and Tillmanism never pitted small landowners or sharecroppers against large landowners. Tillman himself belonged to the latter group, for he owned over 2,000 acres.

Following their chief's lead, the Farmers' Association convention of November, 1886, adopted a resolution demanding that the legislature revamp the Agriculture Bureau. The convention called for a ten-member board to control any state agency or projected agency that concerned agriculture. Not the legislature but the convention should choose the members of the board, which would have the power to elect its own secretary in place of the commissioner. A. P. Butler would be eliminated.

A bill embodying these demands was introduced in the House on November 30, 1886, by Clarendon county Representative James Tindal, a member of the Farmers' Association executive committee. The bill faced little real opposition in the House, and Tillmanites voted for its passage even after addition of some amendments. The

29. *News and Courier,* December 1, 1885, and January 19, 1887.

most important change reserved to the legislature the right to elect the ten board members but, at the same time, it required each of the ten men to be an active farmer. In addition, the bill required the board to hold in Columbia an annual meeting with five delegates from each county farmers' organization and five each from the Grange and the state Agricultural Society.[30]

The bill received quite different treatment in the Senate. Passing the House on December 13, it did not come out of the Senate Agriculture committee until December 21, and then without any recommendation. Senator L. W. Youmans, a farmer and chairman of the committee, considered the bill so revolutionary in its total effect that he suggested continuing it to 1887 because it could not possibly receive a full discussion in the few days remaining in the 1886 session. W. J. Talbert, from Tillman's home county, argued that the bill was overdue the farmers; it should be brought up, discussed, and passed. A strong Conservative, C. St. George Sinkler of Berkeley county, supported Talbert against Youmans, who declared that though he too was a farmer, he could not agree with them. Thereupon, he moved that the bill be continued until the next session, and his motion carried 21 to 14.[31]

Disgusted with the Senate's action on his bill to reorganize the Agriculture Bureau, Tillman castigated lawyers who had once again prevented the enactment of legislation beneficial to farmers. To be sure, lawyers voted yea on Youman's motion to continue, but seven of the fourteen farmers in the Senate joined them in dooming Tillman's project.[32]

The Conservative strength in the legislature had stopped Tillman's drive to make the Agriculture Bureau a vehicle of his Farmers' Association, but it could not silence his cry that the will of the people (i.e., of the farmers, who comprised 75 per cent of the people) had been subverted by politicians and lawyers. The Agriculture Bureau and Colonel Butler continued to serve as targets for his verbal arrows. He never ceased to tell his followers and listeners that their state Agriculture Bureau had done nothing to improve their condi-

30. *Ibid.*, December 1 and 14, 1886.

31. *Ibid.*, December 22, 1886. When the legislature convened in 1887, the reorganization bill duly reached the floor. But when Youmans and his associates finished amending it, the original Tindal bill was unrecognizable. In fact, the old Bureau remained. *Ibid.*, December 10, 1887. For the 1887 law itself, see South Carolina *Statutes at Large*, XIX, 802–3; for the original bureau, cf. *ibid.*, XVII, 72–76. For a possible explanation of Sinkler's behavior see below, n. 44.

32. *News and Courier*, January 6, 1887; *Senate Journal* (1886), pp. 310–11.

tion. Because their condition failed to improve, many continued to heed their Moses.

IV

Although Tillman spent much time decrying the state government's extravagance and incompetence, he did express positive reform ideas centered on two practical and educational aids to farmers. Stressing the ignorance of farmers about their profession, he advocated agencies and institutions that would improve their knowledge of agriculture and their ability to reap rewards from the soil.

The lesser of his two programs called for the establishment of an agricultural experiment station which, through scientific investigations, would advise farmers on new crops, different varieties of seeds, and numerous other questions. The Farmers' Association convention of November, 1886, wrote into its platform a plank requesting the legislature to create such an agency. Noting the Hatch bill pending in Congress, the convention asserted that its $15,000 annual appropriation would suffice to operate the proposed station.[33]

The South Carolina House of Representatives on December 16, 1886, debated a bill embodying the Farmers' Association recommendation. James Tindal led the agrarian forces and received support from William Brawley, a powerful Conservative from Charleston. Brawley insisted that the House must pass this bill because the enlightenment of farmers had to precede any true return to prosperity in a state as agricultural as South Carolina. Such assistance insured the bill's passage, but before the final vote Conservative strategy became clear. Having blocked the Tillmanite-backed reorganization of the Agriculture Bureau, they feared both the popular reaction to complete defeat of the Farmers' Association program and the chance of a single agricultural experiment station growing into the agricultural college that they opposed. Thus, the Conservative Representatives pushed through an amendment setting up two stations, one in the up country and one in the lowlands. Neither of the two stations could grow larger nor into a college without antagonizing the other.[34]

33. *News and Courier,* November 11, 1886. The Hatch Act, passed by Congress in 1887, provided an annual appropriation of $15,000 to each state to defray the expenses of an agricultural experiment station.

34. *Ibid.,* December 18 and 24, 1886, and *Statutes at Large,* XIX, 732–33; Joseph J. Lawton, " Benjamin Ryan Tillman and Agricultural Education: the ' Farmers' Col-

The establishment of an agricultural college, the chief reform demanded by Tillman, became the major political issue in South Carolina between 1886 and 1889. Tillman did not intend for the experiment station to grow into a school because he wanted both an experiment station and an agricultural college. From his speech at Bennettsville in the summer of 1885 to the final passage of the Clemson College bill in December, 1889, agricultural education remained foremost for the agrarian reformer. With Tillman on the offensive for most of the four years, the Conservative regime spent much time attempting to thwart his hopes.

Initially Tillman did not demand a separate college. At Bennettsville, he ridiculed the agriculture school at South Carolina College but revealed no aspirations for another college. One of the resolutions he offered at the close of his address proposed making South Carolina College into "a real agricultural institution." By the middle of November Tillman assured Luther Ransom that he felt "perfectly satisfied [that] we will either force the S. C. College to become an agl. college or get one of our own." [35]

Shortly after the letter to Ransom, Tillman dropped all talk of building up the agriculture school at South Carolina College. Correspondence with Stephen D. Lee, a former South Carolinian then president of the Agricultural and Mechanical College of Mississippi, convinced Tillman that separate agricultural colleges emphasizing practical training offered much more to farmers than did institutions giving different kinds of instruction. President Lee confided that "literary professors" had little use for the study of agriculture. Easily persuaded, Tillman labelled South Carolina College's agricultural school a "pitiful, contemptible, so-called agricultural annex" and accused the College of duplicity. "It is agricultural and mechanical when money is to be received; it is classical and literary when money is to be spent." Convinced of the strength of his agitation, he admonished the trustees of the College to give up their claim to the Morrill funds "before the storm, which is brewing, shakes the foundations of their beloved College, and perhaps, topples it to the ground." [36] Tillman convinced each Farmers' Association

---

lege' in South Carolina Politics, 1885–1889" (unpublished Senior thesis, Dept. of History, Princeton University, 1954), p. 48.

35. *News and Courier*, August 7, 1885; Tillman to Luther [Ransom], November 17, 1885, Clemson History File, CUL.

36. Simkins, *Tillman*, p. 96; *News and Courier*, November 19 and 30, 1885. The Morrill Act (1862) was named for Senator Justin S. Morrill, who introduced

convention to adopt as its first plank "the establishment of a real agricultural college, separate and distinct from the South Carolina College." [37]

Ironically, the Farmers' Association obstructed the implementation of its own platform. Along with an agricultural college the Association repeatedly called for retrenchment, often a hindrance to creation of the college. A close student of the college issue has argued that in the legislative elections of 1886 the county farmers' organizations stressed the economy issue much more than the agricultural college. In two Tillman strongholds, Laurens and Greenville, county farmers' conventions advocated retrenchment but made no mention of the college. The Spartanburg county Farmers' Association convention even explicitly rejected the separate college idea.[38] The Senate defeat of plans for reorganizing the Agriculture Bureau left increased taxation as the only source of revenue for the proposed college. Farmer legislators backed away from recommending any increases; thus they killed any possibility for a college.[39] Swept under by the University proposal in 1887, the separate college scheme drew only four Senate votes. Explaining his negative vote, Senator W. J. Talbert, a prominent Tillmanite from Tillman's own county, said that he could vote for new expenditures only when the people had approved the appropriation in advance.[40]

The principal state officers decided to ignore the furor originated by Tillman. In his message to the legislature in 1885, Governor Thompson made no mention of an agricultural college while praising the work of South Carolina College and the Citadel. Tillman claimed that Senator Butler had promised to endorse his agricultural

---

the original bill in Congress. By its terms, states were offered 30,000 acres of public land for each Congressional representative to which they were entitled, the proceeds to be used for education in agriculture, engineering, and military science. In some states, the lands were given to existing institutions; in others, they provided endowment for new agricultural and mechanical colleges.

37. *News and Courier*, November 11, 1886; cf. *ibid.*, May 1, 1886, and December 2, 1887.

38. Lawton, "College Issue," p. 45; Spartanburg *Carolina Spartan*, July 21, 1886.

39. Lawton, "College Issue," pp. 48–49. The Farmers' reorganization plan would have given to the Bureau for the agricultural college the Morrill and the Hatch funds, plus the license tax on all fertilizer sold in the state. According to the Tillmanites, these moneys would have been sufficient to operate the college. Under the old system which prevailed, the Morrill funds went to the agriculture school at South Carolina College, the Hatch appropriations went to the experiment stations, and the license tax supported the work of the Bureau.

40. *Senate Journal* (1887), p. 254.

college, but no word came from Washington. Governor Sheppard, in his legislative message of 1886, did mention the separate college as an idea of some merit; he refused to take sides, however, and insisted that only the General Assembly could make any decisions on the college issue. In December, 1886, newly elected Governor John P. Richardson completely ignored Tillman's demands in his inaugural address which praised " the South Carolina College and the State Military Academy [the Citadel], as the capstones to a perfected system of common schools . . ." [41]

Despite their public silence on the college issue, the Conservatives did not shrug off Tillman and his campaign as ephemeral. The Conservatives could not disregard any attack on the South Carolina College, certainly not one so vigorous as Tillman's. The farmers in his native Orangeburg county alarmed James F. Izlar, a powerful member of the state Senate, because they opposed—and " the opposition was decided "—anyone who supported the South Carolina College rather than the separate agricultural college. To his close friend, the prominent Conservative leader General John Bratton, Robert Means Davis, a professor of history at South Carolina College, deplored the Farmers' Association campaign. Bratton answered Davis in a tone of helpless resignation, " How can you help it or how can I ? " Professor Davis also criticized Francis Dawson for publishing items in the News and Courier favorable to the separate college; to Davis, such a policy meant enmity to South Carolina College. Claiming to be only open-minded, Dawson warned Davis that " it remains to be seen whether the small circle of College men are as strong as they think they are, and can see as clearly as those who are without the charmed limits." [42]

Unlike General Bratton and Professor Davis, Dawson based his position on practical politics, not ideology. He told Davis that " if the farmers really want an agricultural college . . . they will have it." From the beginning of Tillman's agitation, Dawson had tried to accommodate to the reformer and his program. Since December, 1885, he had given editorial support to the separate college plan; he had even worked for the adoption of the reorganized Agriculture

41. *Journal of the House of Representatives of the General Assembly of the State of South Carolina* (1885), pp. 15–18; Tillman to Luther [Ransom], November 17. 1885, Clemson History File, CUL; *House Journal* (1886), pp. 37–39, 118.

42. Izlar to Robert M. Davis, July, 24, 1886; Bratton to Davis, April 26, 1886; Dawson to Davis, August 1 and 16, 1887, all in Robert M. Davis Papers, SCL.

Bureau bill by the 1886 General Assembly.[43] No partner to a one-sided agreement, he induced Tillman to cease his opposition to the Citadel, important prey in the 1886 Tillman platform, but absent from later ones.[44]

Revealing the same fragmentation of Conservative opinion, local newspapers—such as the Columbia *Daily Register* and the *Darlington News*, edited by Governor Thompson's son—advocated Tillman's college, but only so long as it cost the state no extra money. Their reasoning seemed to support the separate college but in reality worked against it, for they argued strongly against tampering with existing institutions. Without the federal funds for agricultural education then given to South Carolina College, the new institution had little chance. On the other hand, the Georgetown *Enquirer* entreated its readers to let the farmers have their college, and the Orangeburg *Times and Democrat* believed there could be no objection to the college with " such a strong element of our population demanding it." [45]

Disturbed both by the divided opinion in the Conservative press and the momentum of Tillmanism, the trustees of South Carolina College, a group containing a significant number of powerful Conservative leaders,[46] and the institution's president, John M. McBryde, determined in 1887 to wrest the initiative from Tillman. McBryde had previously battled Tillman on the agricultural education issue. Insisting that technical training could be taught most effectively in combination with the liberal arts, he pointed to institutions like Cornell and the University of California where, he argued, the best agricultural work was being done. In the autumn of 1887, he worked

43. Dawson to Davis, August 16, 1887, *ibid;* News and Courier, November 20 and December 4, 1885, November 12, 1886, and January 6, 1887; Dawson to Tillman, May 13, 1886, Dawson Papers, Duke.

44. Tillman to Dawson, June 22, 1886, Dawson Papers, Duke. The support of Brawley in the House, and Buist [Charleston] and Sinkler [Berkeley, a neighbor of Charleston] in the Senate for certain Tillman proposals such as the reorganization bill suggests that Dawson did work in Tillman's behalf, for he was a dominant figure in Charleston county politics.

45. *Daily Register,* December 6, 1885, and *Darlington News,* September 30, 1886; Georgetown *Enquirer,* May 19, 1886, and Orangeburg *Times and Democrat,* May 6, 1886.

46. Conservative leaders—like John Haskell, John Bratton, Charles Simonton, James F. Izlar, Johnson Hagood, and, ex officio, Governor Richardson—sat on the College Board of Trustees. Minutes of the Board of Trustees of the University of South Carolina, IX and X, SCL.

out a plan that would transform South Carolina College into a university. Among its various schools would be a strengthened agricultural one; funds for the new school would include those from the Morrill Act and the Hatch Act, both eagerly sought by Tillman for his college.[47]

The trustees approved McBryde's plan and organized a phalanx of Conservative leaders to obtain public support for the new University. General Bratton in a public letter to the *News and Courier* threw his influence behind a "centralized unified system" of education. John Haskell, a legislator and Hampton's son-in-law, addressed the 1887 Farmers' Association convention, where in the midst of Tillman's most devoted followers, he warmly advocated the university idea because it would mean better agricultural education for the state's farmers at less cost than a separate college. In his message read on the opening day of the session, Governor Richardson put all the influence of his office behind the University bill and called it a step forward in the state's educational program.[48] Dawson, "encouraged" that the new plan offered "a way out of the agricultural college difficulty," turned his editorials away from Tillman's college to the University.[49]

With the passage of the University bill by the 1887 legislature, the Conservatives seemingly had ended the threat of Tillmanism. Angry with Dawson for "desert[ing] us just at the critical time," Tillman argued that with the continued support of Dawson's powerful pen "success would have crowned our efforts."[50] Embittered, the Edgefield Reformer withdrew from the contest in January, 1888, with a formal statement in the *News and Courier*.[51] In this farewell

47. Daniel Walker Hollis, *College to University*, Vol. II: *University of South Carolina* (Columbia: University of South Carolina Press, 1951, 1956), pp. 136, 139, 145–46; "Report of the Board of Trustees of the University of South Carolina," *Reports and Resolutions* (1886).
    The Hatch Act funds would still be used for an experiment station, but under McBryde's plan the station would be an integral part of the University's new agriculture school.
48. *News and Courier*, November 29 and December 2, 1887; *Senate Journal* (1887), pp. 10–11.
49. Dawson to Davis, September 27, 1887, Davis Papers, SCL. From this letter, it seems that Professor Davis had been trying to reach an understanding with Dawson on the university idea.
50. Tillman to Dawson, December 12, 1887, Dawson Papers, Duke. Dawson's decision to support the University bill ended his alliance with Tillman. Even though Dawson did not vigorously oppose the Clemson College bill in 1888, the breach with Tillman was never healed.
51. *News and Courier*, January 26, 1888.

letter, he returned to ideas propounded at Bennettsville when he called the legislature an assembly of " political harlots " and " how-dye-do statesmen " trapped by the same Conservative snares of generals, colonels, and personal attention. He warned the friends of the University to " crow lustily over the great victory they [had] won " because he would return and humble the " lordly planters " by building a separate agricultural college for the farmers.

Tillman had a short retirement. On April 2, 1888, Thomas G. Clemson, son-in-law of John C. Calhoun, died, leaving his Fort Hill estate in up-country Oconee county and a cash endowment of more than $80,000 to the state of South Carolina for the establishment of a separate agricultural college. Clemson had long been interested in scientific agriculture, and as early as 1883 had decided to leave his estate to support an agricultural college. In 1886 he had invited Tillman to Fort Hill to discuss changes in the will that would strengthen Clemson's proposed college.[52]

Fully realizing the weapon Clemson's bequest gave him, Tillman hurriedly called a meeting of the Farmers' Association executive committee so they could take appropriate action immediately. Only three weeks after Clemson's death, the committee issued an address " To the People of South Carolina," that called on the state to accept " the munificent bequest of Mr. Clemson." [53] Because the Clemson will provided both the land and the money for building the college, the address declared, there remained only the question of revenue for its operation. Aware of their retrenchment demands, the committee carefully pointed out that over $50,000, more than enough to operate the school, was readily available from the license tax on fertilizers which rightfully belonged to the farmers and from the federal grants given to the agricultural school at the University of South Carolina. These sources precluded any need for additional taxation to finance Thomas Clemson's college. The address closed with an appeal to elect to the legislature men who would ensure the state's acceptance of Clemson's will. Farmers should shun any candidate who refused openly to support the separate college.

Just as the Farmers' Association executive committee desired, the Clemson legacy became a major topic in the 1888 canvass. From the

52. Alester G. Holmes and George H. Sherill, *Thomas Green Clemson: His Life and Work* (Richmond: Garrett and Massie, 1937), pp. 157–79, 193–201.
53. *News and Courier*, April 26, 1888.

stump, Tillman demanded that the state accept the bequest. To ensure that the lawyers and politicians not take the gift away from the farmers, Tillman solicited election of a legislature pledged to a separate agricultural college.[54]

John Bratton's remark " that old Clemson's expiring spark has set the woods on fire " aptly described the political temperature in South Carolina between April and December, 1888. The *Laurensville Herald,* a Tillman paper in a Tillman stronghold, termed the bequest " a glorious gift." The *Herald* also noted that local candidates, and not in Laurens county alone, were " greedily swallowing that unadulterated dose [the Farmers' Association platform] that, only two years ago, seemed to be so nauseating to their stomachs." Popular support for Clemson's bequest loomed large in that political shift. Normally Conservative papers from Spartanburg to Georgetown advocated acceptance. The Edgefield *Chronicle* summarized widespread opinion on the Clemson will when it argued that lack of funds to establish a separate college had been a legitimate reason for not doing so, but Thomas Clemson's generosity destroyed this legitimacy; therefore, the state had to accept the gift.[55]

Many Conservative leaders refused to join that chorus. They seldom advocated total rejection of the bequest; instead, they so qualified its acceptance as to make it impossible to establish a separate college. The University's trustees again made policy for the regime; they decided to fight the Clemson issue by proscribing any changes in existing institutions. Governor Richardson disagreed with the action of the trustees but remained silent while Congressman Samuel Dibble and former Governor Hagood voiced the trustees' decision.[56]

A letter in the *News and Courier* on May 21, 1888 presented another line in the Conservative defense. Gideon Lee, a Northerner, in a public letter on behalf of his daughter Floride Isabella Lee—

54. *News and Courier,* July 21 and August 2, 1888.
55. Bratton to Davis, May 2, 1888, Davis Papers, SCL; *Laurensville Herald,* April 27 and August 17, 1888; Edgefield *Chronicle,* May 2, 1888; for similar opinions, see Spartanburg *Carolina Spartan,* April 25, 1888, Newberry *Herald and News,* May 3, 1888, and Georgetown *Enquirer,* May 2, 1888.
56. Richardson to W. A. Ancrum August 24, 1888, Richardson Letterbook Personal, Executive File, South Carolina Archives, cited hereafter as SCA; Lawton, " College Issue," p. 62; *News and Courier,* August 14, 1888. Newspaper support for the trustees' policy came from the *Daily Register,* December 15, 1888, and the *Darlington News,* December 20, 1888.

Clemson's granddaughter and John C. Calhoun's great-grand-daughter—accused Clemson of denying Calhoun's heir her rightful heritage of the ancestral acres. He called Clemson an egotistical, unbalanced old man who only wanted to erect a monument to his own name. Appealing to South Carolinians' sentiment and their reverence for Calhoun, Lee begged the legislature to reject the bequest. In November, 1888, he also filed suit in Federal Court contesting Clemson's will.[57]

When the bill accepting the Clemson bequest reached the floor of the General Assembly in December, Conservatives stretched their ingenuity in an attempt to prevent its passage. The will had stipulated that the college be run by thirteen trustees, seven of whom would be trustees for life. Clemson himself chose the first seven and required that the initial seven chose their own successors. Representative B. L. Abney of Richland county feared that such a system allowed the state too little control over a state institution. John Haskell pointed to the suit filed by Gideon Lee and asked whether the legislature wanted to involve the state in litigation; acceptance of the bequest would entangle the state in the suit. In the Senate, E. B. Murray, realizing the futility of open opposition, argued that the will gave the state three years in which to accept the gift; therefore haste was unnecessary. He called on the Senate to postpone its action until after the court decision on the contested will. Groping for weapons, Conservatives made allusions to Clemson's sanity and morals in a desperate attempt to discredit him and create sympathy for his granddaughter.[58]

With a struggle the legislature passed the Clemson College bill. Though vocal opposition occupied much of the House debate, the bill got through the lower chamber with relative ease. In the Senate the Conservatives put up a stiff fight, and it took the tie-breaking vote of Conservative Lieutenant Governor William L. Mauldin of Greenville county to pass the College bill.[59] Even though Conservatives Mauldin, William Munro of Union county, and Marion Moise of Sumter voted with the Clemson forces, the great majority of Conservative senators such as Senate leaders Augustine Smythe of Charleston, Edwards Murray of Anderson, James Izlar of Orangeburg, and Fitz-William McMaster of Richland voted nay.

57. *News and Courier,* 21 May 21, 1888.
58. *Ibid.,* December 15 and 19, 1888.
59. *Ibid.,* December 14, 15 and 19, 1888.

Two crucial Senate votes ended in a tie with Mauldin breaking both in favor of Clemson. The anti-Clemson vote was decidedly sectional, with opposition centered in the low country. The new college would be in Oconee county, in the extreme northwestern part of the state; a trip from Hampton or Williamsburg to Oconee in the 1880s presented many obstacles. Doubtless, the belief that upper counties would derive more benefit from Clemson influenced some votes. But more important, especially in Charleston and Richland, were loyalty and allegiance to the University of South Carolina. There Clemson appeared as unwanted competition and as an intruder on the preserve of the University as the only legitimate state institution, always with the Citadel, for it too had ante-bellum origins.

After Clemson College had received the legislature's approval, Governor Richardson had to make the final decision. A unique constitutional provision allowed the Governor to withhold until the next session his signature on any bill that reached his desk not more than three days before the adjournment of the legislature. Saying he wanted to give John C. Calhoun's great-granddaughter her day in court, Richardson chose that course. This delay opened him to criticism from newspapers inclined toward Tillman. The *Florence Farmer's Friend* denounced him as " the figurehead who sits in the gubernatorial chair and obeys the bidding of the bosses "; the powerful *Greenville News* more charitably only accused the Governor of fence straddling. But generally the press followed the lead of Dawson, who termed Richardson's action " eminently judicious." With no intention of refusing to sign the bill in 1889, Richardson on several occasions expressed to some of the college's most ardent advocates his firm support of Clemson.[60] When the General Assembly began its 1889 session, the Governor forwarded the acceptance act with his signature.

The failure of Lee's suit ensured that the legislature of 1889 would take the steps necessary to make Clemson College operational.[61] The 1888 act only accepted the bequest; it made no

---

60. *Florence Farmer's Friend,* cited in the *News and Courier,* January 8, 1889, and *Greenville News,* cited in Holmes and Sherrill, *Clemson,* p. 186; *News and Courier,* December 27, 1888, and Edgefield *Chronicle,* January 9, 1889; Richardson to R. W. Simpson [Clemson's attorney and executor of his estate], July 14, 1888, and Richardson to W. A. Ancrum, August 24, 1888, both in Richardson Letterbook Personal, Executive File, SCA; also J. S. Verner [state comptroller general] to R. W. Simpson, November 19, 1889, R. W. Simpson Papers, CUL.

61. The United States Circuit Court ruled against Lee in May, 1889; upon that decision, he appealed to the United States Supreme Court. That Court's ruling against

appropriations for the maintenance of the new college. Such a law readily passed the 1889 legislature, but not without opposition from a few die-hard Conservatives. In their futile fight this small group went over the same ground covered in 1888, but with a greater attempt to mark Thomas Clemson as an agnostic and insane old man who stole the birthright of Calhoun's great-granddaughter.[62]

With the final passage of the Clemson bill by the legislature of 1889 and Governor Richardson's signature, the college issue descended from the pre-eminent position it had occupied since 1885. In his victorious political campaign of 1890, Tillman made little reference to the issue that had already well served him and his movement. Tillman's cries had been one-sided and at times inaccurate and cruel, but no one could deny that South Carolina needed stronger agricultural education. That did come in the University bill of 1887, but by then the propitiousness of Clemson's will and Tillman's own political aspirations prevented him from viewing the reforms at the University of South Carolina with objectivity.

V

The political tranquility following the Clemson College Act lasted less than one month. Carrying out a decision made in 1889, the Tillman forces published on January 23, 1890, a political manifesto stating their intention to contest actively for the Democratic gubernatorial nomination of that year. The Manifesto signed by G. W. Shell, president of the Farmers' Association, set the tone and defined the issues that would guide Tillman's efforts to capture the governorship.[63]

The Shell Manifesto displayed the language of vituperation and

---

him came in a unanimous opinion in April, 1890. For the case's legal history, see Lee v. Simpson, 33 Law Ed. United States Supreme Court Reports 1038.

62. News and Courier, December 14–15 and 20–21, 1889. On final passage, no recorded vote occurred in the House; in the Senate, the bill's opponents could find few supporters, and lost by a two-to-one margin. For the Clemson bill itself, see Statutes at Large, XX, 299–302, 689.

63. For the Manifesto, see the News and Courier, January 23, 1890. The political decisions and activities in this instance and all other facets of the 1890 campaign will be treated in detail in the following chapter.

Supposedly Shell, who signed it, composed the manifesto that bore his name, but few doubted that Benjamin Tillman wrote it. The following notation, in William Watts Ball's handwriting, appears on a typed copy of the Manifesto in the W. W. Ball Papers, Duke. "B. R. Tillman wrote it. I heard him say so. WWB." See also Ball, The State that Forgot, p. 219.

invective that had been Tillman's trademark since his Bennettsville speech five years earlier. It accused the Conservatives of resorting to political machinations to defeat the farmers, who had the support of a majority of the people. The Manifesto declared that " ring bosses " had dominated South Carolina politics through " cajolery, threats and . . . rage." Turning to the legislature, Shell's document asserted that " bamboozled and debauched " legislators had forgotten the needs of the people.

The Manifesto appealed to the people to overthrow the aristocrats who ruled the state. Congratulating the people for defeating " the aristocratic coterie who were educated at and sought to monopolize everything for the South Carolina College," the Manifesto praised them for establishing Clemson College. Since the days of the Lords Proprietors, the state had been governed by " an aristocracy under the form of Democracy " which had always succeeded in subverting any " champion of the people " through bribery or slander. Calling on " the common people who redeemed the state from Radical rule," the Manifesto challenged: " Can we afford to leave it [the state government] longer in the hands of those who, wedded to ante-bellum ideas, but possessing little of antebellum patriotism and honor are running it in the interest of a few families and for the benefit of a selfish ring of politicians? "

The Manifesto made little effort to present a positive political program. Aside from the biting language accusing aristocrats of refusing to allow popular rule, the Farmers' Association battle-order did no more than list numerous abuses of the state government. The state Senate, dominated by " Charleston's rich politicians " and the bastion of the aristocrats, headed the list. General charges of extravagance and incompetence in state officials, similar to Tillman's earlier cries, pervaded the document.

The Conservative reaction was immediate and hostile. Calling the Manifesto " harsh and unwise," the Edgefield *Chronicle* rebuked the Farmers' Association. To the *Greenville News* the Manifesto revealed that reform had sold out to politics. The Columbia *Daily Register* denounced the entire document as a slur on the name of South Carolina. The *News and Courier* " regret[ed] the temper of the Manifesto " because it appealed to emotion, not " to the sober judgment " of the people. More specifically, Conservatives deplored " the sweeping accusations . . . against State officers and legislators."

The Newberry *Herald and News* "[did] not like to see grave charges preferred against those who are in office unless the charges [were] substantiated by the facts." The Orangeburg *Times and Democrat* thought the document suffered from its unwarranted attack on the integrity of state legislators.[64]

The Manifesto charge that the state had always been ruled by an aristocracy incited repeated denials. In a thoughtful editorial, the Anderson *Intelligencer* asserted that in South Carolina " power ha[d] always been with the people." [65] Defining the Manifesto's indictment as " too wholesale," the *Intelligencer* challenged the Farmers' Association to prove the veracity of their charges, then declared this proof would never come, for " our dear mother State " had never harbored " an aristocratic oligarchy."

While denying its allegations, the Conservatives convinced themselves that the Manifesto would ultimately work to Tillman's disadvantage. The *Darlington News* predicted that the document would undermine public confidence in Tillman. General Bratton, a candidate for Governor, did not " think it possible that our people " would condone such practices. Voicing faith in the people, Senator Matthew Butler wrote from Washington, " The great body of farmers are not going to sustain such an extravagant arraignment as that [Shell Manifesto]." [66]

VI

The 1890 campaign quickly substituted the hustings for the newspapers. The state Democratic Executive Committee had ordered for gubernatorial hopefuls a public speaking tour to include engagements in every county in the state. This system afforded greater public exposure than had the 1888 practice of holding one meeting in every congressional district. Aware of his ability as a political speaker, Tillman prepared to enter the verbal lists with his two Conservative opponents, General John Bratton and Joseph Earle.

In overwhelmingly rural South Carolina the arrival of " speaking

64. Edgefield *Chronicle*, January 29, 1890; *Greenville News* quoted by *Daily Register*, March 5, 1890; *Daily Register*, February 2, 1890; *News and Courier*, January 24, 1890; Spartanburg *Carolina Spartan*, February 5, 1890; Newberry *Herald and News*, January 30, 1890; Orangeburg *Times and Democrat*, January 29, 1890.

65. Anderson *Intelligencer*, January 30, 1890.

66. *Darlington News*, January 30, 1890; Bratton to R. M. Davis, May 9, 1890, Davis Papers, SCL; Butler to John C. Hemphill [editor of the *News and Courier*], February 2, 1890, Hemphill Family Papers, Duke.

day " aroused a holiday spirit and a carnival atmosphere. Thousands of the local " yeomanry . . . assembled under the spreading branches of a live oak," or journeyed to nearby hillsides to listen to the solicitors for office.[67] But these farmers and storekeepers did more than just listen; they participated, cheering their hero or, at times, displaying even greater enthusiasm. At Winnsboro four of Tillman's followers carried him in their arms; a reporter thought this scene " quaint, but not pretty." Some partisans made Tillman's speech at Florence more comfortable by " brushing flies off [him] with a stalk of green corn." In one county, " pretty young ladies " gathered around General Bratton's carriage and serenaded him with " a sweet soprano shout . . . while from fair young hands a rain of flowers beat in to the . . . vehicle." Earle marched to platforms behind the banner, " Straightout Democracy–1890–For Governor, Jos. H. Earle." [68]

In the canvass Tillman employed the tactics that had characterized his crusade from Bennettsville to the Shell Manifesto. With abusive language he tried to convince hard pressed farmers that they represented a forgotten class for whose welfare the Conservative aristocrats had no interest. To undermine public confidence in the regime, he repeated unsupported charges of extravagance by officials in the state government.

Supposedly the tribune of the farmers, Tillman offered few positive ideas for pulling the state out of its agricultural depression. Instead, he spent his time denouncing the incompetent and corrupt officials that ran the state Agriculture Bureau.[69] He indicted the Bureau for abusing and neglecting the farmers of South Carolina but presented no program for their economic advancement other than his own election. Personal attacks similar to those he had made on Commissioner of Agriculture Andrew P. Butler highlighted his assault. His whole program for agriculture in 1890 followed closely the strategy he had employed in the 1880s. He took a condition—

67. *News and Courier*, July 5 and 19, 1890. For the campaign speeches, I used this paper because it gave the most complete coverage. For a pro-Tillman view, see the Charleston *World*.

The following analysis is based on intensive study of the speeches at nine meetings. I took three speeches from each section of the state so that any specifically sectional issues would be apparent. I found none; and the absence of any particular sectional appeals by any of the candidates enabled me to refrain from cluttering the text with place names.

68. *News and Courier*, July 2, 3, 10, and 11, 1890.

69. *Ibid.*, July 2, 10, 12 and August 2, 1890.

agricultural depression—and blamed the state government for its existence. Except for the abolition of the lien law, no economic suggestions dulled his speeches. Unlike other Southern agrarian radicals, Tillman did not espouse the platform of the Farmers' Alliance, a more nationally and economically oriented organization, which his movement kept in the background in South Carolina.[70]

Instead, he focused on "the moral cowardice and political leprosy" that infested the Conservative regime. To Tillman "the fight [was] between those in power who believe there's nothing wrong in South Carolina and those who want Reform." And those who said "there's nothing wrong" he considered not well-meaning men who happened to disagree with him, but a corrupt, oligarchical ring.[71] As had the Shell Manifesto, he directed most of his volleys against the state Senate and its cardinal sin—refusal in 1887 to reapportion the state.[72] The senators who had voted against reapportionment, all Conservatives, "were rotten and [had] perjured themselves." The treacherous Senate "was the great bulwark against reform." Tillman summed up this charge with a withering accusation: "Brother Democrats had robbed brother Democrats of their rights." [73]

In fact, according to Tillman, he himself represented the true Democrat. He condemned the existing party hierarchy as selfish, aristocratic, and unaware of the people's needs. His opponents, Bratton and Earle, "represent[ed] their ambition only" while he "represent[ed] all classes." [74] Tillman openly made a class appeal, though not a very narrow one. Everyone not connected with the "oligarchy of office seekers, a codfish aristocracy based on money and brass" belonged to "the masses of the people." [75] These people should support Tillman, the true Democrat "arraying Jefferson's

70. Tillman was not an Alliance candidate, and those who see the Alliance supporting him and his victory as a victory for the Alliance program err, e.g., Simkins, *Tillman*, pp. 147–48, and C. Vann Woodward, *Origins of the New South, 1877–1913*, Vol. IX of *A History of the South*, ed. Wendell Holmes Stephenson and E. Merton Coulter (Baton Rouge: Louisiana State University Press, 1951), p. 204. Contemporaries recognized that Tillman did not stand on the Alliance platform. *News and Courier*, April 23, 1890.

71. *News and Courier*, July 3 and 5 and August 2, 1890

72. *Ibid.*, July 10, 19, 30, 1890; supra, chap. ii.

73. *Ibid.*, July 5 and 12, August 6, 1890.

74. *Ibid.*, July 10, 1890.

75. *Ibid.*, July 5, 10, 30, and August 1–2, 1890. The rank and file of the Conservative regime drew such epithets as "pimps, bootlickers, satellites and flunkies." *Ibid.*, July 19, 1890.

dogmas against aristocracy," and Tillmanism, the true democracy, granting equal rights for all white men.[76] Yet with these class appeals, however broad, Tillman offered no platform intended to arouse class against class. During the 1890 canvass, the radicalism of Benjamin Tillman simply amounted to an indictment of his enemies as aristocrats.

Tillman's " aristocrats " tried to wrest the initiative from him by shifting the discussion to national issues. Replying to a Tillman speech at Ridgeway in May, state Senator L. W. Youmans pointed out that " the fight should be on the National and not the State Government." Bratton continually underscored the oppressive nature of the Republican-dominated federal government. In his mind " South Carolina [was] quarreling over one grain of wheat while the whole barn was burning." In the iniquitous tariff and the threat of the Force bill which proposed federal supervision of congressional elections in the South, Bratton argued: " The same dangers of Reconstruction still face us. The Federal Government is as hostile as when, by military force, they imposed that power upon us." [77] Refusing to discuss national questions, Tillman denounced the tactic of blaming troubles on Washington as simply an attempt to bamboozle the voters. Tillman declared that as a contender for Governor he stood before the people to discuss state issues, not national politics.[78]

Rebuffed in their efforts to engage Tillman on the tariff and the Force bill, the Conservatives returned to their familiar role of denying Tillman's accusations. Replying in similarly general terms, Bratton and Earle hastened to defend their comrades and their Democratic Party. General Bratton urged his hearers to stand behind the Conservative Democrats " which had won [in 1876] and preserved our liberties." [79] Earle pronounced Tillman's charge of corruption " a vile slander." Instead of greed and extravagance, " the intelligence and virtue of the State had controlled." [80]

Attempting to convict Tillman of abusing his state and of lacking faith in the Democrats, Earle stressed the goodness and nobility of the Conservatives and the greatness of South Carolina. " That a South Carolinian should charge that the Democratic party was guilty

76. *Ibid.*, July 2, 5, 1890.
77. *New York Times*, May 4, 1890; *News and Courier*, July and 19, 1890.
78. *News and Courier*, July 5 and 12, 1890.
79. *Ibid.*, July 30, 1890; see also *ibid.*, July 4, and 9, and August 2, 1890.
80. *Ibid.*, July 10 and 12, 1890.

of robbery" surprised and shocked him. Forthrightly, Earle proclaimed that his "State stood at the head of the list in honor and loyalty." The men of the Democratic party governing the state "were true to themselves, they kept their pledges and have given the State pure, honest and economical government." In Earle's opinion, Tillman had "no right to rise to power on the ruined reputations of good and true men. Most of them were brave soldiers; they fought with Lee and Jackson, and many of them bear on their bodies scars received in defense of their country." Tillman and his followers, Earle countered, were "ringsters" worse than Republicans in blaspheming the honor of men "as high and noble as any in South Carolina."[81]

When the canvass closed in early August, General Bratton hoped in vain that it had served "as enlightenment of our people as to their public matters." In few instances did any meaningful discussion of issues occur; the speeches, in fact the entire campaign, focused on personalities. The Newberry *Herald and News* observed, "The prejudices of the people have been so aroused that it is almost useless to say anything in soberness, or direct a line to their reasoning." An outside reporter described Tillman's major activity on the stump as "reckless abuse of honest men." Tillman's biographer similarly evaluated the canvass: "Little attention was paid to program and principles; his noisy cohorts preferred banter and personalities."[82]

Professor Simkins pointed to one issue that did receive a complete hearing—Tillman himself. He so dominated the canvass that Simkins judged it "one-sided."[83] He forced his opponents to proceed on his level, and on that level, stump speaking, Tillman had no peer in South Carolina. General Bratton was clearly out of his element; a distinguished Confederate general and planter of fifty-nine years, Bratton proved ineffectual in the face of Tillman's harangues. Earle, a more formidable antagonist, refused to meet Tillman with countercharges. Rather, he castigated Tillman for his lack of civility and repeatedly defended his compatriots in the Conservative Democratic party. On the platform, Earle's dignified appearance proved quite a handicap in a political contest dominated by Tillman's flamboyance.

81. *Ibid.*, July 5, 10, 12, 19, 30, and August 6, 1890.
82. Bratton to R. M. Davis, May 9, 1890, Davis Papers, SCL; Newberry *Herald and News*, July 10, 1890; *New York Times*, June 19, 1890; Simkins, *Tillman*, p. 161.
83. Simkins, *Tillman*, p. 160.

Tillman's proficiency on the platform fomented success. In Camden, Conservatives had pushed close to the speaker's platform and created such confusion that Tillman could not proceed with his speech. Thereupon, he turned directly on his tormentors with " masterly invective " that created " a frenzy" among his supporters who surged forward and displaced the outnumbered Conservatives. In the last month of the campaign, he originated his " hand primary," in which he asked for a show of hands each time he mentioned a candidate's name. Those raised for him dwarfed the number put up for Bratton and Earle. Tillman created even more excitement with his list of perjured senators. When speaking in a county whose senator had voted against reapportionment in 1887, Tillman would publicly denounce that official. Occasionally he was forced to retract his words; often violence was threatened.[84] But Tillman assured himself the attention and the interest of the crowd.[85]

To the end, Conservatives tried to convince themselves that Tillman's tactics would eventually cost him public support. They hoped that " Tillman's failure to prove his charges . . . [had] turned a tide that [would] drown him politically." Tillman's campaign personality disturbed the *News and Courier* and caused it to hope that public opinion would turn on him.[86] Tillman's final test lay in a state convention of the Democratic party of South Carolina. On the outcome of that contest leaned Conservative hopes of freeing their party from " Tillmania." [87]

84. Thomas J. Kirkland, " Tillman and I," Columbia *State*, July 7, 1929, p. 3; *News and Courier*, July 11, June 24, and August 2, 1890.

85. For Tillman, it was essential to draw people to the public meetings because he had not fared well with the press. Only one daily paper, the Charleston *World*, supported him. The three most prominent papers—the *News and Courier* in the low country, the Columbia *Daily Register* in the midlands, and the *Greenville News* in the up country—strongly opposed him. Even the county weeklies stood in great numbers by the Conservative Democrats; the *News and Courier*, April 8, 1890, found only six out of forty weeklies for Tillman. In another poll on April 9, 1890, the Spartanburg *Carolina Spartan* had but six out of twenty-eight for Tillman. The Edgefield *Chronicle*, April 2, 1890, an anti-Tillman paper, felt that 80 per cent of the press was against Tillman. The two most prominent pro-Tillman weeklies were the Edgefield *Advertiser* and the *Laurensville Herald*. My research substantiates the conclusions reached in those contemporary polls. Tillman's smashing triumph in the face of almost universal newspaper condemnation questions the generalizations on the political influence wielded by rural Southern editors made by Thomas D. Clark in his *The Rural Press and the New South* (Baton Rouge: Louisiana State University Press, 1948), pp. 28–30.

86. *New York Times*, June 19, 1890; *News and Courier*, June 12, 1890.

87. " Tillmania " was a contemporary Conservative epithet.

CHAPTER VI

THE CHALLENGE OF TILLMANISM: POLITICS

I

When Benjamin Tillman began his agitation, he denied that he or his movement had any political aspirations. Suggested as a gubernatorial candidate by some newspapers in 1885, he attempted publicly to clarify his status. Avowing " I am not, nor will I be, a candidate for that [the governorship] or any other office in anybody's gift," Tillman hoped to end all talk of high public office for himself. As late as 1888 in a meeting of the Farmers' Association executive committee, he dissuaded the Association from putting anybody in the race for Governor or Lieutenant Governor.[1]

Initially, most Conservatives did not consider Tillmanism a political force and saw no threat in the call for a farmers' convention in April of 1886, but most newspapers agreed with the Anderson *Intelligencer* that " the Convention should not become the tail to the kite of any man or set of men in personal politics." The *Carolina Spartan* of Spartanburg admonished the delegates not to let their convention " get into the hands of farmer demagogues." Anticipating " thoughtful earnest farmers " in control of the convention, the Sumter *Watchman and Southron* knew they would ensure that " political soreheads " made no headway in its deliberations.[2]

Even while attacking the state government, Tillman realized accusations that he wanted to wreck the Democratic party and build up class antagonism might alienate the mass of farmers. He boasted that he had never deviated from a true Democratic path. As late as the 1888 nominating convention, he moved to make John P.

1. Charleston *News and Courier*, December 27, 1885; Tillman to Francis W. Dawson on May 17, 1886 (in Francis W. Dawson Papers, Duke University Library, cited hereafter as Duke); Edgefield *Chronicle*, July 18, 1888.
2. Anderson *Intelligencer*, April 29, 1886; Spartanburg *Carolina Spartan*, April 23, 1886; Sumter *Watchman and Southron*, March 30, 1886. For similar opinions, see the Georgetown *Enquirer*, May 19, 1886, and the Orangeburg *Times and Democrat*, May 6, 1886. The Fairfield *News and Herald*, March 17, 1886, dissented.

Richardson's nomination unanimous after his own candidate had lost;[3] he wanted to leave no doubts of his allegiance to the Democratic faith.

The Farmers' Association supported Tillman's pledge of allegiance. The first resolution adopted in the April convention " solemnly avowed " that the convention had no intention of " creat[ing] a new party, or bring[ing] about dissensions or trouble in the Democratic party." The resolution expressed faith that reforms advocated by the convention would " result advantageously to the tiller of the soil, in common with every other class of honorable citizens in South Carolina." The November, 1886, convention promised to remain " within legitimate bounds " and not to attempt the creation of a new party. Repeating the oath of Democratic loyalty, the 1887 convention defined the object of the Farmers' Association as twofold: development of the state's resources, and advancement of its agricultural interests. The executive committee address opened the 1888 campaign by soliciting the " support and aid of our Democratic fellow-citizens in the coming election "; it invited " all persons in sympathy with our aspirations " to join the Association.[4]

Perhaps Tillman at first had no political ambitions, but from the beginning he desired an organized movement. He wanted local agricultural clubs in all counties and all sections of the state. These clubs would form a state association to promote legislation beneficial to the farmer. The local agricultural societies, while maintaining " disinterestedness " in county politics, should support and work for any candidate who pledged himself to stand by their program.[5] In addition to one delegate from each county agricultural society, the call for the April convention requested the farmers of each county " to send five delegates over and above those from organized societies, and to effect this . . . suggested that those in sympathy with the movement call a mass meeting or county convention of farmers in their respective counties to appoint said delegates."[6]

The April, 1886, convention appointed a committee to recommend

3. Columbia *Daily Register,* September 7, 1888.
4. *News and Courier,* May 1 and November 11, 1886; December 2, 1887; April 26, 1888.
5. Tillman expressed these views in a letter to the Farmers' Club of Beech Island read on November 7, 1885. Farmers' Club of Beech Island [Aiken county] Minutes: 1846–93, South Caroliniana Library, University of South Carolina, cited hereafter as SCL.
6. Edgefield *Chronicle,* March 17, 1886.

proposals for the permanent organization of a Farmer's Association. The committee drafted a plan that closely followed the structure of the Democratic party: a state convention elected by county conventions, in turn elected by local farmers' clubs. The state convention would meet annually and write a platform embodying the movement's programs. Tillman added an amendment intended to increase the political effectiveness of his movement during the coming campaign. It permitted the president of the Association to appoint an executive committee, which included one member from each county who would direct county organization until after the November elections.[7]

Commenting on the April convention, the Orangeburg *Times and Democrat* noted that Tillmanism had aroused the interest of the farmers from one end of the state to the other. In March, 1886, the Jalapa Farmers' Club (the only one in Newberry county), issued a call through the local newspaper for a county farmers' convention; on the appointed day 300 to 500 delegates appeared, representing every township in the county. A short notice in the Anderson *Intelligencer* signed by twenty-five men filled the courthouse for the county convention. The Fairfield county report that " farmers are organizing pretty generally " with one or more clubs in each township summarized the general activity, especially in the midlands and up-country counties in the spring and summer of 1886.[8]

Although any organization of farmers for the expressed purpose of influencing legislation affected politics in a state so predominantly agricultural as South Carolina in the 1880s, the proliferation of farmers' clubs did not necessarily foretoken trouble for the local Conservative political organizations, provided the two organizations remained separate. But two instances in 1886 pointed to the possibility either of farmers' clubs dominating the Democratic party clubs or of the two merging into one. Edgefield county chose its delegates to the county farmers' convention which would elect representatives to the state convention, not through local farmers' clubs, but in the Democratic clubs in the different townships. In October, the executive committee of the Darlington county Farmers' Association decided to back a full ticket both for county offices and the legislative delegation. When the county Democrats met to nominate candidates,

7. *News and Courier*, May 1, 1886.

8. Orangeburg *Times and Democrat*, May 6, 1886; Newberry *Herald and News*, March 31, 1886; Anderson *Intelligencer*, March 25 and April 8, 1886; *Daily Register*, July 4, 1886. See also the *News and Courier*, April 6, 1886.

"the whole thing was 'cut and dried.' The 'farmers' movement men' certainly captured the convention." The vice-president of the county Democratic convention held the same post in the Farmers' Association.[9]

Immediately after the April, 1886, convention, the professedly non-political Tillman began corresponding with Francis Dawson about the state Democratic convention that would choose a new slate of officers in August.[10] Remembering the powerful editor's willingness to publish his letters and even to support his major proposals, Tillman hoped that the two of them could remold South Carolina politics. On May 17, he informed Dawson that "the movement has grown far beyond my intention or expectation;" the April convention had "put the people in a ferment," which caused "a scramble" among politicians "to get on the agl. wagon." Tillman believed that Reform men would dominate the state Democratic convention; whether or not they captured complete control of it they would certainly have the power to veto the nomination of any candidate considered unfriendly to their cause.

Although Dawson doubted Tillman's "estimate of the present effective strength of the farmers' movement," he did not underestimate its political potential. Hoping to modify Tillman's program and to make him a pillar of the Conservative regime, Dawson accepted Tillman's invitation for a consultation "about a state ticket [for 1886]" that would eliminate "the old Bourbon aristocrats and fogies . . . and inject new blood into the body politic." On June 2, the two met in Augusta, Georgia, to review the South Carolina political scene and the programs advocated by Tillman and his movement.

In that meeting and in subsequent corresponding, they reached general agreement on issues and on their public attitudes toward each other. Dawson agreed to support Tillman's demand for an agricultural college and other reforms in state agricultural agencies; Tillman agreed to drop his anti-Citadel campaign and make his supporters do likewise. Tillman told Dawson that "it [would] be

9. Edgefield *Chronicle,* March 31, 1886; *Darlington News,* October 14, 1886.

10. This analysis of the attempt of Dawson and Tillman to reach an understanding on South Carolina politics is based on the file of correspondence between the two men in the Dawson Papers at Duke. The major items include letters from Tillman to Dawson (all in 1886), on May 11 and 17, June 22, on July 7, 29, and an undated fragment, and those from Dawson to Tillman on May 13 and June 28, in the Letterbook 1884–87. The Benjamin Tillman Papers in the Clemson University Library (cited hereafter as CUL) contain no Dawson-Tillman material.

advisable for you once and a while to give me or the ' movement ' a punch . . ." He went on to say that he would " understand [Dawson's] motives and regard them [the punches] as love licks." [11] Mention of various state tickets the Democratic convention might nominate in August frequently appeared in their correspondence. After discussion, Tillman and Dawson agreed to back for re-election Governor John C. Sheppard, an Edgefield lawyer who had been Lieutenant Governor since 1882, and Governor since June, 1886, when Governor Thompson resigned to accept a position in Grover Cleveland's administration.[12]

Both Tillman and Dawson worked for Sheppard with limited success. In a summer letter to Dawson, Tillman had acknowledged that lack of organization in the Farmers' Association might hinder his directing the movement and might prevent its capturing control of the convention.[13] When the Clarendon county Democratic convention met to endorse the candidacy of Clarendon county farmer John P. Richardson (who came from a family with four past governors), James Tindal, a member of the Farmers' Association executive committee, announced his support of Richardson. The Edgefield *Chronicle* thought that Richardson had more strength among farmers than Sheppard.[14] Possibly fearing an adverse reaction among farmers' movement men who looked upon his paper as the voice and Charleston as the citadel of the regime, Dawson never openly advocated Sheppard's nomination, but indirectly he supported Sheppard's candidacy. As the campaign ended and the convention approached, the *News and Courier* reported Sheppard to be making gains at Richardson's expense. By July 28, it declared that Sheppard had replaced Richardson as the front-runner. On the eve of the convention, Dawson's paper informed its readers that Sheppard " has developed far more strength than was anticipated and is unquestionably in the lead."[15]

That Dawson and Tillman had reached a mutual understanding on the state Democratic convention of 1886 became a major reason for their candidate's defeat. As the delegates assembled in Columbia

11. Tillman to Dawson, August 24, 1886, Dawson Papers, Duke.
12. Tillman to Dawson, July 7, 1886, *ibid.*
13. Tillman to Dawson, June 22, 1886, *ibid.*
14. *Manning Times,* August 4, 1886; Edgefield *Chronicle,* July 21, 1886.
15. *News and Courier,* July 28 and August 4, 1886; also see Sheppard to Dawson, July 14, 1886, and Dawson to his wife August 6, and esp. August 24, 1886, Dawson Papers, Duke.

on August 3, the day prior to the convention's opening session, they favored either Sheppard or Richardson, but neither candidate had a clear lead.[16] By 8 o'clock that evening, "a report became current among delegates and visitors" that Tillman and Dawson had made a deal to put Sheppard across. Tillman's part of the bargain, according to the report, included having the delegates who supported his movement endorse Sheppard.[17] On the morning of the convention, Tillman called a caucus of Farmers' Association supporters in the Richland county courthouse. The approximately 120 delegates attending refused to accept Tillman's resolution to put themselves on record as supporting the nomination of Sheppard. Instead, they adopted a meaningless statement that declined to endorse anyone because no candidate seemed "fully in accord with the farmers' movement."[18] When the rumored deal came into the open, Sheppard's fortunes waned.[19] A reporter covering the convention sensed that all doubt as to the outcome had vanished with the tremendous ovation greeting the nomination of Richardson. Needing 160 votes for nomination, Sheppard never exceeded 80; when on the third ballot Richardson received 172 and the nomination, Dawson and Tillman could manage only 50 for their candidate, who fell to third place.[20]

Tillman did not remain quiet in the face of charges that he and Dawson had been in collusion on the state convention; he wrote a letter to the *Greenville News* denying such allegations. He admitted that he had met Dawson at Augusta, but only to discuss "the work of the farmers' convention." According to this public letter, reprinted in other papers across the state, Tillman and Dawson had never discussed politics. In private, however, Tillman revealed more; he wrote Dawson that he regretted "poor Sheppard ['s being] immolated upon the altar just because of the meeting of ours in June." Reflecting upon the adverse publicity of that meeting, he informed Dawson that the two of them "must *never, never, never,*

16. *News and Courier*, August 4, 1886, and *New York Times*, August 4, 1886.
17. Greenville *Enterprise and Mountaineer*, August 11, 1886.
18. *Daily Register*, August 1886.
19. Greenville *Enterprise and Mountaineer*, August 11, 1886. Other papers carried the same story, e. g., *Daily Register*, August 4, 1886, Fairfield *News and Herald*, August 11, 1886, and Spartanburg *Carolina Spartan*, August 11, 1886.
20. *Daily Register*, August 5, 1886. Richardson's nomination received unanimous support across the state; the Georgetown *Enquirer's* August 11, 1886, remark that the ticket had "dignity" summarized the general opinion.

meet again to arrive at such understanding." They still could " understand one another," although only by letter.[21]

The failure of the Farmers' Association delegates to endorse Sheppard did not come from any significant opposition to Tillman's domination of the Association. Rather, it signified the reluctance and refusal of a young organization to back its leader when he dramatically reversed his public position on the gubernatorial contest. Farmers' Association men, supposedly in an organization dedicated to agricultural reform and nothing more, found it difficult to accommodate that idea to their leader's alliance with Dawson, the voice of Charleston, the city condemned by Tillman as the bastion of the farmers' enemies.

Following his setback in the state Democratic convention of 1886, Tillman became even more determined to increase and tighten his control over the Farmers' Association. Heeding Tillman's cry that " organization must be our watchword," the local farmers' clubs endeavored to gain control of the political machinery in the counties.[22] In August, 1887, the farmers' club and the Democratic club in Sandy Spring in Anderson county began meeting jointly; soon, instead of two groups, only one existed. The next month a speech defending Tillman in the Kershaw county Democratic convention swept the delegates, and the speaker " became absolute dictator as to who should attend the state [Democratic] convention." The Tillman movement in Orangeburg county took over the Democratic county convention and brusquely shoved aside all who opposed it. Included in the defeated group, state Senator J. F. Izlar expressed alarm at the Tillmanite strength. None of the former Conservative county leaders remained in Laurens county. Chief Justice William D. Simpson grumbled to a friend who had requested his assistance in his native county, " Old Laurens had greatly changed since I left there. Tillman has set his power in there deeper than in almost any other county, and entirely new men have come to the front; men with whom I would not have the slightest influence." [23]

21. *Greenville Weekly News*, August 31, 1886; Tillman to Dawson, August 24, 1886, Dawson Papers, Duke.

22. *News and Courier*, November 10, 1886.

23. Anderson *Intelligencer*, September 1, 1887; Thomas J. Kirkland, " Tillman and I," Columbia *State*, June 6, 1929, p. 40; Izlar to William A. Courtenay, August 28, 1888, William A. Courtenay Papers, SCL; Simpson to John Bratton, May 15, 1888. William D. Simpson Papers, *ibid*.

By 1888 Tillmanism had become a recognizable force in the Democratic party at the local level, but this success within the existing Democratic machinery did not satisfy Tillman. Convinced that a state-wide primary would be a great boon to his movement, he ardently advocated the adoption of that system. He reasoned that the more citizens became politically active the more his movement would gain strength. No doctrinaire, Tillman was willing to accept Dawson's advice to drop his agitation for a state-wide primary provided that the convention system underwent changes to represent townships instead of counties. Feeling that such a change would produce a convention too large for meaningful deliberations, Dawson refused to accept Tillman's idea.[24]

In 1886 when up-country forces initiated a campaign for a state-wide primary, Tillman had remained quiet and let J. L. Orr, Jr. and W. L. Mauldin wage a losing battle in the Democratic state convention;[25] but two years later at the state convention, he himself led the fight for the primary. Tillman proclaimed that he represented " a call from the people of the State for a voice in the government." Denouncing the convention system as undemocratic, he warned the Conservatives that if they refused to " go before the people and discuss this thing [they] are only laying up wrath." Turning to one of his favorite tactics, he branded the " politicians " who voted down his proposal as enemies of the people.

John C. Haskell defended the Conservatives. He denied that the convention was either undemocratic or filled with politicians who had no interest in the people, and he challenged Tillman to produce specifics, " not come here with vague charges, wild demonstrations, and glittering generalities." After Haskell's speech, the primary resolution was brought up, voted on, and again defeated by 207 to 83.[26]

24. Francis B. Simkins, *Pitchfork Ben Tillman: South Carolinian* (Baton Rouge: Louisiana State University Press, 1944), p. 224; Tillman to Dawson, June 22, 1886, and Dawson to Tillman, June 28, 1886, Letterbook 1884–87, both in Dawson Papers, Duke.

25. *Daily Register*, August 6, 1886, and *News and Courier*, August 6, 1886. The primary fight in 1886 consisted more of civil war in the Conservative camp than of a Tillman demand. It was truly a sectional issue with only three midlands and low-country delegations voting for primaries, and only one of those unanimously. From the up country came eight unanimous, and two majority, votes. The 1888 fight would reveal changes.

26. *Daily Register*, May 18, 1888. On this vote, the up country cast the great majority of yea ballots, but that section was not so strongly united as it had been two

The state Democratic convention frustrated Tillman's hopes for a primary, but at the same time added to the state party constitution an amendment that pleased him. The new amendment proposed by E. B. Murray of Anderson county, required, prior to the nominating convention in September, at least one meeting in every congressional district at which candidates for Governor and Lieutenant Governor should present their views to the people. The executive committee of the Farmers' Association looked upon the new rule as an opportunity for their leader to make his appeals before the largest possible audience.[27] Because Tillman alleged he was gagged in the convention, he challenged his opponents to meet him before the people, where he had every intention of capitalizing on the opportunity afforded him. Tillman foresaw that taxpaying farmers suffering from the agricultural depression composed the bulk of the audiences, and so, to court the voter though not to campaign for Governor, he charged into the canvass demanding Clemson College and tilting at extravagance and incompetence in the state government.

Having no match for Tillman on the stump, the Conservatives had no choice but to remain on the defensive. Senator Butler advised Conservative leaders not to " engage in a controversy on the stump with him [Tillman]. He is so thoroughly reckless in his statements " that such a course could only consist of " endless recrimination." Having broken with Tillman over the University bill in 1887, Dawson decided to try the silent treatment; from New York he wrote his assistant James C. Hemphill not to " allow his [Tillman's] name to appear in the *News and Courier* when it is possible to avoid it." [28] Governor Richardson, who had to face Tillman on those dispiritingly hot summer days in rural South Carolina, wrote Senator Hampton that he and Mauldin, the incumbent Lieutenant Governor, " were met, not by candidates for their positions as contemplated by the changed constitution—but by B. R. Tillman and Col. E. B. Edwards representatives of the ' Farmers' Movement ' who demanded division

---

years earlier. Only five up-country delegations voted unanimously for a primary; on the other hand, low-country Marion joined the primary forces, and the reform picked up strength in the midlands. By 1888, the demand for primaries had been generally identified with Tillmanism, which broadened its support, though a few Conservatives voted for it.

27. *Daily Register,* May 18, 1888; *News and Courier,* April 21, 1888, and the Edgefield *Chronicle,* July 18, 1888.

28. Butler to Dawson, August 17, 1888, Dawson Papers Duke; Dawson to Hemphill, September 11, 1888, Hemphill Family Papers, *ibid.*

of time." Richardson's surprise that " our party managers " agreed
to Tillman's demands offered a telling commentary on the influence
of Tillmanism in local Democratic affairs. Lamenting his inability
to choose the issues for discussion, the Governor told Hampton that
he had to spend all of his time defending his administration against
Tillman's charges. According to Richardson, Tillman had discarded
the mask of non-partisanship and had become the candidate of his
faction. Richardson warned Hampton that " it will take all the wisdom, power and influence of our best and truest men to preserve the
unity and harmony of the Democratic party." [29]

Tillman's potential strength in the nominating convention also
worried Richardson, who importuned Hampton: " I must frankly
say that I urge your presence and influence here as of infinite importance." [30] A possible visit from Hampton was only one line in the
Governor's defense. He wrote his lieutenants and supporters in all
sections of South Carolina to make special efforts in his behalf. The
party and the regime faced mortal danger, he warned, as he bid
them come to Columbia, even if not convention delegates, because
the influence of any man might be vital. [31]

Tillman, confident that he had had the best of the campaign meet-
ings, moved into the nominating convention determined to name the
next Governor of South Carolina. Although no formal opponent
to Richardson's renomination had come forth, the incumbent
Governor's popularity and influence had waned during the summer. [32]
Tillman and his supporters decided to throw their strength behind
Joseph Earle of Sumter, the state's Attorney General. They informed
Earle of this decision just prior to the convention, but the Attorney
General spurned their overtures and refused to allow the Farmers'
Association men to present his name before the convention. [33] In
spite of Earle's wishes, two prominent Tillmanites, D. K. Norris of

29. Richardson to Hampton, August 27, 1888, Richardson Letterbook Personal,
Executive File, South Carolina Archives, cited hereafter as SCA.

30. Ibid.

31. Many letters during July and August, 1888, ibid., substantiate my generalization. See especially two to William L. Mauldin, a candidate for renomination as
Lieutenant Governor, on July 10 and August 18.

32. Richardson to G. W. Shell, July 6, 1888, ibid; Fairfield News and Herald,
July 4, 1888; Orangeburg Times and Democrat, August 15, 1888; Newberry Herald
and News, September 1, 1888.

33. Earle had also assured Richardson that he, Earle, would under no circumstances
allow his name to go before the convention. Richardson to Major P. H. Nelson,
August 30, 1888, Richardson Letterbook Personal, Executive File, SCA.

Anderson and Dr. Samson Pope of Newberry, placed his name in nomination with the argument, " This is a case of the office seeking the man, and not the man seeking the office." Earle, fearing Till-manite intransigence, had prepared for that contingency. Immediately after his nomination, a delegate from Sumter county rose, and upon Earle's authority, withdrew the Attorney General's name. Even so, the first delegate to respond to roll call cast his ballot for Earle. That vote brought to his feet Dr. T. T. Earle of Greenville, the Attorney General's brother, to repeat " that my brother is not a candidate, and that he will not serve if elected." That incident left no doubt of Earle's position. But still the Tillmanite delegates insisted on voting for him, and at the close of the balloting, Joseph Earle had received 116 votes to Governor Richardson's 190.[34]

In the face of Tillman's growing power between 1886 and 1888, no Conservative commander emerged to fill the post left vacant when Hampton gave up active direction of the Democratic party. In 1886 Dawson failed to generate much enthusiasm or support for his efforts to accommodate Tillman. When Dawson's strategy of accommodation miscarried, the Board of Trustees of the University of South Carolina, men who had refused to assist Dawson, determined to wreck Tillman on the Clemson College issue. Not only did the Board's policy fail, in trying to align the Conservative regime against a popular issue, it increased the opponents of both the University and the regime.

Without central direction, Conservative leaders divided on the major issues Tillman raised. While Dawson advocated a separate agricultural college, Governors Thompson, Sheppard, and Richardson either ignored Tillman's demand or refused to take a stand on this, the major public question in the state. Most Conservatives opposed Tillman's college, but in the Clemson debate some Conserva-

34. For the 1888 convention, see the *News and Courier* and the *Daily Register* for September 7, 1888.

Earle's vote shows Tillman's increasing power within the Democratic organization. Back in 1886, Tillman and Dawson could manage a high of only 25 per cent of the vote for Sheppard, and on the final ballot that percentage dropped to 16; but for a man in 1888 who adamantly refused to be a candidate Tillman obtained 38 per cent of the vote. Richardson was especially strong in the nine low-country counties which gave him 81 votes and Earle but 11. Voting in up-country and midlands delegations broke evenly, with Richardson polling 109 to Earle's 105. These figures show that by the fall of 1888 Tillmanism had become a major threat to continued Conservative domination in two-thirds of the state.

tives became important advocates of Thomas Clemson's bequest. Although up-country Conservatives, chafing at what they considered their minority position in the party, had opened the battle for a state-wide primary, Tillman quickly took command. Both in 1886 and in 1888, the majority of delegates in the state convention opposed the new electoral system, yet in 1888 even Bratton and Duncan voted with Tillman.

More than the absence of leaders or the lack of unity on issues, the erosion of Conservative strength in local Democratic organizations hurt their immediate political fortunes. The takeover of Conservative Democratic clubs by farmers' clubs, or the merging of the two into one unit controlled by Tillmanites, went unchecked. That Tillman could deliver almost 40 per cent of the vote to Joseph Earle in the 1888 nominating convention offered indisputable evidence of his power and influence in the party at the county level. The Conservatives, however, contented themselves with a press campaign condemning anyone who might break up the party and with reassuring public statements from leaders insisting that Tillmanites would never turn against the Democratic party, the house of their fathers. Tillman never did and never intended to; instead, he began to occupy that house.

II

The Shell Manifesto of January, 1890, exploded the deceptive political calm in South Carolina. Little had been heard from Tillman in 1889, and many predicted his movement would dissipate. The year 1890 brought a gubernatorial contest, but the two candidates most frequently suggested, former governors Hagood and Sheppard, had no connections with Tillman or his movement.[35] The Manifesto, a public address signed by G. W. Shell, president of the Farmers' Association of South Carolina, sounded a call to arms. Condemning the Conservative regime as " an aristocratic oligarchy," it called not for a college or a primary, but for a March farmers' convention to nominate a full state ticket. To circumvent the one-party fetish and the political danger of being branded independent, Shell's statement stipulated that the Association's nominees be " put in the field for

35. *Greenville News,* quoted by the *Daily Register,* March 30, 1890; *News and Courier,* August 14, 1889; R. C. Watts to W. A. Courtenay, June 29, 1889, and Theodore Jervey to Courtenay, December 12, 1889, Courtenay Papers, SCL.

ratification or rejection by the next Democratic State Convention." Moreover, Shell pledged " to abide the result, whether that is for or against us."

Publication of the Manifesto made Tillmanism an active political faction overtly seeking to control the Democratic party. In calling for a Farmer's Association nominating convention, the Manifesto publicly announced that Tillman felt strong enough to risk side-stepping normal party procedure. With the March convention as a springboard, Tillman could enter the gubernatorial race far ahead of any Conservative rival.

Both the decision to make the race and the choice of methods took place in Edgefield in the spring of 1889. According to John L. M. Irby, Tillman's 1890 campaign manager, leading Tillmanites meeting there resolved the course of action: a Farmers' Association convention would nominate Tillman and a full ticket of state cabinet officers, then put this ticket before the party and the public.[36] A few months later, at a gathering in Pendleton, Tillmanite chieftains voiced final approval to the spring plans. In November, the executive committee of the Farmers' Association formally sanctioned the idea and directed its chairman, G. W. Shell, to publish the address that carried his name.[37]

As Tillman had done earlier, the Manifesto invited " those Democrats who sympathize with our views and purposes " to join the farmers in Columbia on March 27. In still another attempt to broaden the base of the March convention, Shell's address suggested that rather than the Farmers' Association organization, " a mass meeting or convention " elect delegates from each county. Thirty of the state's thirty-five counties held conventions and elected delegates to the March convention. Certain counties, such as Chester, followed Shell's advice, and a large group of farmers and non-farmers met to discuss the question and elect representatives to Columbia. For the most part only farmers and, at that, Farmers' Association members attended the county meetings. Their small size suggests that only active Farmers' Association men or others interested in the political success of Tillman participated in the county conventions.[38]

---

36. Irby gave this information in a letter to the editor of the *News and Courier*, published in that paper on February 26, 1895.

37. Spartanburg *Carolina Spartan*, August 21, 1889; *News and Courier*, August 13, 1889, and March 28, 1890.

38. *News and Courier*, January 23, February 25, and March 4, 1890.

Primarily, the county deliberations debated the wisdom of nominations by the March convention, for nomination, even suggestion, of a state ticket outside a Democratic party convention was a serious move. Many Tillmanites anxious for their leader's political triumph shied away from such a step. The Conservative press and the regular party continually emphasized the danger for white rule in any political activity outside the Democratic party. The results of the county conventions, the election and the instruction of delegates to the state convention formed no clear pattern; almost everyone agreed with the *Greenville News* that " apparently the majority will not be great either way." [39]

President Shell, aware of the fears of nominations outside the party and of the uncertainty shown by the county elections, reiterated one week before the convention that the farmers had no intention of bolting the party. He revealed that the Farmers' Association executive committee had decided the March convention should suggest, not nominate, candidates for Governor and Lieutenant Governor only. The Association would then submit its suggestion to the state Democratic convention, the final arbiter. Shell hoped these changes would dispel fears and win over any doubters on the question of nominations.[40]

If Shell obtained a favorable vote on nominations, the Tillman leaders would be able to select a nominee. For Shell and his associates, the purpose of the March convention was nomination of Benjamin Tillman for Governor. But a general feeling that Tillman had turned a legitimate reform movement into a political machine forced Shell to deny any Tillman connection with the Manifesto or desire for the nomination. Tillman himself, in a public letter to a supporter, confirmed Shell's announcement that he should not be considered a candidate.[41] Even though they worked for Tillman, farmer leaders had to anticipate the possibility, however unlikely, that Tillman would not receive the convention's nomination. As their alternate candidate the evidence points to William A. Courtenay, a former mayor of Charleston who had fallen out with the Conservative hierarchy in that city. They knew that Courtenay no longer supported the regime and that he had helped to found the Charleston

---

39. *Ibid.*, February 25 and March 4, 1890; *Greenville News*, quoted in the *Daily Register*, March 5, 1890.
40. *News and Courier*, March 20, 1890.
41. *Ibid.*

World, the state's only daily newspaper favoring the March convention.[42]

Facing these uncertainties, the Tillman leaders left little to chance. In Shell's hotel room the day before the convention opened, they planned their tactics. Shell and Tillman were chosen orators and Irby floor manager for the pro-Tillman forces. Aware of the number of undecided delegates, the caucus appointed agents to woo the doubtful.[43]

When the convention opened on March 27, the Tillmanite speakers accented their loyalty to the Democratic—the white man's —party.[44] To reassure any wavering delegates, President Shell, in his opening address, asserted that in the convention sat only loyal Democrats, but Democrats who had the right to meet and discuss issues. Pointing to Tillman's record as a Democrat, Shell allowed, " All this talk about our dividing the party is bosh." Tillman himself rose to denounce charges that his movement smacked of independentism. The self-proclaimed " simon-pure Edgefield Democrat " challenged anyone to prove that he or his movement intended to bypass the party.

Realizing the importance of nominations to their political future, the Tillman leaders made, just prior to the voting, a final plea for positive action. President Shell told his listeners that if they failed to sanction nominations they would have " to quietly surrender " their four-year struggle for governmental reform. In trying to win delegate favor for nominations, Tillman solicited courage and determination: " I say to you that the reform element of South Carolina have reached the Rubicon. If you don't cross it now, you may as well go home and you had better never come here."

After those appeals the convention, with W. J. Talbert of Tillman's own county as permanent chairman, moved straight to the showdown ballot on nominations. Talbert cleared the hall of everyone but delegates and, just prior to the roll call, added a few words supporting nominations. To the astonishment and dismay of Talbert,

---

42. *Ibid.,* March 27, 1890; T. W. Stanland to Courtenay, March 25, 1890, Courtenay Papers, SCL.

Later, Tillman wrote Courtenay: " I consider myself fortunate in having at the headquarters of the Ring a true friend and wise counsellor." Tillman to Courtenay, September 17, 1890, *ibid.*

43. *News and Courier,* March 27, 1890.

44. *Ibid.,* March 28, 1890; see also the *Daily Register,* and the Charleston *World* for the same day.

Shell, Irby, and Tillman, that roll call tallied 116 votes against nominations and 115 votes for them; apparently one vote had crushed Tillman's hopes. Talbert, for the moment, withheld public announcement of the outcome. In the resulting confusion, he allowed the vote of Spartanburg delegate H. E. Farley to count even though he lived in Laurens. Talbert had previously ruled against voting in any delegation outside one's own county, so when he counted Farley's vote for nominations, pandemonium set in. Almost simultaneously with Talbert's decision on the Farley vote came a cry that Beaufort cast two votes for nominations; Talbert counted them even though no Beaufort delegates had been officially seated. Irby, circulating among the delegates, called out to Chairman Talbert that certain delegates changed their vote from nay to yea; Irby, never the delegate, announced these changes. After some time, the chair announced the final result as 121 for nominations and 114 against nominations. Tillman's lieutenants manufactured a seven-vote victory out of a one-vote defeat. Following Talbert's declaration, Irby placed the names of Tillman for Governor and James C. Coit for Lieutenant Governor before the convention, and obtained acceptance from that body with neither a roll call nor a vote by acclamation. The chair simply announced the nomination of Tillman and Coit.[45]

An analysis of the vote in the March convention reveals some unsuspected voting patterns. Of the thirty counties officially seated, only seventeen cast the majority of their ballots for nominations; the only area going solidly for nominations was the low country, with all five counties in the Tillman column by thirty-three to nine.[46] This section, continually attacked by Tillman as the center of ring rule and aristocratic control, contributed the votes, including a 75 per cent majority from Charleston, whose citizens Tillman had termed "the most self-idolatrous people in the world," necessary to present John Irby the opportunity for showing his brilliance as a floor manager.[47]

45. The final vote stood 120 to 114, for after the Tillman forces had triumphed, Chairman Talbert ruled that Farley's vote could not count since it violated the rules of the convention. *News and Courier*, March 28, 1890.

James C. Coit, an important Conservative politician from Chesterfield county, was placed on the ticket without his consent. In a public letter printed by the *News and Courier* on April 3, 1890, he declined the nomination.

46. *Ibid.*, March 28, 1890. Of the five counties that did not send an official delegation, four—Beaufort, Georgetown, Hampton, and Horry—were in the low country. Yet in the confusion Chairman Talbert allowed three Beaufort votes to be counted for nominations. Thus, the low country really gave thirty-six votes for nominations to only nine votes against, an 80 per cent majority.

47. *Ibid.*, August 29, 1890.

Doubtlessly these low-country Tillmanites represented disenchanted factions of the regular Democrats that hoped to uproot the established order. Most certainly, the revolt of a submerged agricultural class had no spokesmen among the delegates from Charleston county; selected on twenty-four-hour notice, they included practically no farmers in a group of twenty-eight.[48] They represented the city's Democrats, headed by Courtenay and backed by the Charleston *World,* who had no ties to the regular organization dominated by the county senators and James C. Hemphill.[49]

Their own strength surprised and overwhelmed those delegates opposed to nominations. In all Farmers' Association conventions since 1886 the word of Tillman and his executive committee had completely controlled all deliberations. Anti-Tillmanites, like John J. Dargan of Sumter county, had stood almost alone in previous Farmers' Association state conventions; obviously delegates anticipated the same course in 1890. Evidently Conservative attacks on the evils and dangers of nominations outside regular party channels influenced enough Association men to put the outcome in doubt. But the superbly organized and brilliantly led Tillmanites proved, in the confusion after the roll call, more than a match for their opponents who had neither organization nor recognized leaders.

III

The Shell Manifesto polarized South Carolina politics. Acceptance of the Manifesto and its call for a March convention implied unalterable opposition to the political status quo. On the other hand, members of the regime who had shown interest in Tillman's proposed reforms and even supported certain of them, dissociated themselves from Tillmanism.

48. *Ibid.,* March 27, 1890. William Watts Ball in his "An Episode in South Carolina Politics [Tillmanism]" (1915) in *Pamphlets by and about the Hon. B. R. Tillman and Tillmania in South Carolina, 1890–1918* (n.p., n.d.), p. 30, remembered that no farmers sat in the Charleston delegation. Most of the delegates came from "the streets of Charleston," and anti-Tillmanites called them "'Belgian Block Farmers,' in allusion to street pavements." William Watts Ball, *The State that Forgot: South Carolina's Surrender to Democracy* (Indianapolis: The Bobbs-Merrill Company, Inc., 1932), p. 220.

49. James C. Hemphill, a native of Abbeville county, became editor of the *News and Courier* upon Dawson's death in 1889 (to be discussed below). Although he never had the political power held by Dawson, his position as editor of the largest newspaper in the state gave him considerable influence.

The Conservative friends of Tillman who turned against him after the Shell Manifesto centered in the up country. They had agreed with Tillman's demands for statewide primaries and reapportionment, not to help agrarian interests but to increase their political power. The *Greenville News*, a stanch advocate of those reforms, admitted its error in judging Tillman a patriot rather than a selfish politician. According to the *News*, the farmers' movement " had been twisted into a Tillman movement for Tillman, of Tillman, and by Tillman." Important up-country political leaders who, though not Tillmanites, had materially advanced its cause now spurned their old association. James L. Orr, Jr., who actively supported Tillman demands for primaries in 1886 and 1888, and Lieutenant Governor William L. Mauldin, who cast the deciding ballot for Clemson College, joined the *Greenville News* in pledging their loyalty to the Conservative Democrats.[50]

The Farmers' Alliance refused to back the Manifesto and the March convention even though Tillman served in the Alliance as chairman of the Edgefield county unit. The Alliance's chief periodical, *The Cotton Plant,* denied that a refusal to support the March convention worked against the best interests of the farmers. The Alliance officially chose to stay out of politics but to endorse " as individuals those candidates who favored agrarian reforms." Evidently, fear of the political tactics of Tillmanism overrode any belief that he might back agrarian reforms, for the Alliance remained neutral throughout the bitter contest.[51]

Conservative opposition quickly focused on the specific evil of party disunity. The *News and Courier* initiated one argument when it asked, " If Capt. Shell and his faction really intend to make their fight within the party lines, we fail to see why they should go outside the party lines to make their first attack." The Executive Committee of the regular Democrats in March issued an address warning of the dangers in a divided party. Pointing to the Force bill as evidence of renewed Republican interest in shackling the South, the address

50. *Greenville News,* quoted in the *Daily Register,* March 30, 1890; Ball, "An Episode in South Carolina Politics," p. 28.

51. Simkins, *Tillman,* p. 148, and the Farmers' Alliance of Edgefield county: Minutes 1889–94, SCL; *The Cotton Plant,* quoted in the Charleston *World,* February 8, 1890; Joseph Church, " The Farmers' Alliance and the Populist Movement in South Carolina, 1887–1896 " (unpublished Master's thesis, Dept. of History, University of South Carolina, 1953), pp. 18 and 42.

emphasized " the overmastering necessity . . . to preserve the unity and integrity of the Democratic party in this State." Commenting on the Executive Committee's address, the *News and Courier* warned that the Republican party remained " watchful and vigilant " and " are ready to spare no effort to regain a foothold in South Carolina and are ready to make the most of all dissensions within the Democratic household." [52] Any movement outside regular party channels disturbed General Bratton, a future Conservative gubernatorial candidate, who pronounced it " ill considered and fraught with danger to the best interests of the State." In refusing an invitation to address a political rally not sanctioned by the Democratic party, Bratton asserted that " the sound integrity of our party is of more consequence to our public interests than the selection of any man or set of men for public office." [53]

In an attempt to discredit the new political program of the Farmers' Association, the Conservatives tried to convince the public that the strategy of nominations by the March convention could not possibly succeed. Resorting to logic, the *Greenville News* argued that the best interests of farmers would be served by making no nominations, for defeat of candidates nominated by the March convention could administer a death blow to their cause. A much safer course would try to influence the Democratic nominees, but not in any sense to work outside regular channels.[54] Supplementing logic with supposed facts, the *News and Courier* conducted a straw poll intended to show that Tillman would have trouble winning the gubernatorial nomination. After soliciting opinion across the state in over 1,000 postcards, the *News and Courier* declared Tillman, contrary to the claims of the Farmers' Association, not the people's choice. Counting both the first and second preferences listed by the voters, the *News and Courier* found Tillman third behind John C. Sheppard and Johnson Hagood.[55]

After failing to prevent nominations by the March convention, the Conservatives took more positive steps to show that Tillman

52. *News and Courier,* February 25 and March 22, 1890.
53. Bratton to Richard A. Meares, April 4, 1890, Richard A. Meares Papers, SCL; Bratton to William Hinnant, April 21, 1890, John Bratton Papers, CUL.
54. *Greenville News,* quoted by the *Daily Register,* March 5, 1890; also, see Orangeburg *Times and Democrat,* February 26, 1890.
55. *News and Courier,* March 25, 1890. See also Newberry *Herald and News,* February 20 and March 20, 1890.

still represented only a small portion of the state's Democrats. Because he designated himself the farmers' candidate, the Conservatives proposed to demonstrate that many agrarians had no use for Tillman or the March convention. For that purpose, they called a farmers' conference to meet in Columbia in late April.[56] Although this convention of farmers from twenty-one counties disavowed politics and centered its attention on political education, its object, pure and simple, was to stop Tillman. Even so, the conferees determined to conduct their anti-Tillman campaign on a high level. John J. Dargan, who had opposed nominations in the March convention, sounded the keynote of the Conservative farmers' conference political program, " Our people need political education." [57]

As its major work, the conference adopted an address to the people that defined the dangers in Tillmanism. Echoing early anti-Tillman opinion in judging the March convention " an innovation pregnant with great danger to the unity and harmony of the Democratic party," the document emphasized to the exclusion of practically everything else the sin committed by Tillmanism when, with the March nominations, it had stepped outside the bounds of the Democratic party. At the same time, the conference declared that the farmers who supported Tillman concurred in " a verdict against the Democracy of South Carolina." Confident that the mass of South Carolinians would " arouse itself and . . . support [their] protest," the Conservative farmers' address closed with an appeal to party loyalty and the kinship of the land: " As Democrats, we cannot witness without protest the control of our party by a faction; as agriculturalists, we will not permit our honorable occupation to be degraded into a spoilsmen's ' machine.' "

In the conference's public deliberations on April 23, no one mentioned partisan politics, but that subject received full attention from delegates who remained in Columbia after the conference had adjourned. These men tried to choose a gubernatorial candidate all could and would support. Because public endorsement by the conference would have smacked too much of the Shell convention,

56. J. C. F. Sims to William G. Hinson, April 19, 1890, William G. Hinson Papers, Charleston Library Society, cited hereafter as CLS.
57. *News and Courier*, April 24, 1890. Among the leading delegates were L. W. Youmans from Barnell county, William G. Hinson from Charleston county, T. W. Woodward from Fairfield county, John J. Dargan from Sumter county, and Iredell Jones from York county.

the conferees planned to assure their candidate in private that they pledged everything in their power to assure his success. They decided to back General Bratton, a Fairfield county farmer and a Confederate hero, who had been a prominent Conservative leader since 1877 but had seldom held public office.[58] Thus, Tillman would have difficulty in labeling him a politician; moreover he, too, was a farmer.[59] After their secret decision to work for Bratton, the delegates to the Conservative farmers' conference left Columbia, confident that they had contributed significantly to Tillman's defeat.

That all Conservatives should agree on the candidate or candidates to oppose Tillman became obvious by late April. Tillman and his supporters had persuaded the Democratic state Executive Committee to order that every candidate for Governor must speak in every county prior to the Democratic nominating convention slated for September.[60] This statewide canvass would begin in early June. Remembering Tillman's success in the brief canvass preceding the 1888 convention, Conservative leaders hurriedly debated the proper strategy for stopping Tillman's charge to the Governor's Mansion.

Even though the Conservative farmers' conference had decided on Bratton, and in doing so had followed Congressman Dibble's dictum that the Conservative candidate must come from above Columbia, all Conservative leaders did not think Bratton their strongest man.[61] Many leading Conservatives turned to James L. Orr, Jr., of Anderson, as potentially the most powerful opponent to Tillman; they thought Orr would be particularly effective in the state-wide debate decreed by the state Executive Committee. Orr gained such support that C. St. George Sinkler, senator from Berkeley county and prominent in the Conservative farmers' organization, declared that Bratton and Orr, or at least their agents, should arrange for Bratton to step aside

58. This meeting escaped the newspapers, but a general picture of the proceedings can be garnered in the following correspondence; C. St. George Sinkler to W. G. Hinson, May 29, 1890, and T. G. Barker [Mayor of Charleston] to John Bratton, May 27, 1890 [a copy], Hinson Papers, CLS; also, J. L. Orr to Richard W. Simpson, May 26, 1890, Richard W. Simpson Papers, CUL.
My discussion of Conservative candidate seeking is based on letters from various state leaders to W. G. Hinson, a Charleston county farmer active against Tillman.
59. The *Camden Journal,* quoted by the Fairfield *News and Herald,* June 11, 1890, asserted that Bratton was " a farmer and a farmer's man."
60. Charleston *World,* May 17, 1890; John Bratton to R. M. Davis, May 9, 1890, Davis Papers, SCL.
61. Congressman Samuel Dibble to W. A. Courtenay, May 5, 1890, Courtenay Papers, SCL.

in Orr's favor.[62] These plans collapsed in late May, when Orr announced that he had no intention of running.[63] The farmers' conference men then returned to Bratton.[64] Other Conservatives, however, still preferred another candidate; finally, they selected Attorney General Joseph Earle, who had refused Tillman's overtures in 1888.[65]

During May, the month of selection, the lack of unity in the anti-Tillman ranks troubled thoughtful Conservatives. But by early June, the search for candidates had ended; with the county canvass about to start, Conservatives had to accept two candidates, Bratton and Earle. Two men carried their hopes against Tillman—and such luxury the Conservatives could scarcely afford.

IV

Having picked Bratton and Earle to oppose Tillman in the canvass, Conservatives shifted their political attention from candidates to tactics. Convinced that Tillman had alienated large numbers with his vituperative speeches and aware that their own influence had declined on the county level, the Conservative leaders turned to a weapon they had opposed in 1886 and 1888.

The demand for a compulsory primary for state officers, heretofore a Tillman mandate, the Conservative regime adopted as a possible way to stop Tillman. Joseph Earle challenged his opponents to join him in asking that the state Democratic Executive Committee call a state convention to amend the party constitution to require primary elections for delegates to the nominating convention. Brat-

62. Sinkler to W. G. Hinson, May 29, 1890; James C. Hemphill to Hinson, May 2, 1890; Iredell Jones to Hinson, n.d. [but from its contents sometime in May, 1890], all in the Hinson Papers, CLS.

63. J. L. Weber to Hinson, May 27, 1890, *ibid.* I have found no evidence clearly explaining Orr's reasons for refusing, but see Alan Johnstone to Richard Simpson, August 27, 1890, Simpson Papers, CUL.

64. C. St. George Sinkler to W. G. Hinson, May 29, 1890, Hinson Papers, CLS. Sinkler said, "Matters must not be left in doubt. [We must] rally promptly and loyally around Bratton." He told Hinson that he had written Iredell Jones, who had been president of the April Conservative farmers' conference, that Conservative farmers must secure a "concert of action" for their candidate.

65. I have been unable to discover any materials relating to Earle's decision to make the race except his letter announcing his candidacy, printed in the *News and Courier* on June 6, 1890. That as the campaign developed he showed much more strength than Bratton suggests that leading Conservative politicians in Columbia prevailed on the Attorney General to be a candidate. But without manuscript sources, that explanation can be nothing more than suggestion.

ton readily agreed; Tillman, beginning to doubt the wisdom of a primary in 1890, had to go along or publicly repudiate one of the oldest demands of his movement. Earle forwarded the request of the three candidates to James A. Hoyt, chairman of the Executive Committee, who immediately called that body to consider the matter.[66] Hoyt then requested the candidates to put their petition into writing for the committee. Earle drew up a document that he presented to Bratton and Tillman at Union on June 21. Aware of his organizational strength, Tillman broke with his record and refused to sign Earle's paper. In his defense he called the whole affair " a trick " manufactured by his opponents to ensnare him. Even though Tillman ended the unity among the candidates, the Conservative-dominated Executive Committee granted Earle's request and called a state convention to meet in August to consider the question of primaries.

The Conservative decision to reverse their position and call for a primary revealed serious problems in their traditional source of power. In May the Columbia *Daily Register* had complained that " inaction " of the regular Democratic party in organizational matters left " the opponents of Tillmanism practically without a shadow of organization." The Conservative farmers' conference, recognizing Tillman's primacy in local organization, on July 2 sent out a circular suggesting the formation of " Farmers' Clubs for the present political campaign." " The claim of certain candidates for public office that they represent the farmers of the State," the Conservative circular stressed, impelled the need for " prompt action " by those opposed to Tillman.[67] Still, no central organization directed the effort against Tillman.[68]

66. Chairman Hoyt, in a lengthy interview printed in the *News and Courier* on July 8, 1890, told the detailed story of the primary affair among the three candidates.
67. *Daily Register,* May 11, 1890; a copy of this circular is in the Hinson Papers, CLS.
68. A major blow to Conservative political strength came with the murder of Francis Dawson in March, 1889. After his break with Tillman over the University bill in 1887, Dawson worked in every way to thwart his old ally. His newspaper, especially in the canvass prior to the 1888 nominating convention, headed the Conservative defense against Tillman. Dawson, to be sure, did not directly control Conservative political decisions, but his political experience and sagacity was an invaluable aid to the Conservative cause. He had not filled Hampton's place, but he was missed.
Dawson's death, especially the manner in which he died, created great excitement. (He was shot to death by a physician in an argument over advances the physician allegedly had made toward Dawson's maid, a young European girl.) The *News and Courier,* beginning on March 1, 1889, the day after his death, gives complete coverage to all aspects of the affair.

The Richland county Democratic party provided the main direction. Guided by Alexander C. Haskell, a prominent Columbia attorney who had run the Democratic campaign in 1876, the Democratic Campaign Club of Richland county called a conference of Straightout Democrats to meet in Columbia on July 10.[69] Overtly political, unlike the April farmers' conference, these Conservatives tried to clothe their cause in the aura of 1876 when South Carolina Democrats proudly wore the Straightout mantle. This conference, which became the leader of the anti-Tillman forces, represented the Conservative leadership.[70] The roll call of the 400 delegates, from all but one of the state's counties, read like a list of leading Conservative figures. Former Governors Hagood and Sheppard headed a group of state officials and county leaders of the Conservative Democrats.

The conference designated two main items of business: the issue of primaries and the need for organization in the anti-Tillman ranks. After endorsing the primary plan proposed by Earle, the conference appointed a committee to draft a primary amendment for presentation to the August convention. Turning to organization, the conference elected an executive committee composed of two members from the state at large and one member from each Congressional district " for the purpose of advising and co-operating with those Democrats in the several counties of this State who are in favor of sustaining the Straightout Democratic party." The resolution creating the executive committee also requested " Democrats who are in sympathy with the objects of this Conference . . . as far as possible to conform to the suggestion of said committee."

The executive committee wasted little time in building a strong organization out of the anti-Tillman forces. A directive signed by the committee's chairman, former Lieutenant Governor John D. Kennedy of Kershaw county, and mailed from Columbia on July 17 to important county leaders [71] provided a uniform state-wide basis for organizing anti-Tillman groups. Aware that the Conservatives attacked Tillman for operating outside party machinery and that his

69. *Ibid.*, June 19 and July 3, 1890; for evidence that other Conservative political leaders, particularly Governor Richardson, were involved in Haskell's activities, see W. E. Gonzales [Richardson's private secretary] to M. P. Howell, June 19, 1890, Richardson Letterbook G, Executive File, SCA.

70. *News and Courier,* July 11 and 12, 1890.

71. A copy of this directive can be found in the Hinson Papers, CLS.

faction claimed to be the true Democratic party, Kennedy advocated forming new clubs, but only in the most constitutional manner. The committee urged organization of new Democratic clubs in each precinct " where the County Constitution permits," even if the membership only reached twenty-five. Through these new clubs the Conservatives hoped to gain the voice in county conventions that they had lacked because of such preponderant Tillmanite majorities in certain clubs. The directive asked its recipient to " confer *at once* with prudent men upon these matters." It further requested that county developments be reported promptly and in full to state headquarters in Columbia. This new program was to be " vigorously inaugurated " so that Conservatives would acquire a strong position for controlling the legislature and the county offices and have a powerful voice in the August convention.

The *News and Courier* ardently supported the new organizational campaign conducted by the Straightouts. Calling for a Straightout club " in every election precinct in the State," the paper defined the fight against Tillman as one for " the party and the State." A convention call published by Straightout leaders in Williamsburg county received great publicity and lavish praise from Hemphill. He told his readers, " The Democrats of Williamsburg are moving on the right line," and he challenged " every other county " to join in the crusade that would defeat Tillman.[72]

The Straightout attempt to reorganize within the Democratic party revealed how thoroughly Tillman had done his work in the counties and verified the observation of Chairman Kennedy: " We are aware that it is late to begin work that should have been done weeks ago." In the Newberry county Democratic convention Tillman men planned their strategy in a caucus preceding the convention and completely dominated the proceedings. In Hampton county, Tillmanites overpowered all attempts to censure their candidate or tactics and ended by instructing the county's delegates to vote for Tillman in the nominating convention.[73] Even in Earle's home county of Sumter, Tillmanites had enough strength to block any threatening action by the county convention. There the Conservative chairman, Colonel James D. Blanding, finally obtained a resolution directing the convention to recess for an hour to allow both Tillmanites and

72. *News and Courier*, July 16 and 26, 1890.
73. Straightout Election Circular, Hinson Papers, CLS; Newberry *Herald and News*, July 3, 1890; Orangeburg *Times and Democrat*, June 25, 1890.

Straightouts to elect representatives to the state convention. In Abbeville county, Conservatives failed to contest Tillman's control of the party apparatus; in fact, a Newberry editor aptly described political conditions in most counties when he observed that Conservative opposition to Tillmanites proved, at best, useless.[74]

In his circular, Chairman Kennedy emphasized the formation of new clubs as a method of ensuring the Straightouts a voice in county conventions. Local Conservative leaders adopted this course with some success but found that it failed to guarantee a hearing for their cause on the county level.[75] Tillmanite control of the party machinery in the counties enabled them to dominate county conventions and nullify the actions of the new Conservative clubs. In Clarendon, the home county of Governor Richardson, the Conservatives failed by twenty-four to sixty-one to have representatives from their new clubs seated. The same fight erupted in the Fairfield convention and led to violent arguments and the disruption of the Fairfield Democratic party.[76]

When the state Democratic convention, called in June to consider the feasibility of primaries, met on August 13, 1890, the Tillman leaders quickly took control of the supreme Democratic body in South Carolina.[77] Immediately after calling the convention to order, Chairman Hoyt nominated G. Lamb Buist of Charleston as temporary president. This officer did nothing except preside over the election of a permanent president, which occurred immediately after his own nomination. Traditionally the convention had accepted the state Executive Committee's nominee without a murmur and proceeded on to more important business. But not in August, 1890. The Tillmanites wanted to display their strength within the Democratic party. No sooner had Hoyt spoken than Samson Pope of Newberry county rose to nominate W. Jasper Talbert for temporary president. A parliamentary wrangle resulted. Could the convention elect any officer prior to the call of the roll of delegates? The Conservatives, led by John C. Haskell of Richland and S. D. M. Byrd of Williams-

74. Sumter *Watchman and Southron*, July 30, 1890; Eugene B. Gary to John Gary Evans, June 30, 1890, John Gary Evans Papers, SCL; Newberry *Herald and News*, July 3, 1890.

75. For an example of their success, see the Borough House Papers, Roll and Minutes of the Stateburg Democratic Club, 1890–1910, Southern Historical Collection, University of North Carolina, cited hereafter as SHC.

76. *Manning Times*, August 13, 1890; Fairfield *News and Herald*, August 6, 1890.

77. *Daily Register*, August 14, 1890.

burg, said "no"; for the Tillmanites, Pope and Irby argued affirmatively. After heated debate, Hoyt decided for the Tillmanites and put Talbert's name before the delegates.[78] This time no one doubted who controlled the organization; the motion to put Talbert in carried by 240 to 61.

After this initial show of strength, the Tillman forces maintained control and secured their dominant position in the party. When the majority report of the credentials committee seated the pro-Tillman delegation from Fairfield county, the Straightouts made a fight for the Conservative delegation from that county. They had a good case, for the Conservatives had credentials from the legal county chairman. To the convention this technicality mattered little. The majority report was adopted by 238 to 70. Then a Conservative attempt to force the convention to consider primaries lost by 200 votes. Following that vote, the Tillmanites proposed and elected a new state Democratic Executive Committee headed by Irby. Finally, the convention decided to have delegates to the September nominating convention chosen by the same county conventions that had elected delegates to the August convention. Thus, the Conservative leaders lost control of the vehicle of their power, the Democratic party of South Carolina, to Ben Tillman and his associates.

Tillmanism triumphed in the August convention because it had previously triumphed in the counties. The Conservatives fell before a man who took possession of their own political machinery. To be sure, Tillman's success entailed more than a brilliant victory in the spring of 1890. After 1886, Tillman's power and influence on the county level increased steadily. His candidate before the convention in 1888 polled a substantially larger percentage of the vote than had his favorite two years earlier; by 1890 he annihilated all opposition.

Important to Tillman's success in the county Democratic parties was Conservative failure to combat him effectively. John Haskell thought that Tillman had gained control of the party "while we [the Conservatives] slept." [79] Undoubtedly, the Conservatives neither perceived nor understood the growing strength of Tillman in the party, but in at least two instances Conservative practices aided Tillman's victory. Governor Richardson, even in the summer of 1890, appointed local officials according to the traditional methods; that is, he made

78. James A. Hoyt, Jr., "The 1890 Campaign" (1900), James A. Hoyt Papers SCL.

79. New York Times, August 20, 1890.

no appointments without seeking the advice of the county delegation
to the legislature, especially the county's senator. But advice became
dictation. Governor Richardson made no new departure or attempt
to circumvent the legislative delegation, even when under Tillmanite
control. By failing to do so, he enabled Tillmanism to solidify its
position on the county level.[80]

But the mechanics of county organization penalized the Conservatives more heavily than Richardson's appointment policy. Tight
organizations operating under rigid rules with precise methods of
recruiting and holding Democratic party members did not exist at
the local level. Rather, Conservative chieftains relied on the influence of a prominent man or group of men in each county to ensure
the support of the people. County chairmen and state senators
dominated the Conservative Democrats in their bailiwicks through
force of personality and prestige of name and position. The decline
in that prestige largely accounts for Conservative ineffectiveness
against Tillman in the spring and summer of 1890.[81]

Discussions among prominent Conservative county leaders in the
executive committee of the Straightout conference revealed their
dilemma. One of them, Joseph W. Barnwell of Charleston, remembered that "county after county was called on and almost universally
men who had been prominent in their counties stated that they could
not give a reason but that numbers of good men who had formerly
supported them had told them they could not do so in this
campaign." Former Governor and Confederate General Johnson
Hagood sensed the inevitable triumph of Tillmanism. He had dominated Barnwell county most of his life, but found his influence to
be of no avail.[82]

Although routed by the Tillmanites in the August convention,
Straightouts met again later in the month to discuss whether they

80. Traditionally, senators stood by their colleagues on this issue; but had
Governor Richardson inaugurated a vigorous new program, the bitterness brought on
by Tillmanism could possibly have changed the attitudes of Conservative senators.

For Richardson's actions, see esp. the letter on July 7, 1890, in Richardson Letterbook F, Executive File, SCA, to Senator Henry Meetze of Lexington county, a powerful
Tillman leader who became president *pro tempore* of the state Senate in the first
Tillman legislature; see also the letter to Y. J. Pope of Newberry county on January 15,
1890, *ibid.*

81. William W. Ball suggests this idea in his *The State that Forgot,* chap. xiv. My
research has found this suggestion largely correct. *Infra,* sec. V.

82. Joseph W. Barnwell, "Life and Recollections of Joseph W. Barnwell," unpublished autobiography (typescript dated 1929), pp. 467–68, South Carolina
Historical Society.

could do anything to prevent Tillman's nomination in September. Chairman Kennedy of the Straightout executive committee recommended making some kind of fight in the September convention, but, he counseled, if all failed, Conservatives should "yield as gracefully as we can to . . . the inevitable."[83] Old-line Conservative leaders such as Edward McCrady and Augustine Smythe of Charleston and Comptroller General J. S. Verner of Greenville agreed with Kennedy. Verner simply said that nothing more could be done; Smythe wrote, "I, for one, am prepared to acquiesce in this as a fact [Tillman's nomination]. I would not wish it, but it will come, and I accept it."[84]

These men put the sanctity of the Democratic party above enmity for Tillman; on the other hand, a small group of ultra-Conservatives led by Alexander Haskell placed defeat of Tillman above party loyalty. Joseph Barnwell enounced this position to the August Straightout conference: "Let us swear that B. R. Tillman shall never be Governor of South Carolina."[85] These ultras evinced a willingness to bolt the party and to make a direct appeal to the Negro in an effort to thwart Tillman's victory in November.[86]

That the ultras represented only a token portion of the Conservative leadership became apparent as the Conservatives responded to Tillman's smashing victory in the September nominating convention.[87] The News and Courier set the tone by proclaiming, "There is no appeal from the action of the Democratic Convention yesterday. Capt. Tillman is the duly accredited standard bearer of

83. Ambrose Gonzales [Secretary of the Straightout executive committee] to Gertrude Gonzales [his sister], August 23, 1890, Elliot-Gonzales Papers, SHC.

84. Verner to Courtenay, August 18, 1890; Smythe to Courtenay, August 23, 1890, both in Courtenay Papers, SCL; also see *supra*, n. 81.

85. Ambrose Gonzales to Gertrude Gonzales, August 23, 1890, Elliot–Gonzales Papers, SHC; Barnwell, "Autobiography," p. 468.

86. The ultras did put up a ticket, headed by Alexander C. Haskell, against Tillman in the November general election. In that contest, the regular Democrat Tillman won easily with 80 per cent of the vote. Forty per cent of Haskell's total vote came from Black District counties, with the rest fairly scattered. Because the Republicans endorsed Haskell's candidacy and he ran strongest in heavily Negro counties such as Beaufort and Berkeley, it seems likely that Negroes comprised his greatest source of strength. Moreover, that strong Haskell counties gave more votes proportionately to Benjamin Harrison in 1888 reinforces the idea that the Negroes were supporting Haskell.

For the 1890 vote, see the *Tribune Almanac* (1892), p. 284; *ibid.* (1889), p. 89 has the 1888 presidential vote.

87. *Daily Register,* September 11, 1890, and *News and Courier,* September 11, 1890; see also the *Constitution of the Democratic Party of South Carolina* (1890).

the party. He will be the next Governor of South Carolina." With the succinct phrase, "the whole thing is over," the *Daily Register* exhorted South Carolinians to support Tillman.[88] Senators Butler and Hampton and Governor Richardson announced their support of Tillman as the Democratic nominee.[89] Practically all Conservative newspapers and politicians followed their leaders' course. The greater number of Conservatives had such strong loyalties to the Democratic party and what it represented that they stood, however reluctantly, behind Benjamin R. Tillman.

V

Tillman, by his own account, began his agitation after becoming alarmed at the economic plight of farmers like himself. But his movement adopted none of the economic and social programs of other Southern radical agrarian movements. Unlike them, Tillman paid little attention to Wall Street, the trusts, or any other national issue; he called South Carolina his only concern.[90]

In 1890 and before, Tillman condemned politicians and lawyers as enemies of farmers and talked of the lower classes replacing the aristocrats in the government, but in the platform of his Farmers' Association and his more moderate statements he invited all occupations to join his banner. In the heat of the 1890 canvass, his chief newspaper supporter declared that Tillmanism meant "no proscription of any class, no furious upheaval of the ignorant against the wise." In the mid-1890s Tillman denied any similarity of his crusade to the radical Farmers' Alliance or Populist movements.[91]

In this convention, Conservative opposition was hardly visible. The Tillman forces organized the convention with no difficulty. Although Conservative delegates had no candidate to support, they refused to allow Tillman to be nominated by acclamation. They cast 40 votes against Tillman who won 269. The only counties still in Conservative hands were Charleston, Richland, Sumter, and Beaufort. Issues that had characterized Tillman's agitation, such as his demand for statewide primaries and reorganization of the state Agriculture Bureau, were embodied in the party constitution and the platform adopted by the convention.

88. *News and Courier*, September 11, 1890; *Daily Register*, September 12, 1890. Practically every other South Carolina newspaper I looked at followed suit.

89. Simkins, *Tillman*, p. 166; Manly Wade Wellman, *Giant in Gray: Wade Hampton of South Carolina* (New York: Charles Scribner's Sons, 1949), p. 317. For county leaders of the old Conservative Democrats remaining with the regular nominee Tillman see Ball, *The State that Forgot*, pp. 222–23.

90. Tillman's emergence as a national figure and his concern for national issues came after 1890. In fact, his national period really did not begin until his election to the United States Senate in 1894.

91. Charleston *Weekly World*, June 24, 1890; *Memorial Addresses on the Life*

Tillman's following belied any truly radical movement. Most of his lieutenants were, like their Conservative opponents, well-educated natives of South Carolina born on plantations or in professional environments during the ante-bellum years.[92] Bright young lawyers like John Gary Evans and John L. McLaurin became Tillmanite stalwarts. Tillman himself supported a lawyer over a farmer for Governor both in 1886 and 1888. And Tillmanite leaders participated profitably in South Carolina's growing textile industry.

That almost one-half of Tillman's leaders farmed, as compared to almost 20 per cent among their Conservative counterparts, imported no essential class differences.[93] Tillman never appealed to the landless, either white or black. At the same time, he won the allegiance of many substantial landowners such as John L. M. Irby, James Tindal, and William H. Ellerbe. Tillman spoke truthfully when he declared, " Many of these farmers [his supporters]— thousands of them—are as intelligent and well-educated men as there are in the State, and they own a large share of its wealth." [94]

In fact, Tillmanism cut across economic, social, and even family lines. Sons of formerly wealthy, slave-owning families supported Tillman. The Gary family of Abbeville and Edgefield counties, who " never considered themselves of the common people," stood firmly with him. William Watts Ball recalled that " nearly every family [he knew] was divided." The law partner and the closest friend of Ball's father, the Conservative chairman of the Laurens county Democratic party, and several members of his mother's family became Tillmanites.[95]

Sectionalism, traditional in South Carolina politics, existed in the division between Tillmanites and Conservatives, but not in the stereotyped hills-versus-tidewater division.[96] A majority of the Tillmanite leaders did come from the up country, but on the other hand, Conservative leaders did not cluster in the low country. Most of the Conservatives lived in the midlands, and more came from the

---

and Character of Joseph H. Earle (Late a Senator from South Carolina) Delivered in the Senate and House of Representatives, Fifty-fifth Congress, Second Session (Washington: U. S. Government Printing Office, 1898), p. 55.

92. Appendix A, Tables I, III, and VI. For a comparable analysis of Conservative leadership see chap. i, sec. V.

93. Appendix A, Table II.

94. Earle Memorial Addresses, p. 55.

95. Ball to David R. Coker, June 7, 1929, W. W. Ball Papers, Duke.

96. Appendix A, Table V and map.

up country than from the low country. This alignment arose from both the political control long exercised by the midlands and the growing discontent of the up country.[97]

Politics, of course, aided the growth of Tillmanism. Over two-thirds of the Tillman leadership occupied state political offices before 1890; they held state offices but not state-wide offices. No Governor, no Lieutenant Governor, no United States Senator, no national Representative[98] emerged from their ranks in the 1880s. Though active and successful politicians, they had not reached the pinnacles of state political power. Doubtless, more than one politically aware young man boarded Tillmanism for transportation to high office. Even so, the rise of Tillmanism cannot be described simply as the political " outs " wanting in.

The emergence of a new generation tired of the old shibboleths better explains the disruption of the South Carolina Democratic party in the late 1880s.[99] The glorious past eulogized by Conservative spokesmen had little meaning for Tillmanites. They had been born too late in the ante-bellum era to enjoy its bounty.[100] As young men they had endured the hardships of private soldiers in the Confederate Army[101] or had struggled to build homes in an unstable and war-devastated region.

By 1885 and 1886, many South Carolinians had grown tired of the constant Conservative hymns to the past. Eagerly they awaited something different.[102] A ready audience heard Tillman attack the Con-

97. This shift in political control from the rice aristocracy in the low country to the cotton-oriented midlands, which began about the time of the War of 1812, is discussed by George C. Rogers, Jr. in his *Evolution of a Federalist: William Loughton Smith of Charleston, 1758–1812* (Columbia: University of South Carolina Press, 1962), chap. xiv, esp. pp. 369–74.

98. George Tillman, Ben's older brother, served in Congress throughout the Conservative period, but he did not become a supporter of his brother. In fact, he was beaten in 1892 by a man who had Ben's blessings.

99. Many years ago, Holland Thompson in his *The New South: A Chronicle of Social and Industrial Evolution*, Vol. XLII of *The Chronicle of America Series*, ed. Allen Johnson (New Haven: Yale University Press, 1921), p. 30, noted the prevalence of younger men in the political protests of the late eighties that overturned Conservative regimes in several states.

100. The average Tillman leader (data on 96 per cent) was 45.58 years old; 50 per cent were under 45 (seven of those under 40) while only 29.2 per cent were over 50, with but three men over 60. As a result, most could not even have gone to college in the prewar years. In fact of the 62.5 per cent who attended college, more than half went after the war and few chose South Carolina College. Appendix A, Table VI.

101. Appendix A, Table IV.

102. Letters from South Carolina Republicans trace the growth of this feeling.

servatives for viewing the world "through ante-bellum spectacles" and for allowing an "oligarchy of office seekers based on . . . [Confederate] brass" to govern the state.[103] He and his supporters gave no quarter to men who "worship[ed] the past and [were] marching backwards when they march[ed] at all." [104]

Tillmanism challenged the sanctity of Confederate gray. In 1890 Tillman vigorously condemned General John Bratton as an old man whose "gaze [was] toward the grave." [105] That same year noisy Tillman supporters howled down Senator Hampton, now past seventy, when he invoked Confederate service and honor as a barrier to Tillmanism. Hampton told his audience, "When I saw that a South Carolina audience could insult John Bratton [General Bratton had been prevented from speaking at Laurens], I thought, Good God! have the memories of '61, of '65, have they been obliterated." [106] A triumphant Tillman demanded the defeat of Senator Hampton when the old general came up for re-election to the United States Senate in December, 1890. More saddening to Hampton than defeat was the failure of old soldiers to support him rather than John Irby, who had been a boy of seven in 1861.[107]

The difference in their Confederate experience increased the distance between two generations and underlay the breach in the South Carolina Democratic party. With agricultural depression and political opportunism providing the catalysts, young men protested that neither service in the past nor appeals to its memory could any longer suffice as prerequisites for high office or as determinants for public policy.

For examples, see J. H. Ostendorff to Benjamin Harrison, May 14, 1889, and Thomas P. Vaughan to Harrison, February 25, 1890, both in the Benjamin Harrison Papers, Library of Congress. Also, see the Charleston *Evening Sun,* quoted in the Georgetown *Enquirer,* August 15, 1888.

Certain Conservative leaders seemed to sense this growing dissatisfaction. See Governor Hugh Thompson to E. Croft, June 7, 1886, Thompson Letterbook D, Executive File, SCA, and the speech of Senator Butler before a meeting of the state Agricultural Society in 1888, reported in the *News and Courier,* August 9, 1888.

103. *News and Courier,* June 13 and August 1, 1890.

104. *Ibid.,* November 19, 1885.

105. *Ibid.,* June 13, 1890; see also *ibid.,* April 30, 1886.

106. *Ibid.,* June 28, 1890. That incident occurred in Aiken. The quotation comes from a speech made in Columbia three days previously. *Ibid.,* June 25, 1890. Hampton spoke only twice during the campaign.

107. Hampton to Matthew C. Butler, December 13, 1890, Matthew C. Butler Papers, SCL. Tillman noted the refusal of the "old Confederate soldiers" to vote for their onetime hero. Tillman to Martin V. Calvin, December 11, 1890, Letterbook 1890–94, Benjamin Tillman Papers, CUL.

EPILOGUE

The South Carolina Conservatives attempted to govern their state with few programs or policies designed for the 1880s. They did not envision a future—either distant or near—that held greater benefits, rewards, and challenges for the citizens of South Carolina than had the past. At the same time, they did not preach the sanctity of the status quo. During their fourteen-year hegemony the South Carolina Conservatives tried to re-create the ideals of that polity they esteemed above all other: ante-bellum South Carolina. To achieve an economical government controlled by native whites and dedicated to the generous support of an educational institution that inculcated the values and ideals of the past—a past they almost worshiped—was to accomplish their mission to their state.

While the process of re-creation went forward, the Conservatives, in the absence of traditional political programs, wore their past service to South Carolina as campaign buttons. That they had led the state in 1861–65 and 1876—to fight for independence and then to regain control of her destiny—secured for them the allegiance of most white South Carolinians.

In spite of internal dissensions and rivalries, the Conservative regime successfully pursued its vision until the middle of the 1880s. The emergence of Benjamin Tillman spelled its doom. Tillman capitalized upon the agricultural depression and organized a movement that captured control of the Democratic party. But, ultimately, Tillmanism wrought the political destruction of Conservatives with lack of reverence for the state's Confederate leaders. The ebbing of the spell of the Confederacy withered the prestige of the local Colonel or even General. No longer able to hold in line the majority of Democrats in county meetings, he was often looked upon as an old man, as he normally was, who had impeded the advance of more vigorous, younger men. Stunned by the harsh invective of Tillman, most Conservatives simply clung to their banners; the defeat they met in 1890 was as final as that of 1865.

APPENDIX A

An Analysis of Leadership

This social recruitment analysis of the leaders of both wings of the discordant Democratic party assists in explaining both the nature of Conservatism and the rupture of the Democrats and makes possible definite statements about the characteristics of both Conservative and Tillmanite leaders.

In selecting my leaders, I chose men who held specific offices. I make no claim that these leaders represent all of the top political commanders in both factions, but because of their positions, my groups of leaders most certainly were major political powers in the state.

My leaders held the following positions:

United States Senator
United States Congressman
Governor
Lieutenant Governor
Speaker of the state House of Representatives
President *pro tempore* of the state Senate
Member of the state Supreme Court
Chairman, state Democratic Executive Committee
Legislative leader (other than speaker or president *pro tempore*)
Gubernatorial candidate, 1890
Editor

In analyzing the Tillman leaders, men elected in 1890 to the same state-wide and legislative offices previously held by Conservatives plus Tillman's candidates in 1890 for the state cabinet comprised the nucleus of my group. To these I added:

President of the Farmers' Association
Farmers' Association leader

My major sources for biographical information about the political leaders are (full publication information is in the bibliography):

Samuel Ashe and Edward McCrady, Jr. (eds.), *Cyclopedia of Eminent and Representative Men of the Carolinas*
Biographical Directory of Congress

208

U. R. Brooks, *South Carolina Bench and Bar*, Vol. I

J. C. Garlington (ed.), *Men of the Times . . . Biographical Encyclopedia of Contemporaneous South Carolina Leaders*

James C. Hemphill (ed.), *Men of Mark in South Carolina*

Allen Johnson and Dumas Malone (eds.), *Dictionary of American Biography*

Emily Reynolds and Joan Faunt (comps.), *Biographical Directory of the Senate of the State of South Carolina*

David Duncan Wallace, *History of South Carolina*, Vol. IV

Ezra J. Warner, *Generals in Gray*

CONSERVATIVE LEADERSHIP (43)

D. Wyatt Aiken (Abbeville)—U.S. Congressman

John Bratton (Fairfield)—Chairman, state Democratic Executive Committee; U.S. Congressman; 1890 candidate for Governor

Matthew C. Butler (Edgefield)—U.S. Senator

James S. Cothran (Abbeville)—U.S. Congressman

George W. Dargan (Darlington)—U.S. Congressman

Francis W. Dawson (Charleston)—Editor

Samuel Dibble (Orangeburg)—U.S. Congressman

Joseph Earle (Sumter)—Legislative leader; 1890 candidate for Governor

William Elliott (Beaufort)—U.S. Congressman

John H. Evins (Spartanburg)—U.S. Congressman

Johnson Hagood (Barnwell)—Governor

Wade Hampton (Richland)—Governor; U.S. Senator

William W. Harllee (Marion)—President *pro tempore*, state Senate

Alexander C. Haskell (Richland)—Chairman, state Democratic Executive Committee; Associate Justice, state Supreme Court

John C. Haskell (Richland)—Legislative leader

James C. Hemphill (Charleston)—Editor

John J. Hemphill (Chester)—Legislative leader; U.S. Congressman

James A. Hoyt (Greenville)—Chairman, state Democratic Executive Committee

James F. Izlar (Orangeburg)—Chairman, state Democratic Executive Committee; president *pro tempore*, state Senate

Thomas B. Jeter (Union)—President *pro tempore* state Senate; Governor

John D. Kennedy (Kershaw)—Chairman, state Democratic Executive Committee; Lieutenant Governor

Edward McCrady, Jr. (Charleston)—Legislative leader

Samuel McGowan (Abbeville)—Associate Justice, state Supreme Court

Henry McIver (Chesterfield)—Associate Justice, state Supreme Court

William L. Mauldin (Greenville)—Legislative leader; Lieutenant Governor

James W. Moore (Hampton)—Chairman, state Democratic Executive Committee
William Munro (Union)—Legislative leader
Edwards B. Murray (Anderson)—Legislative leader
Michael P. O'Connor (Charleston)—U.S. Congressman
William H. Perry (Greenville)—U.S. Congressman
John P. Richardson (Clarendon)—Governor
John S. Richardson (Sumter)—U.S. Congressman
John C. Sheppard (Edgefield)—Speaker, state House of Representatives; Lieutenant Governor; Governor
James Simons (Charleston)—Speaker, state House of Representatives
Charles H. Simonton (Charleston)—Legislative leader
William D. Simpson (Laurens)—Lieutenant Governor; Governor; Chief Justice, state Supreme Court
Augustine T. Smythe (Charleston)—Legislative leader
Hugh S. Thompson (Richland)—Governor
George D. Tillman (Edgefield)—U.S. Congressman
William H. Wallace (Union)—Speaker, state House of Representatives
Alfred B. Williams (Greenville)—Editor
Isaac D. Witherspoon (York)—President *pro tempore*, state Senate
Lawrence W. Youmans (Barnwell)—Legislative leader

TILLMAN LEADERSHIP (25)

W. T. C. Bates (Orangeburg)—State ticket
W. Christie Benet (Abbeville)—Legislative leader
Octavus Cohen (Charleston)—Editor
Berryman W. Edwards (Darlington)—Legislative leader
William H. Ellerbe (Marion)—State ticket
John Gary Evans (Aiken)—Legislative leader
Hugh Farley (Spartanburg)—State ticket
Eugene B. Gary (Abbeville)—Lieutenant Governor
John L. M. Irby (Laurens)—Chairman, state Democratic Executive Committee; Speaker, state House of Representatives; U.S. Senator
George Johnstone (Newberry)—U.S. Congressman
Ira B. Jones (Lancaster)—Speaker, state House of Representatives
Asbury C. Latimer (Abbeville)—U.S. Congressman
John L. McLaurin (Marlboro)—Farmers' Association leader; U.S. Congressman
William D. Mayfield (Greenville)—State ticket
Henry A. Meetze (Lexington)—President *pro tempore*, state Senate
Daniel K. Norris (Anderson)—President, Farmers' Association
Samson Pope (Newberry)—Farmers' Association leader

Young J. Pope (Newberry)—State ticket

George W. Shell (Laurens)—President, Farmers' Association; U.S. Congressman

Richard W. Simpson (Anderson)—Legislative leader

Jefferson A. Sligh (Newberry)—Legislative leader

Eli T. Stackhouse (Marion)—U.S. Congressman

W. Jasper Talbert (Edgefield)—Legislative leader

Benjamin R. Tillman (Edgefield)—Governor

James E. Tindal (Clarendon)—Legislative leader, state ticket

BIOGRAPHICAL STATISTICS

TABLE I

SOCIAL AND ECONOMIC BACKGROUND

(*Father's occupation*)

Father's occupation	Conservatives (Data on 81.4 per cent)	Tillmanites (Data on 76.0 per cent)[1]
Professional soldier	—	5.3, one man
Planter [2]	42.9	47.4
Lawyer	17.1	21.1
Merchant	5.7	10.5
Farmer [2]	5.7	5.3, one man
Professor	2.9, one man	—
Doctor	11.4	10.5
Minister	5.7	—
Editor	5.7	—
Mechanic	2.9, one man	

Note: 80 per cent of the Conservatives and 84.3 per cent of the Tillmanites came from either planter or professional backgrounds.

1. The percentage in parentheses at the top of each table represents the percentage of leaders about whom data were gathered.
2. Use of terms "farmer" and "planter" was determined by the biographical data leaders gave about themselves.

TABLE II

OCCUPATIONS

Occupations	Conservatives (Data on 100 per cent)	Tillmanites (Data on 100 per cent)
Lawyer	67.4	44.0
Planter	14.0	28.0
Farmer	4.6	16.0
Doctor, editor, educator	14.0	12.0

TABLE III

PLACE OF ORIGIN

Place of origin	Conservatives (Data on 100 per cent)	Tillmanites (Data on 100 per cent)
South Carolina	93.0	88.0
Another state (in South)	4.7	8.0
Foreign born	one man	one man

TABLE IV

CONFEDERATE SERVICE

Confederate service	Conservatives (Data on 100 per cent)	Tillmanites (Data on 96.0 per cent)
In service	79.1	50.0
Officer [1]	88.2	33.3
Enlisted man	11.8	66.7

1. Seven Conservatives were general officers.

TABLE V

SECTIONAL DISTRIBUTION

Location in state	Conservatives (Data on 100 per cent)	Tillmanites (Data on 100 per cent)
Low Country	23.2	12.0
Midlands	39.6	32.0
Up Country	37.2	56.0

TABLE VI

EDUCATIONAL BACKGROUND

Educational background	Conservatives (Data on 100 per cent)	Tillmanites (Data on 96.0 per cent)
Attended college	88.4	62.5
in South Carolina	78.9	66.7
college student before the Civil War	86.8	46.7
college student after the Civil War	13.2	53.3
South Carolina College	55.3	12.5
	(only 1 after Civil War)	(only 1 before Civil War)
Professional school (law or medicine)	7.9	16.7

Note: In instances where a man attended more than one college, I used the school last attended.

RESIDENCE OF CONSERVATIVE LEADERS

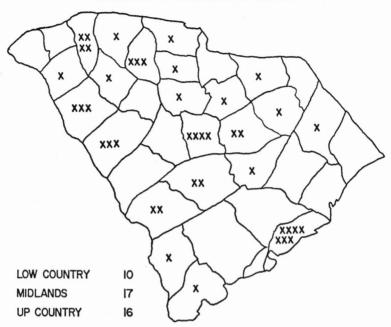

LOW COUNTRY   10
MIDLANDS   17
UP COUNTRY   16

RESIDENCE OF TILLMAN LEADERS

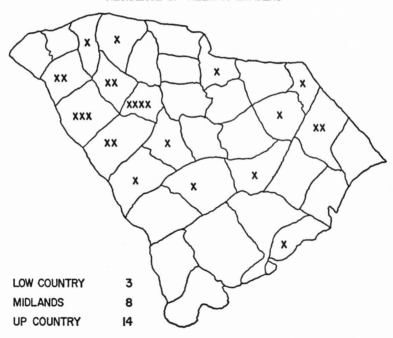

LOW COUNTRY   3
MIDLANDS   8
UP COUNTRY   14

APPENDIX B

In 1878 Wade Hampton received 119,550 votes—27,289, or 19.6 per cent more than in 1876; 213 were scattered. Whether or not that increase came from Negroes voting the Democratic ticket is difficult to prove. On the face of the returns, it seems that substantial numbers of Negroes did switch their political loyalty between 1876 and 1878.

The ten counties that had the highest Republican percentage in 1876 gave Hampton 30,077 votes in that year,[1] two years later he won 48,298 votes in those counties. In fact, 66.8 per cent of the Democratic increase between 1876 and 1878 came from those counties. According to the state census of 1875, only 22,757 white males 21 years and older lived in those counties. Thus, for the Democratic vote to reach the figure for 1878 some of the 55,078 Negro males 21 years and older residing in those same counties seemingly would have had to vote for Hampton.[2]

Of course, the undoubted frauds practiced in 1876 and in 1878 make any definite statements based on the official returns unsatisfactory at best. Still, that the Republican party failed to run a candidate in 1878 coupled with the public support of Hampton announced by several Republican leaders suggests that more Negroes voted for Wade Hampton in 1878 than in 1876.

1.	Counties	Republican percentage in 1876
	Beaufort	75.4
	Georgetown	72.2
	Charleston	63.1
	Sumter	61.8
	Richland	61.3
	Orangeburg	60.7
	Colleton	58.2
	Williamsburg	58.2
	Clarendon	56.7
	Newberry	55.7

Only four other counties—Darlington, Fairfield, Chester, Kershaw—voted Republican in 1876.

2. For the 1876 vote and the information from the state census, see U.S., Congress, Senate, *South Carolina in 1876, Senate Misc. Doc. 48, 44th Cong., 2d Sess.* (Washington: U.S. Government Printing Office, 1877), III, 73 and 85; for the 1878 election, see *Reports and Resolutions of the General Assembly of the State of South Carolina* (1878), p. 436.

APPENDIX C

Negro Voting

Precise statements about Negro voting pose many difficulties. Federal District Attorney Samuel Melton thought that the registration in May and June of 1882 disfranchised 75 per cent of the Negro voters.[1] Negroes nevertheless did register,[2] sometimes in sufficient numbers to frighten the Democratic leadership. As late as 1888, the number of Republicans at the polls in the Black District disturbed Governor John P. Richardson.[3] To pin down Negro activity in Democratic primaries remains all but impossible. There can be no doubt that rules such as those discussed in the text effectively and sharply curtailed that activity. The Republican party put no state ticket in the field after 1876, but Republican presidential candidates appeared on the ballot. Hayes polled 92,000 votes in the corrupt election of 1876; Garfield, in 1880, got 58,000; in 1884, Blaine netted only 22,000; by 1888, Benjamin Harrison gathered but 14,000.[4] In twelve years, the Republican presidential vote dropped by 66 per cent. By 1888, educational and registration requirements, political passivity, and lack of strong Republican effort to get out the vote coupled with a Democratic determination to limit Republican strength had drastically reduced the party's voting power.

1. Samuel Melton to Benjamin Brewster, December 20, 1882, Source Chronological File of the Justice Department, Record Group 60, National Archives.
2. Charleston *News and Courier*, June 27, 1882 and November 14, 1887.
3. Richardson to James W. Moore [chairman of the state Democratic Executive Committee], June 5, 1888, Richardson Letterbook Personal, Executive File, South Carolina Archives.
The Republican or Negro vote in the Black District had increased from 5,750 in 1886 to over 7,000 in 1888. *News and Courier*, November 19, 1886, and November 23, 1888.
4. U.S., Bureau of the Census, *Historical Statistics of the United States: Colonial Times to 1957* (Washington: U.S. Government Printing Office, 1960), p. 688.

APPENDIX D

Economics of Cotton Farming in South Carolina

My evidence for this generalization consists of computations of cost and income for an average acre of cotton. Because production costs were available for 1880 but not 1890, my figures are for the former year. They are probably close to the 1890 totals because any reduction in cost per acre would probably have been offset by lower production per acre and lower cotton prices. Those two facts would tend to negate any improvements from increased acreage. My figures can only be approximations, but they have sufficient accuracy to suggest the prosperity (or lack of prosperity) on the average cotton farm in South Carolina.

To obtain cost per acre for the state, I averaged the several figures given by Harry Hammond for production costs in different sections.[1] Hammond's figures come from various farmers across the state. It cost $28.42 to grow an average acre of cotton in 1880.

The average income per acre can be calculated by multiplying the price per pound by the pounds of lint per acre. Using that procedure, I arrived at $18.23 as the income the average farmer could expect. Thus, in 1880 he lost $10.19 an acre.

But to make that figure more accurate, I computed the value of the cotton-seed each acre produced. Using the cottonseed figures and the normal price mentioned by Hammond, I added $3.40 to the per acre income.[2] With this addition, the farmer still lost $6.79 per acre. However, the ratio of 65 pounds of seed to 35 pounds of lint used in *Cotton* does not, in my opinion, give a large enough proportion of seed to lint. Hammond's calculation of 1,000 pounds of seed to 450 pounds of lint seems more correct.[3] Also, Hammond had intimate knowledge of cotton in South Carolina. Using his ratio, seed would yield the average farmer more than $4.00 per acre. That seed value would bring the average loss per acre in 1880 down to around $6.00.

Of course some farmers made more than 186 pounds of lint per acre. The highest county average Hammond found in 1880 was 267 pounds in Marlboro county, the "central cotton belt of Carolina."[4] That much lint would give an income of $26.17 per acre. Adding nearly $6.00 for seed would give a profit of approximately $3.50 per acre in Marlboro county.

1. South Carolina, State Board of Agriculture, *South Carolina, Resources and Population, Institutions and Industries*, ed. Harry Hammond (Charleston: Walker,

Evans and Cogswell Printers, 1883), pp. 63–64, 95, 163. Cited hereafter as *Handbook* (1883).

2. U.S., Department of Agriculture, Agricultural Marketing Service, *Cotton and Cottonseed*, Statistical Bulletin No. 164 (1955), p. 9; Handbook (1883), p. 63.

3. *Handbook* (1883), p. 63.

4. *Ibid.*, p. 81.

BIBLIOGRAPHICAL ESSAY

Manuscripts

Collections in the South Caroliniana Library at the University of South Carolina comprised my most important manuscript sources. The richest collection in that depository was the Martin Witherspoon Gary Papers, which contain a full record of Gary's political activities between 1877 and 1880. The correspondence relating to Gary's 1878 campaign for the United States Senate is particularly informative; a major reason for the completeness of this collection is the presence of many original letters from Gary to his political confidant, Hugh Farley, who read law with Gary after 1878.

Several collections in the South Caroliniana Library have significant material on Tillmanism. The papers of Robert Means Davis, professor of history at South Carolina College, clarify the Conservative efforts against the establishment of Clemson College and contain many rewarding letters from John Bratton on various aspects of Tillmanism. Many leading Conservatives, especially Charlestonians, informed William A. Courtenay of events; Courtenay also—as his papers reveal—shared the confidence of Benjamin Tillman. The minutes of the Farmers' Club of Beech Island [Aiken county], 1846–93, contain an important early Tillman letter on organization; the Minutes of the Farmers' Alliance of Edgefield county, 1889–94, relate Tillman's formal connections with that organization. Although disappointing on political developments, the John Gary Evans Papers document the diverse activities of a young Tillmanite stalwart. The William Dunlap Simpson Papers are thin, but there is a noteworthy letter on Tillman's growing strength on the county level. In the small collection of Matthew C. Butler Papers is a revealing Hampton letter regarding his failure to be re-elected to the U.S. Senate in 1890. I also found helpful material in both the Richard A. Meares Papers and the James A. Hoyt Papers.

On economic issues, the Milledge Luke Bonham Papers present a full picture of Bonham's activities on the Railroad Commission and the fight for a strong commission in 1882 and in 1883; the typescript of an unpublished biography of Bonham by his grandson Milledge Louis Bonham, "The Life and Times of Milledge Luke Bonham," is also in the Bonham collection. It relates everything Bonham ever did, but is little more than a lengthy calendar of events. The John C. Haskell Letterbook, 1883–87, has some interesting letters on the plans of the Richmond and Danville Railroad. The Minutes of the Patrons of Husbandry: First State Grange of South Carolina, 1873–1905, have little material of any interest except to record the organization's weakness.

The Hugh Smith Thompson Papers help to illuminate the gubernatorial contest of 1882. The John S. Richardson Papers have material on the Greenbackers and the Redistricting Plan of 1882; a memorandum on the plan is in the Williams-Chestnut-Manning Papers, along with a thought provoking letter about Gary written by Senator Butler.

The activities of one local Democratic club can be followed in the Minutes and Scrapbook of the Richland Democratic Club, 1876–80.

Other collections that had useful items include: the Wade Hampton Papers, the Narcisco G. Gonzales Papers, the Benjamin Stuart Williams Papers, the Benjamin F. Perry Papers, the Yates Snowden Papers, and the Minutes of the Trustees of the University of South Carolina (microfilm).

Probably the richest manuscript source for my purposes was the Francis Dawson collection in the Duke University Library. Especially valuable was the file of correspondence between Dawson and Benjamin Tillman between 1886 and 1888, when the two men worked as political allies. Besides the Tillman letters, the Dawson Papers also have invaluable material on the relationship of Dawson with Hampton and with the Democratic party, both on a state and national level, as well as several items relating to the negotiations between Columbia and Washington on the Ellenton Cases.

Also at Duke are the Hemphill Family Papers; the Hemphills were an important up-country family centered in Abbeville and Chester counties. Information on the Hampton-Gary feud and letters to James C. Hemphill when he worked on the News and Courier comprise its most helpful items. The George Gage Papers cast light on the activities of South Carolina Republicans, especially in the Black District. The Wade Hampton Papers contain Hampton's famous 1867 letter on the Negro. In the William Watts Ball Papers, letters written by Ball on various aspects of the 1877–90 period reveal the same flair for interpretation found in his published works.

In the Southern Historical Collection at the University of North Carolina I found information in the Elliott-Gonzales Papers on Wade Hampton, the Railroad Law of 1883, and Conservative efforts against Tillman in the summer of 1890. Correspondence between William Porcher Miles and Charles Simonton on South Carolina College is in the William Porcher Miles Papers. The William Mauldin Diary, although erratically kept, is informative about Greenbackers and the Democratic gubernatorial nomination in 1882, among other things. In the Borough House Papers (microfilm) are the Roll and Minutes of the Stateburg Democratic Club, 1890–1910, which detail the activities of an anti-Tillman club in the summer of 1890.

The William G. Hinson Papers in the Charleston Library Society is the only collection with any significant manuscript materials on the Conservative search for a candidate to oppose Tillman in 1890. Hinson, a James Island farmer, was active in Conservative efforts to stop Tillman.

In his unpublished autobiography, "Life and Recollections of Joseph W. Barnwell" (typescript, 1929), held by the South Carolina Historical Society, Joseph Barnwell tells of the plans and difficulties faced by the Straightout Executive Committee (he was a member) in August, 1890. The James Conner Papers in the same depository afford valuable glimpses into the activities and character of Wade Hampton as well as Francis Dawson.

The Benjamin Tillman Papers in the Clemson University Library were my biggest disappointment. This huge and uncatalogued collection has nothing of any value prior to Tillman's becoming Governor in December, 1890; during his two terms as Governor the collection remains sketchy, but it becomes voluminous after his election to the United States Senate in 1894. Although I found practically nothing in the Tillman Papers, the Clemson History File yielded four letters written by Tillman in the autumn of 1885 that spoke of his conception of his role at that early period. Both the John Bratton Papers and the Richard W. Simpson Papers had Tillman items. The Mississippi Department of Archives and History turned up in its collection of L. Q. C. Lamar Papers a Hampton letter on election disturbances.

The papers of certain national leaders, held by the Library of Congress, were of great assistance to me. The Morrison Waite Papers had materials on the negotiations of the Ellenton Cases; particularly useful were letters, written from South Carolina by Waite to his wife, about conditions in the state. South Carolina Republicans told Washington of their woes and reported—at times with perception—Democratic activities; many helpful letters are in the Benjamin Harrison Papers. Democrats evidently did not report to Washington, but the Grover Cleveland Papers contain several interesting pieces. There are also some Hampton letters in the Thomas F. Bayard Papers. The Wade Hampton Papers (Personal Miscellaneous File) contain a 1889 letter on race policy.

Archival materials were invaluable to me. The Source Chronological File of the Justice Department, Record Group 60, in the National Archives contains a rich source of information on Democratic tactics toward Republicans and Negroes, especially the Democratic determination not to allow Negroes to vote Republican. Most of the material consists of letters and reports to the Justice Department from the federal District Attorney and the United States Marshal in South Carolina. The Nominations File in the Records of the United States Senate, Record Group 46, assists in charting President Hayes's appointment policy.

The Executive File in the South Carolina Archives was another exceedingly valuable source. This file contains the letterbooks and incoming correspondence of all governors from Hampton through John P. Richardson. The letterbooks provide information on appointment procedure and the role of the governors in many events. The incoming correspondence—when I examined it—was of relatively little use to the historian because the Archives had not made much headway toward organizing that mass of material.

Newspapers

In parentheses after each newspaper I have placed dates for which I used the paper; "scattered" is used when there are no long continuous runs.

The single most important newspaper—in fact the basic source for this book—was the Charleston *News and Courier* (1877–90). Edited by Francis Dawson, and after his death in 1889 by James C. Hemphill, and a stanch supporter of the Conservative regime, the *News and Courier* was the largest and most influential newspaper in South Carolina. As the chief newspaper in the state, it gave full coverage to local news and reprinted excerpts from local newspapers.

The Conservative regime also had the backing of the Columbia *Daily Register* (1877–90). The *Greenville News* (scattered) championed the grievances of the up country but remained loyal in the battle against Benjamin Tillman. The Charleston *Journal of Commerce* (1877–78), which suspended publication in July, 1878, stood by Hampton in his feud with Martin Gary. Beginning publication in 1887, the Charleston *World* (1887–90) became the only daily in the state to support Tillman's gubernatorial campaign.

Local newspapers—all weeklies—provide an intimate glimpse into county political history and local feelings on various issues. The best of the weeklies are the Anderson *Intelligencer* (1877–90), the Edgefield *Chronicle* (1881–90), the Spartanburg *Carolina Spartan* (1879–90) and the Winnsboro *News and Herald* (1877–80), which became the Fairfield *News and Herald* in 1881 (1881–90). Others that I read included: the Yorkville *Enquirer* (1877–90); the *Laurensville Herald* (1877–79, 1884–90, scattered); the Newberry *Herald* (1877–84); the Newberry *Herald and News* (1884–90); the Barnwell *People* (1877–78); the *Manning Times* (scattered, 1888–90); the Bennettsville *Marlboro Democrat* (1885–90); the *Darlington News* (1886, 1888–90); the Spartanburg *Herald* (1877–79, scattered); the Orangeburg *Times and Democrat* (1881–90); the Greenville *Enterprise and Mountaineer* (scattered); the Georgetown *Enquirer* (1880–89); the Kingstree *Williamsburg Herald* (1882); the Port Royal *Palmetto Post* (1882–90); the Sumter *Watchman* (1878–79); the Sumter *True Southron* (1878–80); the Sumter *Watchman and Southron* (1881–90); the Edgefield *Advertiser* (scattered). The *Advertiser* was the chief press supporter of Gary and—along with the Charleston *World*—of Tillman.

Much information on South Carolina affairs, especially between 1877 and 1880, can be found in the *New York Times* (1877–90).

Publications of the United States Government

Publications of the United States Bureau of the Census provided essential statistical data. Volumes that I used included: *Compendium of the Tenth Census: 1880. Part I; Tenth Census: 1880. Statistics of Agriculture; Compendium of the Eleventh Census: 1890. Part I. Population; Eleventh Census: 1890. Statistics of Agriculture; and Historical Statistics of the United States: Colonial Times to 1957.*

Several other items assisted my research: James D. Richardson, *A Compilation of the Messages and Papers of the Presidents, 1789–1897* (Washington: U.S. Government Printing Office, 1898); U.S., Congress, Senate, *South Carolina in 1876. Testimony as to the Denial of the Elective Franchise in South Carolina at the Elections of 1875 and 1876,* Sen. Mis. Doc. 48, 44th Cong., 2d Sess. (Washington: U.S. Government Printing Office, 1877); U.S., Department of Agriculture, Agricultural Marketing Service, *Cotton and Cottonseed,* Statistical Bulletin No. 164 (1955); *Lee v. Simpson,* 33 *Law Ed. United States Supreme Court Reports,* 1038.

Publications of the South Carolina State Government

Three publications chart the course followed by the state legislature. Roll call votes, reports of committees and state agencies, and resolutions of the legislature can be found in the *Journal of the House of Representatives of the General Assembly of the State of South Carolina,* the *Journal of the Senate of the General Assembly of the State of South Carolina,* and *Reports and Resolutions of the General Assembly of the State of South Carolina.*

For the legal documents and legal history of the period, see South Carolina, *Constitution* (1868); South Carolina, *Statutes at Large; Code of Laws of South Carolina, 1902;* and *South Carolina Supreme Court Reports.*

Two statistical volumes, one prepared by the state Board of Agriculture in 1883 and the other in 1907 by its successor, the Department of Agriculture, Commerce and Immigration, are filled with informative material. The earlier effort: *South Carolina. Resources and Population, Institutions and Industries* (Charleston: Walker, Evans and Cogswell Printers, 1883), ed. Harry Hammond is more complete, especially on agriculture, than the *Handbook of South Carolina* (Columbia: The State Company, 1907).

Memoirs, Printed Letters, Pamphlets, and Speeches

The most important autobiographical volume used was *The State that Forgot: South Carolina's Surrender to Democracy* (Indianapolis: The Bobbs-

Merrill Company, 1932) by William Watts Ball. The son of a Conservative county leader, Ball was a long time editor in South Carolina and a keen student of South Carolina history, especially of Tillmanism. His comments about Tillmanism are fresh and stimulating.

Thomas J. Kirkland, an early follower of Tillman, wrote a series of colorful articles recounting his memories of Tillman and Tillmanism. Entitled "Tillman and I," the articles appeared in the Columbia *State* on June 30 and July 7, 14, 21, and 28, 1929.

I also found useful: Mary Doline O'Connor, *The Life and Letters of M. P. O'Connor* (New York: Dempsey and Carroll, 1893); Rupert Sargent Holland (ed.), *The Letters and Diary of Laura M. Towne: Written from the Sea Islands of South Carolina, 1862–1884* (Cambridge, Mass.: The Riverside Press, 1912); Duncan Clinch Heyward, *Seed from Madagascar* (Chapel Hill: University of North Carolina Press, 1937).

Edward McCrady set forth his political philosophy and his theory of the ballot in two pamphlets: *The Necessity of Education as the Basis of Our Political System: an Address Delivered before the Euphemian Society of Erskine College* [June 28, 1880] (Charleston: Walker, Evans and Cogswell, Publishers, 1880), and *The Necessity of Raising the Standard of Citizenship and the Right of the General Assembly of the State of South Carolina to Impose Qualifications upon Electors* (Charleston: Walker, Evans and Cogswell, Printers, 1881).

Two important documents that show the change in Conservative racial policy are: *Free Men! Free Ballots!! Free Schools!!! The Pledges of General Wade Hampton, Democratic Candidate for Governor to the Colored People of South Carolina, 1865–1876,* published by the state Democratic Executive Committee in 1876, tells of the brief courtship paid the Negro by the Democrats. "The Race Problem," *Arena* II (1890), 132–38, where Wade Hampton expressed his views on Negro emigration, shows just how much Conservative thinking on race had changed.

Speeches by Senators Wade Hampton and Matthew Butler illuminated Conservative thinking on several topics. Those that assisted me most included: *Speech of the Hon. Wade Hampton of South Carolina, in the Senate of the United States, on Senate Bill No. 398 to Aid in the Establishment Ane* [sic] *Temporary Support of Common Schools, March 27, 1884* (Washington, 1884); *Negro Emigration. Speech of Wade Hampton, a Senator from the State of South Carolina, in the Senate of the United States, Thursday, January 30, 1890* (Washington, 1890); several speeches by Senator Butler in *The Negro Problem* (n.p., n.d.); and the *Address of Hon. M. C. Butler at the Laying of the Corner-Stone of the Confederate Monument at Orangeburg, S. C., on the 12th Day of April, 1892* (Orangeburg, S. C.: Times and Democrat Job Print, 1892).

Miscellaneous

Two annual publications contain pertinent information. *Appleton's Annual Cyclopedia* covers a variety of topics; the *Tribune Almanac and Register of Political Events* published state election results.

The various constitutions of the South Carolina Democratic party offer a clear picture of the mechanics and rules of the party.

SECONDARY SOURCES

General Histories

For competent, up-to-date introductions to the literature on the Bourbon era, see Paul M. Gaston's " The ' New South,' " in *Writing Southern History: Essays in Historiography in Honor of Fletcher M. Green*, ed. Arthur S. Link and Rembert W. Patrick (Baton Rouge: Louisiana State University Press, 1965), pp. 316–36, and Jacob E. Cooke's " The New South," in *Essays in American Historiography: Papers Presented in Honor of Allan Nevins*, ed. by Donald Sheehan and Harold C. Syrett (New York: Columbia University Press, 1960), pp. 50–80.

Professor C. Vann Woodward, the most eminent historian of the post-Reconstruction South, has written three volumes that are indispensable to any student of the Bourbons. His *Origins of the New South, 1877–1913*, Vol. IX of *A History of the South*, ed. Wendell Holmes Stephenson and E. Merton Coulter (Baton Rouge: Louisiana State University Press, 1951) is the best general survey. In one of his most influential books, *The Strange Career of Jim Crow*, Galaxy edition (2d ed. rev.; New York: Oxford University Press, 1966), Woodward argues that statutory segregation generally came after Conservatives had been defeated by agrarians. His *Reunion and Reaction: The Compromise of 1877 and the End of Reconstruction*, Anchor edition (New York: Doubleday and Company, Inc., 1951), emphasizes the economic pressures for reconciliation.

Even though Woodward's *Origins of the New South* has become the standard volume, an older book by Holland Thompson, *The New South: A Chronicle of Social and Industrial Evolution*, Vol. XLII of *The Chronicles of America Series*, ed. Allen Johnson (New Haven: Yale University Press, 1921), still has valuable insights.

The three most notable discussions of the Bourbon era in other Southern states are Albert D. Kirwan's excellent *Revolt of the Rednecks, Mississippi Politics: 1876–1925* (Lexington, Ky.: University of Kentucky Press, 1951) ; Allen J. Going, *Bourbon Democracy in Alabama, 1874–1890* (University, Ala.: University of Alabama Press, 1951) ; and Judson Clement Ward, Jr., " New Departure Democrats in Georgia: An Interpretation," *Georgia Historical Quarterly*, XLI (September, 1957), 227–37.

Other useful volumes that explore different aspects of the post-Reconstruction South are: Thomas D. Clark, *The Rural Press and the New South* (Baton Rouge: Louisiana State University, 1948); William B. Hesseltine, *Confederate Leaders in the New South* (Baton Rouge: Louisiana State University Press, 1950); W. J. Cash, *The Mind of the South*, Vintage edition (New York: Vintage Books, 1960); Robert Penn Warren, *The Legacy of the Civil War* (New York: Random House, 1961); John F. Stover, *The Railroads of the South, 1865–1900: A Study in Finance and Control* (Chapel Hill: University of North Carolina Press, 1955); Thomas D. Clark, *Pills, Petticoats, and Plows: The Southern Country Store* (reprint, Norman: University of Oklahoma Press, 1964); idem, "The Furnishing and Supply System in Southern Agriculture since 1865," *Journal of Southern History*, XII (1946), 24–44; Maxwell Ferguson, "State Regulation of Railroads in the South" in *Columbia University Studies in History, Economics and Public Law*, LXVII, No. 2 (New York, 1916); M[atthew] B[rown] Hammond, *The Cotton Industry: An Essay in American Economic History, Publications of the American Economic Association, New Series, No. 1* (New York: The Macmillan Company, 1897); Theodore Saloutos, *Farmer Movements in the South, 1865–1933*, Bison Books edition (Lincoln: University of Nebraska Press, 1960).

Studies of various aspects of national development and biographies of national figures after Reconstruction enabled me to view my materials in a broader setting. The major ones included: Vincent P. DeSantis, *Republicans Face the Southern Question, 1877–1897* (Baltimore: The Johns Hopkins Press, 1959); Stanley P. Hirshson, *Farewell to the Bloody Shirt: Northern Republicans and the Southern Negro, 1877–1893* (Bloomington, Ind.: University of Indiana Press, 1962); Rayford W. Logan, *The Negro in American Life and Thought: the Nadir, 1877–1900* (New York: The Dial Press, Inc., 1954); Allen J. Going, "The South and the Blair Bill," *Mississippi Valley Historical Review*, XLIV (1957), 267–90; Paul H. Buck, *The Road to Reunion, 1865–1900*, Vintage edition (New York: Vintage Books, 1959); Earle D. Ross, *The Liberal Republican Movement* (New York: Henry Holt and Company, 1919); Carter Goodrich, *Government Promotion of American Canals and Railroads, 1800–1890* (New York: Columbia University Press, 1960); Fred A. Shannon, *The Farmers' Last Frontier: Agriculture, 1860–1897*, Vol. V of *The Economic History of the United States*, ed. Henry David et al. (New York: Farrar and Rinehart, 1945); B. U. Ratchford, *American State Debts* (Durham: Duke University Press, 1941); C. Peter Magrath, *Morrison R. Waite: The Triumph of Character* (New York: The Macmillan Company, 1963); Harry Barnard, *Rutherford B. Hayes and His America* (Indianapolis: The Bobbs-Merrill Company, Inc., 1954).

An outstanding work on political parties that carefully delineates the one-party system is Maurice Duverger, *Political Parties: Their Organization and Activity in the Modern State* (New York: John Wiley and Sons, Inc., 1955).

South Carolina: General Histories

Two works by David Duncan Wallace, the late dean of South Carolina historians, offer a good introduction to the study of the state's history. His four-volume (Vol. IV is a biographical volume) *History of South Carolina* (New York: American Historical Society, Inc., 1934), and a one-volume abridgement, *South Carolina: A Short History, 1520–1948* (Columbia: University of South Carolina Press, 1961) are marked by an intimate knowledge of material and wealth of information. A recent volume by Ernest M. Lander, Jr., *A History of South Carolina, 1865–1960* (Chapel Hill: University of North Carolina Press, 1960) is best on industrial development but lacks the thoroughness and depth of Wallace's work.

Ante-bellum South Carolina

For a general study that focuses on what the South thought about itself and said about national developments during the decade and a half preceding the Civil War, see Avery O. Craven, *The Growth of Southern Nationalism, 1848–1861*, Vol. VI of *A History of the South*, ed. Wendell Holmes Stephenson and E. Merton Coulter (Baton Rouge: Louisiana State University Press, 1953).

These books provided background material and offered challenging interpretations on the influence of sectionalism in the development of the state. William A. Schaper in his "Sectionalism and Representation in South Carolina," *Annual Report of the American Historical Association* (1900), I, 237–463, has made an admirable study of this important issue in the state's political history. *Evolution of a Federalist: William Loughton Smith of Charleston, 1758–1812* (Columbia: University of South Carolina Press, 1962) by George C. Rogers, Jr., has particularly valuable comments on the shift in political power from the rice aristocracy in the low country to the cotton-oriented midlands. Also helpful was Harold S. Schultz's careful work, *Nationalism and Sectionalism in South Carolina, 1852–1860* (Durham: Duke University Press, 1950).

Alfred Glaze Smith, Jr. has written a thorough account of ante-bellum economics in his *Economic Readjustment of an Old Cotton State: South Carolina, 1820–1860* (Columbia: University of South Carolina Press, 1958).

Reconstruction and the Hampton-Gary Conflict

" South Carolina Recontruction Historiography," *The South Carolina Historical Magazine*, LXV (1964), 20–32, by Neill W. Macaulay, Jr. is a convenient guide to a diverse literature. Two of these volumes proved most helpful: Francis Butler Simkins and Robert Hilliard Woody, *South Carolina during Reconstruction* (Chapel Hill: University of North Carolina Press, 1932) and John S. Reynolds, *Reconstruction in South Carolina, 1865–1877* (Columbia: The State Company, 1905).

Reconstruction had hardly ended before the Hampton-Gary feud threatened to destroy Democratic unity. Each contestant has had his defender. In *Wade Hampton and the Negro: the Road Not Taken* (Columbia: University of South Carolina Press, 1950) Hampton Jarrell with emphasis on race policy presents Hampton as the wise, moderate leader who towered over all his contemporaries, especially Gary. William Arthur Sheppard's polemical defense of Gary, *Red Shirts Remembered: Southern Brigadiers of the Reconstruction Period* (Atlanta: The Ruralist Press, 1940), asserts that Hampton kept Gary from attaining the rewards due him as the man chiefly responsible for the Democratic victory in 1876. For a definitive statement on one aspect of the Hampton-Gary argument, see David D. Wallace, " The Question of the Withdrawal of Democratic Presidential Electors in South Carolina in 1876," *Journal of Southern History*, VIII (1942), 374–85, which proves beyond any doubt that Wade Hampton did not agree to the withdrawal of the Democratic electors.

Biographies of Hampton add little material of value. Edward L. Wells' eulogistic *Hampton and Reconstruction* (Columbia: The State Company, 1907) focuses on the war years and has little on post-1877 developments. The only full length study, *Giant in Gray: a Biography of Wade Hampton of South Carolina* (New York: Charles Scribner's Sons, 1949) by Manly Wade Wellman is thin, superficial, and based on secondary sources.

As the decade of the 1880s began, Edward Hogan wrote with perception about social conditions in South Carolina in " South Carolina To-Day," *The International Review*, VIII (1880), 105–19.

The Negro

The question of the Negro, which divided Hampton and Gary and which has always been a central issue in South Carolina, has drawn two detailed studies that cover the years between the Civil War and 1900. George Brown Tindall in his *South Carolina Negroes, 1877–1900* (Columbia: University of South Carolina Press, 1952), argues that Conservative racial policy was generally a moderate interlude between slavery and the harsh racist policy of the 1890s. In a recent book, *After Slavery: The Negro in South Carolina During Reconstruction, 1861–1877* (Chapel Hill: University of North Carolina Press, 1965), Joel Williamson has challenged Tindall's thesis. Williamson feels that the harsh racist policy of the 1890s existed even during Reconstruction and that there was never any period of moderation. For reasons expressed in my text, I feel that Williamson has somewhat overstated his case.

For an excellent treatment of the South Carolina Republican party, the party of the majority of Negroes, see James Welch Patton, "The Republican Party in South Carolina, 1876–1895," *Essays in Southern History* ed. Fletcher Melvin Green in the *James Sprunt Studies in History and Political Science*, XXI (Chapel Hill: University of North Carolina Press, 1949), 91–111. In the same volume, on pp. 112–23, Fletcher Melvin Green comments on the relative lack of harshness in South Carolina's convict lease system in his "Some Aspects of the Convict Lease System in the Southern States."

Industry and Agriculture

Useful items pertaining to different parts of the economic story of South Carolina in the 1880s include: Samuel Melancthon Derrick, *Centennial History of South Carolina Railroad* (Columbia: The State Company, 1930), which emphasizes the financial condition of that road; the *History of the State Agricultural Society of South Carolina, 1839–1916* (Columbia: R. L. Bryan Company, 1916), prepared by a committee of the society, is more a memorial than history; R. H. Taylor documents the spreading use of commercial fertilizers in his "Commercial Fertilizers in South Carolina," *South Atlantic Quarterly*, XXIX (1930), 179–89.

Two pamphlets that provide excellent introductions to the South Carolina phosphate industry are: Philip E. Chazal, *The Century in Phosphates and Fertilizers: a Sketch of the South Carolina Phosphate Industry* (Charleston, 1904), and Charles A. Shepard, Jr., *South Carolina Phosphates and their Principal Competitors in the Markets of the World* (Charleston: Laboratory for Analytical Chemistry, 1880).

Several theses and dissertations proved most valuable for my treatment of economic affairs. "Cotton Manufacturing in South Carolina, 1865–1892" (unpublished Ph.D. dissertation, Dept. of History, The Johns Hopkins University, 1954) by Gustauvus Galloway Williamson, Jr., is a thorough study of an important subject. Willie Frank Putnam's "An Analysis of Public Aid to Railroads in South Carolina, 1865–1900" (unpublished Master's thesis, Dept. of Economics, University of South Carolina, 1957) documents the interest shown by localities in obtaining railroads. William Herman Patterson's "'Through the Heart of the South': A History of the Seaboard Air Line Railroad Company, 1832–1950" (unpublished Ph.D. dissertation, Dept. of History, University of South Carolina, 1951) relates the history of a major road, and shows the eagerness displayed by local areas to get Seaboard tracks in their communities. Albert Neely Sanders, "The South Carolina Railroad Commission, 1878–1895" (unpublished Master's thesis, Dept. of History, University of North Carolina, 1948), and "State Regulation of Public Utilities by South Carolina, 1879–1935" (unpublished Ph.D. dissertation, Dept. of History, University of North Carolina, 1956) give, in full detail, the activities of the most important state regulatory agency. Edward Delos

Beechert, Jr., discusses with insight what Southerners thought about industrialism in his "Industrialism in the Southeast, 1870–1914" (unpublished Ph.D. dissertation, Dept. of History, University of California, Berkeley, 1957).

Tillmanism

The student of Tillmanism should consult two books by Francis Butler Simkins. His first book *The Tillman Movement* (Durham: Duke University Press, 1926) has been superseded by his later biography of Tillman; in the early volume he holds to a strong class interpretation of Tillmanism that has been tempered in the biography. The biography, *Pitchfork Ben Tillman: South Carolinian* (Baton Rouge: Louisiana State University Press, 1944), is fairly complete but Simkins's treatment of the years between 1885 and 1890 is unanalytical and based on limited sources.

A valuable, but neglected, commentary on Tillmanism is William Watts Ball, "An Episode in South Carolina Politics [Tillmanism]" (1915) in *Pamphlets by and about the Hon. B. R. Tillman and Tillmania in South Carolina, 1890–1918* (n.p., n.d.). Tillman offered his personal interpretation of his movement in an address eulogizing Joseph H. Earle in *Memorial Addresses on the Life and Character of Joseph H. Earle (Late a Senator from South Carolina) Delivered in the Senate and House of Representatives, Fifty-fifth Congress, Second Session* (Washington: U.S. Government Printing Office, 1898).

Especially helpful on the agricultural college issue was Joseph J. Lawton's excellent "Benjamin Ryan Tillman and Agricultural Education: the 'Farmers' College' in South Carolina Politics, 1885–1889" (unpublished Senior thesis, Dept. of History, Princeton University, 1954). See also Alester G. Holmes and George R. Sherrill, *Thomas Green Clemson: His Life and Work* (Richmond: Garrett and Massie, Inc., 1937).

An important article on the industrial interests of Tillman's lieutenants is Gustauvus G. Williamson, Jr., "South Carolina Cotton Mills and the Tillman Movement," *The Proceedings of the South Carolina Historical Association* (1949), pp. 36–49, which shows that leading Tillmanites were directly involved in the burgeoning textile industry.

In his "The Farmers' Alliance and the Populist Movement in South Carolina, 1887–1896" (unpublished Master's thesis, Dept. of History, University of South Carolina, 1953) Joseph Church traces the development of the Alliance and its relations with Tillmanism.

Biographical Directories

Because many of my characters were state officials who never gained prominence outside South Carolina, biographical directories supplied much essential information. The more well-known of them received space in Allen Johnson and Dumas Malone (eds.), *Dictionary of American Biography* (New York: Charles Scribner's Sons, 1928–58). Especially helpful, because it contains sketches of numerous Tillmanite leaders, was Samuel A. Ashe and Edward McCrady, Jr. (eds.), *Cyclopedia of Eminent and Representative Men of the Carolinas of the Nineteenth Century* (Madison, Wis.: Brant and Fuller, 1892). Others include: *Biographical Directory of the American Congress, 1774–1949* (Washington: U.S. Government Printing Office, 1950); J. C. Garlington (ed.), *Men of the Times: Sketches of Living Notables: Biographical Encyclopedia of Contemporaneous South Carolina Leaders* (Spartanburg, S. C.: J. C. Garlington Publishing Company, 1902); James C. Hemphill (ed.), *Men of Mark in South Carolina* (Washington: Men of Mark Publishing Company, 1907); U. R. Brooks, *South Carolina Bench and Bar* (Columbia: The State Company, 1908), I; Emily Bellinger Reynolds and Joan Reynolds Faunt (comps.), *Biographical Directory of the Senate of the State of South Carolina, 1776–1964* (Columbia: South Carolina Archives Department, 1964); Ezra J. Warner, *Generals in Gray: Lives of the Confederate Commanders* (Baton Rouge: Louisiana State University Press, 1959).

Special Subjects

Educational institutions that influenced the state's leaders have been discussed in Daniel Walker Hollis's excellent *University of South Carolina* (2 vols.; Columbia: University of South Carolina Press, 1951, 1956) and John Peyre Thomas, *The History of the South Carolina Military Academy* (Charleston: Walker, Evans and Cogswell Co., Publishers, 1893).

J. H. Easterby's "The Granger Movement in South Carolina," *The Proceedings of the South Carolina Historical Association* (1931), pp. 21–32, provides an adequate introduction to an organization that had lost its impetus by 1877. Frank S. Logan, "Francis Warrington Dawson, 1840–1889: South Carolina Editor," *The Proceedings of the South Carolina Historical Association* (1953), pp. 13–28, is practically the only work on this influential editor.

INDEX